# of Squash

By the same author

The Tennis Set
and (with Leslie Hamer)
Teach Yourself Squash Rackets

Rex Bellamy

The Story of Squash

Cassell
London

CASSELL LTD.
35 Red Lion Square, London WC1R 4SG
and at Sydney, Auckland, Toronto, Johannesburg,
an affiliate of
Macmillan Publishing Co., Inc.,
New York.

First published 1978

ISBN 0 304 29766 6

Typeset by Inforum Ltd., Portsmouth.
Printed in Great Britain by
The Camelot Press Ltd.,
Southampton

Contents

Illustrations

between pages 120 and 121

*Pakistan International Airlines

Acknowledgements

This book could not have been as comprehensive as it is but for the co-operation of many people from whom I sought information or merely opinions. Some provided that help in unlikely places: an aircraft flying from Karachi to Peshawar, the garden of a pub in the Chilterns, the back of a taxi in Paris, a Manhattan hotel room at three in the morning, or by post from Riyadh. My association with squash did not begin until the closing years of the Khan era, so I am particularly indebted to those whose knowledge of the game stretches back farther.

In a wider sense I am grateful to my wife, to *The Times*, and to Pakistan International Airlines. My wife had to run a home single-handed during the four months in which I was at grips with a typewriter and a mountain of notes. Much of the material here was gathered while I was working for *The Times*, and 'The Man on Flight 326' is a revised version of a feature published in that newspaper in April, 1976. The practical assistance of PIA enabled me to write at first hand of the land that produced the great Khans.

The individuals who contributed to *The Story of Squash* included many Khans: Hashim, Azam, Roshan, Torsam, Hidayat and Shah Jahan, and a fellow journalist, Abdul Majid. Others who took the time and trouble to help included Sherif Afifi, Abdel Fattah Amr, Jonah Barrington, Simon Berry, Stewart Brauns, Claire Chapman, Michael Corby, Jean Couvercelle, Alex Cowie, Bill Emmett, Trish Faulkner (*née* McClenaughan), Ted Friel, Tony Gathercole, Jack Giles, Dick Hawkey, Ken Hiscoe, John Horry, Geoff Hunt, Leslie Hamer, Sheila Macintosh,

Dugald Macpherson, Dan Maskell, Heather McKay, Roy McKelvie, Muneer Ahmad, Sajjad Muneer, Michael Oddy, Brian Phillips, Ahmed Safwat, Janet Shardlow, Roy Wilson, and Ian Wright, honorary custodian of records of the Squash Rackets Association. The staff of two magazines, *The Squash Player* and *Squash World*, were equally helpful.

The SRA, the Women's SRA, and the Lawn Tennis Association kindly allowed me to browse freely through their bookcases. The books consulted included *The Badminton Library of Sports and Pastimes* edited by the Duke of Beaufort, *The Book of Jonah* by Jonah Barrington and Clive Everton, *Brewer's Dictionary of Phrase and Fable*, *The Encyclopedia of Sports* edited by Martin Tyler, *Geoff Hunt on Squash* edited by Alan Trengove, *Harrow School Yesterday and Today* by Dr. E.D. Laborde, *India and the Passing of the Empire* by Sir George Dunbar, *The Lonsdale Library* edited by Lord Aberdare, *More About Squash Rackets* by Susan Noel, *Newer Angles on Squash* by R.B. Hawkey, *The Oxford Companion to Sports and Games* edited by John Arlott, *Play Better Squash* by John Beddington, *The Racquet Game* by Allison Danzig, *Squash Rackets* by J.H. Giles, *Squash Rackets* by Hashim Khan and Richard E. Randall, *Squash Rackets* by Gerald Pawle, *The Squash Rackets Annual* edited by Hubert Winterbotham and *The Squash Rackets Association Handbook*.

All these made *The Story of Squash* a better book than it might have been. They played their parts in giving the game the recorded history it deserved. Finally my thanks to all the players who created that history — and gave so much pleasure while doing so.

R.B.

Introduction

This was an exciting but difficult book to write. Exciting because it was original. Difficult because it meant picking one's way through a historic labyrinth that had never been fully explored. There has been no previous survey, at this length, of a game that probably existed in a primitive form 150 years ago and has suddenly — in the past decade — leapt to prominence as one of the most popular recreations in the middle-class communities of the Anglo-Saxon world. Its rapidly increasing popularity within these traditional boundaries has been accompanied by an accelerating advance elsewhere. The International Squash Rackets Federation, an organization there was no pressing need to create until 1967, already has twenty members. The European SRF, formed as recently as 1973, has attracted eleven others. In addition to these thirty-one officially established squash-playing nations, there are many more with playing facilities that, modest though they may be, contain the seeds of a future harvest.

Since 1970, when Jonah Barrington and Pakistan International Airlines organized a five-man missionary tour of the East, the game has also acquired a world-wide professional circuit: highly trained, jet-set sportsmen competing for prizes of up to £3,000. There can be no doubt that professional squash will continue to be an expanding segment of the entertainment industry, with more and more sponsors realizing the vast extent of this new market for their products. Nor can there be any doubt that the artificial distinction between professionals and amateurs will gradually be eroded as commercial interests move into the game.

In 1976, for the first time, there were official world open

championships for men and women. Both were won by Australians — Geoff Hunt and Heather McKay. Bruce Brownlee became the first New Zealander to win the British amateur championship and Lars Kvant the first Swede to reach the semi-finals. Now in 1977-8 we celebrate the Golden Jubilee of the Squash Rackets Association, formed in 1928, and two tenth anniversaries: because 1967 was the year in which the ISRF was born and Barrington completed his first historic 'double' by winning the British open and amateur championships in the same season (in those days both were regarded as 'world' titles because the real thing did not exist, though the inaugural ISRF amateur championships were promoted later the same year). When Barrington repeated the feat the following season, one of the players he beat was another public schoolboy who was to become a world champion — James Hunt, who won the 1976 Grand Prix series in motor racing.

The only other squash player to achieve the 'double' was Abdel Fattah Amr, who dominated the game in the 1930s. He and Barrington were both open champions for six years, a record surpassed only by Hashim Khan. These three men have had an enormous influence on the game. Amr raised squash to a level of efficiency that had never before been attained. Hashim was interesting because of his romantic background and the fact that he won his championships between the ages of thirty-five and forty-two. Barrington's personality inspired widespread interest in squash, and he pioneered the professional circuit as we know it today.

This is the most exciting period in the game's history. Yet although squash is in the midst of change, one can look back and feel that all the important threads in its development are assuming a consistent pattern. Among other things squash has proved that a major participant sport (as opposed to a spectator sport) can grow and flourish without the benefit of massive publicity and thousands of spectators. In both areas squash has been restricted by its intimate nature, though the advent of glass walls and the introduction of television are enabling more people to watch it. Squash has not been vigorously and widely promoted. It has assumed its present stature because of its obvious advantages for those who play games as distinct from those who watch them. It offers enjoyable, concentrated exercise for the entire family at any time of day all the year round and has the great virtue of simplicity. It can be as easy or as difficult as you want to make it. The margin for error is huge enough for any duffer. Conversely, the scope for improvement is almost limitless, not least in such teasing qualities as bluff and deception. The essence of squash could, with care, be written on the back of a postage stamp. But one can spend a lifetime failing to master it.

There are, of course, flaws in every success story. The obvious flaw in squash is that both players are in one court, which creates a traffic problem. The most controversial rule in the book insists that when a player has hit the ball he must get out of the way and give his opponent a fair view and the freedom to play a proper stroke. Throughout the world the interpretation of that rule is inconsistent — the ensuing lets and penalty points disruptive and irksome. The referee's level of competence too often falls below that of the players he is trying to control. Not that the players are blameless. 'There are blokes who just hit the ball and stand there,' says Ken Hiscoe. 'It's about time the bloody referees got stuck into 'em and applied the rules.'

A more worrying international problem, because it is probably insoluble, arose from the fact that the game developed simultaneously on both sides of the Atlantic before standard playing conditions had been established. The North American court is narrower, the racket a little heavier and stronger. The ball is bigger, heavier, harder and faster. The scoring system is different. The real villain of the piece is the ball. It is pointless to try finesse with the skidding American version, and softball specialists have to discard a few shots in order to control it. The American's task in a softball country is more difficult because he needs shots that are unfamiliar to him.

Both games are thriving and neither faction is going to abolish expensive courts to build new ones in the cause of compromise. The narrower courts suit the hardball games and the wider courts suit softball. Both sides are happy with the game they have and any drastic change in the ball would be damaging. In short, the two games cannot be happily married. And they know it.

The United States (which has roughly the same number of courts and players as Great Britain) considers that the ISRF have not given the hardball game the consideration it deserves. Unless the ISRF create separate sections for the two games the USSRA will almost certainly organize an independent governing body for themselves, Canada, Mexico, El Salvador and Guatemala. Meantime the entrepreneurs of the much larger softball game are casting envious eyes on the rich US market and preparing to compete with hardball squash on its own territory. So far there has been no sign that the US would welcome such an initiative.

But the international game has two things in its favour. One is the fact that whereas Canada and the US used to compete primarily with each other and be content with that, both are now eager to take part in the ISRF championships and other major fixtures on the softball calendar. Canada, indeed, promoted the 1977 ISRF championships. The second encouraging feature for those who hope to bring North America within the framework of the softball game is that the groundwork has already been done in Canada and, to some extent, in Mexico.

The Canadian dilemma is the worst of all. They have separate seasons — and separate championships — for the hardball and softball games and the latter is making better progress. But they are stuck with a predominance of American courts, though any new construction tends to incorporate an international court because no one knows what is going to happen in the future. The confusion is such that in one area softball is played on American courts, in another it is played on international courts, and in a third the hardball game is played on American courts. In other words, Canada is being torn in two directions. Because of this lack of coherence, squash is losing potential recruits to racket ball (a threat throughout North America) and platform tennis.

Except for regretting Canada's embarrassment, there is no need to be gloomy about what is likely to be a permanent division within the game. The important thing is that wherever we look, more people than ever before are playing squash and enjoying it. North America, incidentally, has one source of pleasure that is denied to international squash. Doubles is a popular form of the game there, at all levels, and is particularly useful for players who are too old for the rigours of singles. But in the rest of the world it has never been customary to include the larger doubles court in the designs for a new club. And the only approved dimensions, those used in North America for hardball doubles, might be unsuitable for softball.

The difference between the two versions of squash cannot destroy the *camaraderie* that exists throughout the world game. Though this book traces the origins and progress of squash, it is primarily about people — particularly about those who have made the game what it is and those who are still giving us so much pleasure. By the time you put it down you will know them better and may feel, as I do, that the cosmopolitan cast of squash are worthy of the beautiful if demanding game they are playing.

One

The Man on Flight 326

The elderly man in the window-seat is small, deep-chested, paunchy. His self-assurance, and that bulging but firm torso, belie the lack of inches and the thinning grey tonsure. He exudes the kind of authority that does not need advertising. In repose, the eyes are hooded, inscrutable. Even when he talks, the agreeably animated public man obviously keeps a private man in reserve. The cliché about the tip of the iceberg would be inexact. He has too much warmth for that. The power below the surface is more like a faint rumble from a distant engine-room.

He wears an American lightweight suit and comes from Denver. But this is PIA Flight 326 from Karachi to Peshawar. Hashim Khan is going to see his mother and browse through the pages of a half-forgotten youth. He, himself, had twelve children, he says — seven boys and a girl (four others had been 'lost'). Seven still live at home and the youngest is only eight. Hashim grins, proud of his virility. He is sixty, he says. But a doctor has told him that, physically, he could be ten years younger. It is an April morning in 1976. The sap is rising.

This man, Hashim Khan, has become a legend. He hails from Nawakilla (a Pushto word meaning 'new village') on the edge of Peshawar. Seven times he won the British open championship, recognized as the unofficial world championship. No one else has done that. He gave Nawakilla, Peshawar, the Pathans, Pakistan — and squash — a sporting renown none had previously known. He raised the softball game to a new level of excellence. Then he went to North America and did the same thing with the hardball game. Inspired by his example, others of his family succeeded him. Because of all this it is Peshawar, rather than Harrow in England, that has assumed the stature of a Mecca for the devotees of squash. And we are on the way.

A long-robed stewardess swirls up the gangway holding a tray crowded with native goodies. Hashim chooses carefully, recommends this and that. 'If I can't eat, I get tired. If I eat, I can't run . . .' To the west — swelling through the clear air like gigantic, dun-coloured beasts sleeping in the sunlight — are the mountains of Baluchistan.

'In short time squash is best exercise,' says Hashim. 'Fun game. Just follow ball and forget everything. Can play anywhere, any time.'

What qualities does the good player need?

'First thing is, should be fit. Second is quick think. Third is quick footwork. Fourth is quick handwork — to hit soon is best, not from behind. And must keep eyes on ball all time. If you make error you beat yourself. If you hit back to opponent you are in trouble.' Modern players, he adds, begin too fast. 'Not necessary all time. Must be able to play faster, change gear, every game if necessary.'

Hashim says he was thirty-five when he won his first British open championship, forty-three when he won his last.* 'If I begin at Barrington's age I win British open not seven times, but twenty-seven times!' An exaggeration, but let it pass.

He still plays for three hours or more a day. 'One day, 1975, they send me players long way, from other cities. I play for nine hours, to help. If health is all right, should play for ever. If stop, health not too good. The good squash players, they play almost every day. I never see them die young . . . I still play any championship they invite. Sons, Sharif and Gulmast, talk to me to stop, because I want to run faster than young. But I love to play. I give lessons. But I like to play championship. I don't care get tired or get beaten. I can't play two matches a day. By second or third round, play Sharif or Mohibullah and get tired. Ten times win US veteran championship. Last winter I play exhibition with Heather McKay in Toronto. First time I play English game for sixteen years. Before exhibition she told me she took lesson from me, Canberra, when she was beginner, and I tell her she would be best in

*According to Hashim's own book, he won his last British open championship at the age of forty-two.

world. She beat all the men down there, Toronto. She can't beat me. 9-5, 9-3 (best of three games — I was playing some American exhibition after that). She's smart and she's in good shape. If you win, it's all right. If you lose, you change game. She tried to keep me back, lost game. Second game she play short; but I think a little tired.'

During his peak years, Hashim's stamina produced some extraordinary spectacles during practice.

'I play Azam five games, Roshan five games, Abdul Bari five games. Anyone who want to play, after that. Mohibullah. I play four. No rest. I did not go out from court. Between fifteen and twenty-five I was 105lb to 110lb. I was not heavy like now. New Zealand, 1952, I play 350 games one week. Three places one day. Five people every place. Every day fifteen different people. Final day I just can't swing shoulder.'

We land at Lyallpur in the Punjab, stretch our legs, and look at the day. Nothing is happening. Just silence. And a wide stillness. Edward Thomas could have written an 'Adlestrop' here:

'No one left and no one came
On the bare platform.'

Another take-off. Another new horizon.

'Big things for me. One, from beginning I never go for B or C class. Always big championship. And 1944 to 1956 I never lost match in English game. Two, nobody wins these in my age. Like forty-three nobody win British open. Nobody win seven times. Three, in same year win every championship in world in different game. These three things so far is impossible.'

Squash, I suggest, is not widely played in Pakistan. So how have they produced so many outstanding players?

'Reason, specially, all from one village, one family. Close cousin, far cousin. Chance to start playing each other from young age and chance to play all year round. Chance to go to England, good living, good money, if make it at squash. After the partition, first time I go to England my brother Azam was just playing squash for fun once in a while. Not really serious. Believe it or not, I haven't anyone in Peshawar to play with. I practise with myself and I go to England and win every championship. After couple of years, I trained Azam and told him he was going to England. First day, one game. He say it is enough, you kill me. Second day, two games. Third day, three games. Same year he play me in final of

British professional championship. They say who is he? — we never heard of him. He play with tall man, Brian Phillips, for trial. He beat him easily, so they say he can play in open championship. And I think if anything happen to him I need another man. So I train Mohibullah . . .'

The aircraft swoops. Seat belts on. Cigarettes out. Beyond the green fields are mountains and clouds and, tucked among them somewhere, the Khyber Pass and Afghanistan.

'But I go to America. Azam retire and live London. Roshan retire. Mohibullah settle in Boston. After that Pakistan hadn't got good player to play in British open. After we left, Air Marshal Nur Khan made the game. At that time he was C.-in-C. in Air Force. He built coaching centre in Peshawar (800 people can watch — biggest in world). He told coaches to get poor boys from village. Rich boys can't do it. Too soft. Not tough. They don't want to run too much. Easy life — don't want hard work. And from beginning it's hard work. So give poor boys a racket. Mohibullah*, Zaman, are from that centre. Still looking for poor boys.'

Through the window we can see the hazy bulk of the hills. They remind me of days that tasted like wine, days with my brother and assorted friends (one a memorably muscled chimney-sweep) among the crags of the Peak District, Snowdonia, the Lake District, the Alps, even the Zagros Mountains of Iran. Hashim, too, must feel an affinity with high places. He has pursued his profession from the Himalayas to the Rockies, by way of Detroit. The move from Detroit to Denver, he says, helped to cure his wife's rheumatism.

We land at Peshawar — among brown, quiet men with far-seeing eyes, flowing garments, and Pathan hats, like Balaclavas rolled up and loosely flattened on top. These are mostly the lowland Pathans — the big fellows are up in the mountains. They scrutinize the mob streaming across the apron from the perched plane. Some embrace Hashim affectionately, with instant remembrance. A great man has come home. His American suit suddenly seems out of place, a concession to the conventions of another world.

We drive to the Peshawar Club, its grandeur fading now. The original red-brick building, which rose from the ground in 1862, is

*Hashim here refers to Mohibullah Junior — unrelated to Hashim's nephew, the 1962 British open champion.

still there. But Hashim, by request, goes first towards the weathered walls that contain the roofless, cement-floored courts on which he learned the game. They look old and grey and tired now, but are still used. Constructed in 1901, they replaced two rackets courts. The doors are iron. Hashim, standing again on the court of his youth, looks up and waves a hand, indicating the top of the front wall. As a boy, he says, he used to sit up there with his friend Safirullah. They would jump down and fetch the ball whenever the officers hit it out of court. He smiles. Twice Safirullah fell off through no cause other than drowsiness. Later Safirullah married Hashim's sister (the senior Mohibullah was their son). Hashim played barefoot on these courts. When he went he England he bought his shoes at Woolworth's because the soles were thinner and broader.

In the dining-room of the club, where his father, Abdullah, was head steward, Hashim points out five fireplaces and says it was sometimes very cold. He grins. 'Anyone who give him good tip had table by fire.' When Hashim was eleven his father was killed when thrown from a truck that ran into a wall. Hashim was on the same truck and saw it all.

Down the road is the Air Force officers' club, where Hashim ('In beginning was tennis "pro"') had his first professional post. His only jobs in Pakistan were with the Air Force, at Peshawar from 1942 to 1951 and at Risalpur from 1952 to 1960. We climb the steps to a two-bench gallery and look down on the open-air courts where Hashim coached or simply played. They paid him fifty rupees a month and he married the girl his mother had chosen for him. Life was good. We walk through the flowered gardens to look at Nur Khan's brainchild, the coaching centre Hashim was talking about on the plane. When it was finished in 1967, there was a new beginning for squash in Pakistan. The accommodation around the main court is interesting. In addition to a soaring gallery at the back, there are three recessed galleries — one above the other — on either side. These are like boxes built in the wings of a theatre. But they look down on a squash court rather than a stage.

Hashim's family home at Nawakilla is the next stop on the tour. It is not the old Nawakilla, nor indeed the old home. 'The British come in and decide that is best place to build new cantonment. Move village. Later, need to make big runway for airport. So they take farmland and houses. We build another house. 1963. Mother and sister live here.'

On the site of the original village the railroad crosses the airfield. To control the crossing they built a small station — and they called it 'Hashim's Village'.

The house is cool because of the stone floor, the mud-brick walls and the high ceiling. The reception-room is furnished with an assortment of beds, a few chairs, a table. The beds suggest that when the family gather, they gather in dozens. High on the walls are photographs of the famous squash-playing Khans. They seem out of place here but the truth is, of course, that they are out of place anywhere else. Hashim summons afternoon tea: an intimidating assembly of fattening temptation. Relatives, friends and neighbours drift in. Composed, casual. Imperceptibly the room fills, like the bottom of some vast hour-glass. There are more embraces, together with the laughter of remembered bonds. Hashim excuses himself, exits left for a tête-à-tête with his mother. Then the house empties — and others around it — as Nawakilla's most famous son sets out once more for a world that can only be guesswork and dreams to those he leaves behind in the mud houses and dirt roads of his native village.

First, though, we bump and clatter along for the obligatory tourist trip to the bustling little settlement alongside Fort Jamrud, at the bottom of the Khyber Pass. This is very much a frontier post. Next stop Afghanistan, through a wild land still governed by tribal laws. The men here are watchfully thoughtful. Many carry well-worn rifles, slung from their shoulders, as carelessly as umbrellas. Battered, incredibly congested single-decker coaches trundle through. They are like mobile ant-hills. Passengers cling to protruberances on the bodywork because the interiors are packed to bursting point. Bodies and rifles dangle from every coach.

'You like an orange?' asks Hashim. 'Oranges very good here.'

A passer-by suddenly throws a blanket down on the roadside, and kneels and prays. A private act in a public place. Something inside him had said, 'Here — and now.' Men sit on their heels, knees up, and look at space and mountains.

A notice reads: 'All travellers are requested to cross the Khyber Pass and reach Torkham before the hours of darkness'. Another insists that foreigners should not stray from the Jamrud-Torkham road unless specially permitted. One might as well hang a banner on the north face of the Eiger telling climbers not to jump. With all those gun-toting hillmen on the loose, merging with the landscape, the urge to explore this beautifully bulky land can easily be suppressed. But would it, one wonders, be any more dangerous than strolling through the seedier suburbs of New York?

The Pathans are Afghan tribesmen of the North-West Frontier Province. Their code of honour imposes three duties: the right of asylum, 'an eye for an eye, a tooth for a tooth', and hospitality to all. You can read about it on a slab erected across the road from Fort Jamrud.

The scattered influences that produced Hashim and his kind are slotting slowly into place, like tiles on a roof. The shape and texture of the whole is still vague, incomplete. But it is no surprise to learn that Hashim and Azam have a house in Peshawar, in readiness for their twilight years. A man from the conservative, closely-knit, tribal society of the Pathans may have many houses. But he can have only one home. When Hashim and Azam go back, they may miss the creature comforts of Denver and London — but they may also be content to discard some of the distorted values of western civilization.

We drive back to Peshawar, bounce down a dirt road past primitive open-fronted shops and stop outside a structure that is Hashim's favourite restaurant. To western eyes, it is hardly prepossessing. One's confidence in Hashim briefly wavers but is restored by the food, which is 'finger-licking' good.

Dusk is upon us. We fly back to Karachi. The pilgrimage is over. Hashim looks a little weary, a little older than he did on this morning's flight. It has been a long day. He will be grateful for his bed. But doubtless some inner battery has been recharged.

And you and I know the man and his people better than we did.

Two

From Prison to Public School

After that relaxing yet stimulating trip up the Indus, let us search for the game's more remote tributaries. There is a legend that squash was born in a debtors' prison. This may loosely be true of its parent game, rackets, from which a primitive form of squash later developed. But to confuse the origins of one game with the origins of the other is like confusing the birth of the father with the birth of the son. The legend is valid only in the sense that it indicates a line of descent. We could trace that line back even farther — to the sources of rackets games as a whole. Then, delving more deeply into history, to the development of the ball as an aid to exercise. Finally, to the misty past of all those games requiring some kind of equipment other than the complement of muscles, ball bearings, and locomotive power with which Nature supplied us. But such research is not strictly relevant to our present purpose.

As a starting point we should go back only, as it were, for one generation — to the age when rackets first became popular. It still survives in a limited form, like those scattered clumps of natural woodland that remind us of the forested, dangerous beauty of ancient Britain. But the prime importance of rackets was as the obscure sire of a famous son.

Before going any further we should briefly compare rackets and squash as we know them today. Both are played within four walls and the scoring systems correspond in essence if not in detail. The rackets court measures 60ft by 30ft (18.3 m by 9.1 m), the squash court 32ft by 21ft (9.75 m by 6.40 m). The floor of a rackets court is usually composed of flagstones — as distinct from the wooden surface prevalent in squash — and the walls are black and rock-hard (those in squash are plastered and mostly white). In rackets, the racket is bigger and stronger than a squash racket and the ball is white and solid, whereas its squash counterpart is soft and either dark green or black. The basic difference in playing conditions is that the rackets ball travels much faster — and squash tends to be more strenuous for the players.

The evidence suggests that rackets developed in and around prisons and taverns (which is hardly surprising when you consider that both were amply provided with walled yards and men with time to spare). The earliest period containing any reference to rackets was the beginning of the nineteenth century. The best-known playground of the infant game was the Fleet prison — which used to stand on the eastern side of Farringdon Street, London — and its environs. Rackets was also mentioned in connection with other prisons and taverns, including one inn at Pentonville and another in the Marylebone Road. We may assume that this incipient form of rackets was a rival or companion 'pub' game to skittles. But the game's strongest early associations were with the infamous Fleet.

The Fleet was built in the time of Richard I, the lion-hearted Crusader, at the end of the twelfth century. It was demolished between 1846 and 1848. The prison took its name from a river — later channelled into a pipe — sometimes known as the Fleet Ditch. This flowed from Hampstead to Holborn and joined the Thames at Blackfriars (Farringdon Street follows a similar course). Fleet Street, which took its name from the same source, was formerly renowned for its bookshops and the taverns that served as rendezvous for the literary set. Nowadays, it is better known as the heart of the British newspaper industry. But there are still faint echoes from the past — among them Seacoal Lane, a reminder that as late as the sixteenth century coal barges used to go up the Fleet as far as Holborn.

The Fleet was an unusually interesting prison. Its long-term residents possibly differed from that judgement, but they are not around to pester me with contradictions. In Tudor and Stuart times the Star Chamber (abolished in 1641) sent it some distinguished guests. Then the Fleet assumed notoriety as a debtors' prison in which the inmates were often subjected to cruel treatment. Surprisingly, as prisons go, it became well known as a place where impatient or imprudent lovers — in many cases, minors — could get married with a minimum of fuss and ceremony. No banns, no licence. The scene outside must have been rather like that at a modern football ground, because the imprisoned clergy had touts in the street. Towards the end of Anne's reign (1702-14) these marriages were performed by the Fleet clergy in local taverns and houses. This was possible because of 'the liberties of the Fleet', a saying that referred to the district — immediately around the prison — where some prisoners were allowed to live as long as they respected the prescribed boundaries and did not go wandering off. The marriage racket also gave rise to the saying 'Fleet Book Evidence'. Reasonably enough, this meant 'no evidence at all — the book of the old Fleet prison was inadmissible as evidence of marriage'. This thriving if bizarre business was ruined by the Marriage Act of 1753, which declared such marriages void. As a hastily improvised matrimonial launching pad, the Fleet then ceded its role to Gretna Green. (Until 1856 it was possible to get legally married at Gretna Green without banns, licence, or priest — though even the most hot-blooded recruits to primitive horizontal exercises had time to cool off on the way to Scotland.)

There was a lot going on, though, in and around the old Fleet — the coal barges, the sailors and prisoners passing the time of day, the instant marriages, and Charles Dickens busily taking notes and capturing the flavour of it all for posterity. The place must have been teeming with vitality, though its rich character may have appealed more to casual visitors than to residents. In the midst of this human ant-hill beside the Thames the citizens eventually discovered a new diversion — hammering away with rudimentary rackets and balls in enclosed or partly enclosed yards, often with cobblestones or compressed gravel underfoot and rough walls to hit against (while prisoners on the loose roamed about and maybe barracked this player or that). Children got into the act whenever they could lay their hands on some equipment and find a vacant space where they could enjoy this new game that the grown-ups were playing. The balls used were presumably hard because the recreational possibilities of rubber had yet to be fully explored.

That was the infancy of rackets — a game for the kind of people who lived and loved, worked and played, in the vicinity of a prison (though, as I say, the game was also being enjoyed in tavern yards in other areas of what is now central London). By the time the Fleet was reduced to rubble, it had served its purpose for posterity by facilitating one indoor sport, for the newly wed, and developing another, for anyone.

The next landmark we approach — and remember, we are still travelling along the rackets road, with squash out of sight around the corner — could hardly offer a more startling contrast with the society we have just left. Of all places it was one of the most famous public schools, Harrow, populated by a privileged class who had probably never even heard of the Fleet (and would not admit it if they had). We may note, though, that Harrow was founded seventy years before the Star Chamber ceased sending selected representatives of the gentry to the Fleet. It is possible that a few Harrovians were among them. But such idle speculation must end there, because rackets travelled from the prison to the school, and not in the opposite direction.

How on earth, we may wonder, did the game leap across thirteen miles or so and a social chasm of similar proportions?

History is often inconsiderate, neglecting to leave footprints in the snow. Where such blanks occur we can only test the wind, check the direction of the sun, and calculate the chances. Let us do that. There can be no harm in dallying for a while with the possibilities, and inventing a tale that will unravel the mystery of progress. We are seeking the agent of transition — the man who took rackets from the Fleet district to Harrow. Sherlock Holmes would identify him instantly as a young and energetic chap who taught English at Harrow, supervised the young at play, and liked to let his hair down occasionally (an alternative suspect, of course, would be the close friend of such a man). Let us not suggest that Harrow employed a master formerly familiar with the recreational facilities of a debtors' prison. But it is reasonable, is it not, to picture a man who taught his charges their mother tongue and considered it in the line of duty to pop up to Fleet Street from time to time, plunge into carefully chosen taverns, and find out what the literary giants were discussing in the way of semantics and syntax?

With all that vigour and initiative he would probably be one of the younger members of the staff and, on the quiet, a bit of a 'goer'. Not the kind to turn up his nose at the chance of a few jars in the taverns of London's more colourful nooks and crannies.

Just the man, too, who would sociably join in — with due gentility — any games that happened to be in progress. The city was not far away, after all. He could easily nip up to London on his day off, wash the academic dust out of his mind with a change of scene, and return to his labours all the better for it. Just a question of recharging the batteries.

You see how easy it is to fill in the blanks which history so carelessly left lying about. Here was a man who worked 'on the hill' and knew where to have some fun whenever he was let off the leash. He tried this new game and enjoyed it. He reasoned that if it could turn men into boys it might also do the reverse. So he introduced it at Harrow. And thus was rackets rescued from the oblivion that was already threatening the Fleet. We may even hazard a broad guess at the period — some time between 1815 and 1820, according to the references to rackets that began to seep into Harrovian memoirs. But let me reassure any reader who recognizes our fictitious hero as a respected and long-dead relative. I was just having some fun, deducing in a fanciful way how rackets may have jumped the vast gap between the Fleet and Harrow.

It landed on both feet. This would doubtless have appalled John Lyon, a local landowner who founded the school in 1571. He made special provision for the encouragement of archery and this sport became particularly prevalent at Harrow, though not peculiar to it. The bow and arrow used to be the chief weapon of war. Practice and competition were officially encouraged throughout England — to such an extent that there was an attempt to ban rival sports that might have affected the archers' devotion to duty. A later and more enduring academic prejudice was that in favour of team games, which were reasonably considered to be good for the soul and had the additional advantage of providing more exercise for more pupils in a limited area and a limited time. This prejudice survives, but it has been weakened since Britain ceded the Empire. If the nation has no one to lean on and must stand on its own feet, it is obviously no bad idea if the young are brought up to do the same thing.

The rackets bug that bit Harrow was also taking tentative nips at Elstree, Rugby, and Winchester. At Harrow the game was played in makeshift courts reminiscent of those around the Fleet. All that was necessary was an asphalted base and two walls meeting at right angles, with a line chalked across one of them. The yards outside the Harrow boarding-houses were ideal for the purpose. A favoured spot was 'The Corner', where one of the walls separated the school yard from the precincts of the church and thus served as a tolerably effective barrier between perspiration and prayer.

One day (we know not when, but we can guess why) it was deemed expedient to use a softer, slower, less waywardly lively ball. Whoever thought of that — possibly some curmudgeon objecting to broken windows, or to cranial collisions with whizzing missiles — was responsible for the birth of squash. There was not a great deal of space available for the free flight of a hard ball given a real whack, especially if the whacker's aim strayed from the straight and narrow path of virtue. We may assume that, as the denizens of Harrow have never been particularly obtuse, the advantages of a softer ball were appreciated with reasonable rapidity. The prototype of squash was probably taking shape at Harrow during the 1830s, perhaps even the 1820s. Certainly the game originally played in the yards soon had two names: 'harder' and 'squash', according to the type of ball used. It was then discovered that the soft, rubber ball could be 'squashed' even more easily if punctured. We may imagine how this discovery occurred. Perhaps some bright lad with a bent for science tried a calculated experiment. A more tempting theory is that the two boys playing squash damaged the ball — the only one they had — on some projecting spur in the masonry. But the damaged ball did more than survive. It thrived. Our boys found out that, joy of joys, the ball was even more amenable to discipline when punctured than it was when intact.

You will gather that, once more, speculation has built freely on a modest foundation of fact. But the 'holer' ball — which achieved lasting popularity at Harrow and later at the Bath Club, the game's first spiritual home in London — may indeed have happened by accident. Many of life's most vivid lines are unscripted.

The intrinsic merits of squash, as a game in its own right, were not to be fully revealed for almost a hundred years. They must have been suspected, because the softer, slower ball obviously permitted a greater variety of shots and changes of pace than the hard one. But in terms of recognition squash marked time for about fifty years, in the shadow of rackets. Squash was 'baby' rackets. A training exercise. A poor relation. A substitute. It was easier to play, because of the slower ball, and provided a useful grounding in ball sense, court sense and the manipulation of a racket. We can picture the scene — boys standing about, twitching with suppressed energy as the young do, while waiting their turn for a rackets court. They were full of beans and squash was as good a means as any of getting the lid off. Almost every house at Harrow had its miniature rackets court on which boys sharpened up at squash with the slower ball. By the end of the nineteenth century squash had established a separate identity from rackets and was developing its own technique and tactics, to such an extent that rackets players were discouraged from playing it because it was thought to be bad for their game — a complete reversal in attitude. But in its early years (that hazy period around the middle of the century) the supposed advantages of squash as a preparation for rackets had much to do with its acceptance as part of Harrow's sporting scene.

There was no standard pattern to the primitive open-air courts, except for the fact that none had four walls. Each court had its own peculiarities, challenging the eyes, the reactions and the wrist. We read of one that had a water pipe embedded in the front wall, a ledge halfway up the back wall, protectively wired windows, and a doorway with, on each side of it, a recessed bootscraper. Players served from the right, because there was no wall on that side. It was all part of the fun. Such courts were still in use in the twentieth century. Rugby fives courts turned out to be more popular with squash players.

An important year was 1850, when two roofless rackets courts — one of them had but a single side wall — were constructed at Harrow. The importance of this development was that it clearly separated 'harder', which now had a home of its own, from squash. It was not until 1864 that squash was granted a similar degree of recognition. As part of a general conversion scheme, a covered rackets court was built and four squash courts were installed on the site of one of the 1850 rackets courts. In trying to isolate a year in which the previously embryonic game called squash finally emerged from the womb, we must accept 1864 as odds-on favourite. Later on, the other old rackets court was also converted to squash and in 1897 the same thing happened to the three oldest fives courts. In 1908 the four original squash courts, which were considered to be too small, were remodelled into three larger courts. But long before that the game had spread beyond Harrow and was sinking its roots into society as a whole. From 1864 onwards, the ball was in play and everything began to happen.

Simon Harcourt, who had a great deal to do with the coherent administrative structure British squash acquired in the 1930s, recollects that his father played squash at Harrow in 1850 and later, in 1883, built a court as part of his home on the banks of the Cherwell at Oxford. It was longer than the modern court and had a much higher play-line on the front wall, but was about the same width. After twenty years the house was converted into a women's college, the squash court into bedrooms — the first recorded case of anyone sleeping on court!

Harcourt tells us that on his father's court they played with a black ball, a red one (pink achieved fleeting popularity elsewhere), and also with the renowned 'holer' ball. Those who believe the game should properly be called squash rackets should perhaps think again, because Harcourt reminds us that 'we always called it just squash'.

As the years went by, more and more courts were built in private houses, clubs, schools, universities, business premises and Services' establishments. In many cases the floors and side walls were constructed with planks. Until the 1930s, courts and balls were dazzling in their diversity, though the balls had a common quality in that they were faster than today's. The era of covered courts was ushered in by the example of rackets. The old Prince's Club, opened in 1853, set the trend. For thirty years all the big matches were played there, until the place was pulled down. And Harrow, as we have noticed, built a covered rackets court in 1864. The heyday of the old Prince's Club, by the way, coincided with the dying years of rackets as a game for the *hoi polloi* and the taverns. One by one the old courts fell into disuse. Rackets lost its popular following — and became a game for the well-educated, prosperous minority. They were the only people who could afford it. Rackets was now formalized and sophisticated. The cost of its vast courts and its playing equipment — always under horrid stress because of the nature of the game — was hard on the pocket.

Was there an alternative? There was, indeed. Already, squash was taking over as a more practicable court game for the reasonably well-to-do (it was almost 150 years behind rackets in its appeal to the masses). The squash court was smaller, and easier and quicker to construct. It fitted more conveniently into premises primarily used for other purposes. The soft ball was less easily damaged and less prone to do nasty things to the rackets. In short, squash was the better investment. In any case, reasoned the reluctantly converted rackets players, squash was an amusing substitute and good training (that argument was on its last legs by now, but could still kick up its heels when provoked). To this day, there are rackets players who turn up their noses at any reference to the game's one-time poor relation, especially at those schools where rackets survives. Rackets, they will tell you, is a better game because it is more difficult to play. What arrant casuistry! Because one thing is more difficult to do than another, it is not necessarily better. One might as well argue that the value of music or painting should be measured by the technical virtuosity of the composer or the artist, or that grass-court tennis is better than clay-court tennis because it is faster. Speed, as distinct from a needful momentum, is the enemy of the graces — and no criterion of merit.

We could debate the issue for hours. Advocates of the two games will doubtless continue to do so, whenever they have the time to trot out all the pros and cons under the lubricating influence of a glass or two of the right stuff. But for the moment we will let a barrister sum up for us, because he has the necessary judicial approach — and the weighty additional qualification of having represented Oxford University at both sports (plus three others). I speak of Jonathan Leslie, who in 1975 won Britain's inaugural national amateur squash championship — as distinct from the better known international event. Rackets, he said, was so fast that it demanded a better eye and higher level of ball skill. Superficially, it was more attractive and exciting. But it was mostly played at one pace. Squash was easier for more people to play — and had depths and complexities that were not immediately obvious.

We will leave it there, except for pointing out that as squash is the easier game to play — up to a reasonable level of competence, anyway — and is also less expensive, it is hardly to be wondered at that it has become one of the most widely and regularly played games in Britain, whereas rackets remains a minority sport.

This pattern has been reproduced overseas. Attempts were

made to export rackets to the United States, Canada, and the land since partitioned into India and Pakistan. But there turned out to be a much bigger market for squash. In North America, though, the consequences have in one sense been unfortunate. In 1907 the first meeting of the Tennis and Rackets Association appointed a sub-committee to look after squash, which thus remained under the inhibiting influence of men with other priorities. It was not until 1911 that this committee attempted to introduce standard court dimensions — and not until 1923 that standardization was finally imposed. But the United States association was formed in 1907 and the Canadian in 1911. They swiftly approved rules governing court dimensions and other conditions of play — rules from which those later adopted in Britain differed. The American court was narrower, the play-line on the front wall lower, the ball harder and faster. In those few years before the First World War the brothers born were not twins — and squash was stuck with the clash of personalities. In many ways the North American version was, and remains, closer to the original of both — rackets. It therefore serves as a sort of missing link, a reminder of the days (and the ways) in which the British and international game drew away from rackets. Though it may seem a little unkind to say so, the game played in North America is — for all its virtues — a sporting example of arrested development.

The chief export agents for squash were the Services. Late in the nineteenth century and early in the twentieth, Britain's military commitments demanded garrisons in India (particularly the North-West Frontier Province) and much of Africa. The Services followed the merchants and squash courts followed the flag. Civil administrators, traders and settlers expanded the ranks of those energetic Britons prepared to leap about and raise a sweat at the drop of a racket. Thus were sown the seeds from which sprang — among other things — the great traditions of Egyptian and Pakistani squash (though in neither country has this essentially alien game developed beyond a very small segment of the native community).

The construction of even a limited number of courts presented difficulties. In the 1930s, for example, strange stories seeped out of East Africa. More than one administrator had the cunning idea of requesting official funds for 'a new court'. They got the money because it was assumed — as intended — that the court in question was to be a court of law. This occurred, for example, at a place called Handeni, where the court was blistered onto an old German fort and externally disguised to look like the rest of the place. Then there was the Sumbawanga wangle. A new court was finished except for the plastering. No one was available to do the job. But it was known that, roaming about the district somewhere, was a criminal who was also a mason. So the search for this suddenly useful character was intensified. They caught him, convicted him — and put him to work. Thus, another squash court was added to the list. The lengths some people will go to in order to organize some decent exercise! Some of these courts, mind you, were bizarre structures, for all the ingenuity that went into their making. 'Stubbs' Stubbings recalls one very oddly shaped court — again, part of an old fort — on which, when provincial commissioner at Tabora, he played Colonel Roy Stockwell. The latter's driver, a local lad, was posted atop the front wall to 'spot' for them whenever a miscued shot hurtled towards the bush (lost balls were difficult to replace). At about the same time, a boy called Hashim Khan was performing a similar chore for British officers at Peshawar.

But we dig too deeply into the twentieth century. The purpose of this chapter was to explain how squash grew out of rackets, how it was conceived in the vicinity of a prison and born at a public school. Now it is time to move on, from the game's infancy to the years of its adolescence and maturity.

Three

The Ancient Britons

The story of twentieth-century squash is essentially the story of the people who played it. During the years preceding and succeeding the First World War, while the 'qu' in racquets was quietly being replaced by a 'k', a few of these began to assume shape and substance. They emerged from the mists of history like those Everest mountaineers who were privileged to reach the peak — after others had explored the terrain, selected the most prudent routes, and defied gravity and fatigue by lugging all the gear to handy nooks and hollows in the topography of the Himalayas.

For a time, as we have noticed, the game was better organized in North America — and perhaps in South Africa, where the national association formed in 1910 was the first anywhere to adopt 'British' rules, thus avoiding the trap that ensnared the Americans — than it was in Britain, its birthplace and spiritual home. But Britain was to set the standards, on and off court, from which the international game as we now know it, gradually developed. Lest there be confusion about terms, let us substitute 'softball' for 'international'. The American language is not a library from which one should borrow freely, but it does contain some etymological flowers, proudly prominent in a linguistic vegetable patch. What could be more vividly and crisply explicit than the use of 'hardball' and 'softball' to distinguish their kind of squash from that played everywhere else? Score one for Uncle Sam.

We have noted how rackets began as a game for everyone but, after seventy or eighty years, lost its popular basis and became a game for a privileged minority. By contrast squash began as a game for what we may loosely call the upper middle class and took more than a hundred years to spread to the masses. It moved into the twentieth century primarily as an exercise for those who went to public schools and universities and provided the Services with 'officer material'. Most had played rackets and many still did. It was this segment of society, trained for leadership, who took the initiative by assembling the scattered pieces of the jigsaw called squash, which had been lying around for far too long. They put the pieces into place and made the picture clear. First they approved standards for courts, rackets, and balls. Then they established a code of rules. The years were 1923 and 1924 respectively. How sad it was that during the intervening winter, when the first British touring team invaded North America, the two codes had already taken decisive steps in different directions.

That team consisted of 'Ginger' Basset, Theo Drysdale, Dugald Macpherson, Timmy Robarts and Sam Toyne: the first men to represent Britain. Robarts did not have much to do with the administrative side of the game. The others did. A key figure was Jimmy Tomkinson (later Palmer-Tomkinson). Simon Harcourt shouldered much of the inevitable burden of paper work. Those were the men primarily responsible for organizing softball squash, though many others added a little mental muscle in the right places. Four of the seven were members of the Bath Club, which became the hub of the game — fulfilling, if you like to think of it that way, a role similar to that of Lord's in cricket or Twickenham in rugby.

They used the 'holer' ball at the Bath Club. It had one hole in it and was slightly bigger and much softer than today's (it could be squeezed flat with the fingers). Palmer-Tomkinson was a loyal advocate of the slower ball because he liked to see stroke players doing their stuff. The ball was a controversial issue when Macpherson became technical adviser to the Squash Rackets Association. 'The Bath Club had the 'holer' ball,' he recalls, 'and the RAC had a shiny one, harder and faster than today's and a little smaller. Like a rackets ball. We had to evolve a common ball — and it was a slow one. We quietly make it slower. The average player was against the slower ball and hated it. They played for fun and wanted longer rallies. They said it was being done for the good players — and this was quite true.' But without that slower ball, squash would not be so richly embellished with drops, angles, and lobs. The faster ball was technically restrictive and unduly difficult to kill. The legislators were right.

Rackets were no problem. Their design has not varied much.

A court built at the Bath Club at the beginning of the century was the dimensional model on which the standard court was based. Kenneth Gandar Dower, who won the British amateur championship eight years after first contesting the final, was among those who thought standardization had been imposed at too early a stage in the game's development. A little extra length and width would, he considered, have spared us many tediously long rallies. 'I also wanted the court wider, because of the let problem,' says Macpherson. 'I have always taken the view that squash is a game for exercise and fun and was never good for serious competitive play, because the court is too small. For the first ten years we all played for fun. I played four big matches with Amr and can remember only one let — entirely my fault — in our last match. In those days we used to hit the man. I hit Timmy Robarts three or four times, and he gave it up. Nowadays they don't seem to do that. They claim a let. Perhaps they're too gentlemanly now. I gave up refereeing in the amateur championships because of the lets. The last one I did was Wilson and Amin in the final. There were about ninety lets. Whoever got in front never moved out of the way. In our day, we hit him. We were all rackets players. The only way to solve a let is to put them in a rackets court — these chaps who get in the way would be killed in no time.'

Strong stuff. Let me hasten to remind those who would emulate the Macpherson breed that in squash, unlike boxing, there is no need to hit a man hard in order to make one's point — if, indeed, one needs to hit him with the ball at all.

One final point before we transfer our attention from the court to the players. In the late 1930s there was an attempt to lower the height of the tin by two inches. This proposal was strongly resisted and experiments suggested that a lower tin would merely make the players work harder without improving the game in any way. An effort to introduce a faster ball was equally abortive, for similar reasons.

Palmer-Tomkinson (not to be confused with another all-round sportsman, Sir Geoffrey Tomkinson) was perhaps the first genuine squash player. He moved ahead faster than others who, for years, were basically adapting their rackets craft to squash. Had there been an amateur championship in the first two decades of the century, he would have dominated it — certainly from 1907 onwards. He was as outstanding among the amateurs as Charles Read was among the professionals. According to those who were around at the time, Palmer-Tomkinson was a master of court craft who made his opponents do the running. He had a dagger-thrust of a volley and, like Read, used the reverse angle* (which was an unusual shot in those days and, even now, retains rather flamboyant overtones). Disconcerted by an unfamiliar court (35 ft by 22ft with a 2ft 3 in board) and an extraordinarily fast ball, Palmer-Tomkinson was beaten by Tommy Jameson at Lord's in the final of the first British amateur championship in 1923. Two months later, playing conditions were standardized. Palmer-Tomkinson was runner-up three times in four seasons. He was forty-seven years old — having been at or near the top of the amateur game for almost a quarter of a century — when he finally won the title in 1926. By that time the championship was being played at his own recreational retreat, the Bath Club.

That 1926-7 season had a wider importance. It was the first in which British squash was contested under the present softball scoring system. North America persevered with the old system and still does.

Whether a player should need fifteen points to win a game, as in hardball, or nine points, as in softball, is beside the point. The boiling controversy, which simmers on because it has never been resolved, concerns the allocation of points rather than their total. In softball squash only the server can win a point. Hand-out can win no more than the right to serve. In hardball squash, a point is awarded to whoever wins a rally, whether he is serving or not. Let us summarize the arguments. Uncle Sam's first. The softball system arose from rackets, in which the server has a definite advantage — an advantage denied him by the advent of the slower ball used in squash. In winning the right to serve, a player therefore wins nothing. A player who wins a rally deserves a tangible reward — a point. So the hardball system is more equitable and produces a more genuine reflection of the run of play. The system also suits the American temperament in that it guarantees a continual progression in the score and restricts a match to a more predictable period of time. The main argument for softball scoring is that it encourages greater tactical contrasts and more attrac-

*A reverse angle is a forehand played onto the backhand side wall, or vice versa.

tive squash. The server can take chances in going for his shots without risk of losing a point, whereas hand-out must be discreet to the point of caution. Consequently there is a clear distinction between aggression and containment, a deeper development of tactics and technique, and an instant test of mental agility whenever the service changes hands. Advocates of softball scoring also assert that the hardball system induces a mostly one-pace game, with each player trying to out-hit his opponent without taking too many chances. It is finally and less convincingly argued that the real test is a player's ability to win two successive rallies, whenever the need arises, rather than one.

The debate is inconclusive. All I can add, from personal experience of both games, is that the difference in scoring systems is trivial by comparison with the difference in balls. While gathering the material for this book I played at Manhattan Squash Club with John Beddington, who must be the only Etonian heavily engaged in the promotion of squash and tennis. We played one game with the hard, fast American ball. Then we looked at each other with an instant understanding that needed no words — and, as one, we left the court in search of a slower ball. There is more to music than relentlessly rapid rhythms. What about melody, harmony, counterpoint, and the rest?

But let us get back to Palmer-Tomkinson. Besides being a squash player, he was a gentleman and a sportsman in the old-fashioned sense, taking part in hunting, shooting, and fishing — and of course, lawn tennis and golf. His family later became the biggest names, in both senses, in British ski-ing. After the First World War, as we have noted, he devoted a lot of time to the task of getting squash properly organized, so that players everywhere (North America excepted) would be playing the same sort of game in the same sort of conditions under the same rules. His initiative led to the formation, in 1928, of the Squash Rackets Association — which became, *de facto*, the governing body of the softball game. Six years earlier he had started the Bath Club Cup competition, between the West End social clubs, which gave British squash its competitive impetus. Not that everything the Bath Club did was a success. In 1936 they decided to restrict Cup matches to the best of three games, because the best of five was considered too strenuous for the average businessman. That controversial experiment was eventually discarded. Never mind.

Men who never make mistakes never make anything. In squash, everything was happening at the Bath Club: and Palmer-Tomkinson was mixed up in all of it.

Among the rules he bequeathed to us was that which awards a point to the striker when the ball, travelling directly to the front wall, impinges on the anatomy or accoutrements of his opponent. You and I, of course, are well aware that nowadays (as distinct from Dugald Macpherson's) it is considered bad manners to hit our opponents with anything. But the rule is there, just to deter the ponderous and the bloody-minded from hanging about in the line of fire.

There is a good story about the large and powerful Michael Oddy (whose brother Roland became a professional at Manhattan) and a free-swinging Egyptian, Tewfik Shafik. Built like a prop forward, Shafik was a gentle and amiable man off court but far less congenial company on it. The story goes that in the dressing-room of the Royal Automobile Club, before their 1962 semi-final in the British amateur championship, Oddy warned Shafik that if he brandished his racket under the Scot's nose just once, then Oddy would drill the ball up the Egyptian's backside so hard that an operation would be necessary in order to get it out. But truth, though often stranger than fiction, is seldom as outrageous. Oddy denies the warning — but confesses that he did the deed. On match point, too. Oddy was 9-3, 9-7, and 8-6 up and in hand. 'There was a long rally. Shafik hit the second last shot wildly round the back wall and I hit a crisp backhand straight up his backside. There was no other shot I could play in the situation. I walked up to him, shook hands, and walked off. And he looked up at the referee, appealing.' Having seen plenty of Oddy's 'crisp' backhands I can imagine how Shafik felt.

These were hard men. Squash has never been a game for softies.

But we digress. A few words about Palmer-Tomkinson's fellow pioneers. 'Ginger' Basset was fit, determined, and a fighter. But he was fifty, conceding thirty years, when he played Ian Akers-Douglas in a semi-final of the 1929 British amateur championship. Akers-Douglas led 9-5, 9-1, 8-5. Match point. But he was beaten. Indeed, he scored only seven more points. In view of the immense difference in ages, that has to be one of the most astonishing and admirable feats in the history of competitive squash. Kipling had the words for Basset: 'E's all 'ot sand an' ginger when alive, an' 'e's generally shammin' when 'e's dead.' But Victor Cazalet beat him in the final.

Timmy Robarts won the Canadian and United States amateur championships during the 1923-4 tour. He hit hard and accurately down the side walls and his squash suited the hardball game. The captain of that British team was Sam Toyne, a wristy player with a good touch on angles and drops. He was a player and administrator for more than forty years and found time to excel at cricket and hockey, too. Headmaster at St Peter's, York, he transformed the school into a renowned squash nursery. His best known protégé was Norman Yardley, who was gifted at all games. Yardley had quick eyes, good footwork, and a supple wrist. At the age of twenty he played beautifully to take nine points from Abdel Fattah Amr in a semi-final of the 1935 British amateur championship, and in those days he seemed as likely as anyone to succeed Amr as champion. But he chose to concentrate on cricket and became England's captain in 1947. Not the least of Toyne's many services to the game was his initiative in arranging the first public schools' match: St Peter's against his own Alma Mater, Haileybury, at Queen's Club in 1925.

Macpherson we will discuss in a moment. He was a special case among that small group of player-administrators whose names should be remembered with respect. Posterity owes them something (though posterity seldom pays its debts).

It may be a little invidious to select a few more names from the host of talented amateurs who were hammering squash balls about between the wars. But we will do it anyway. Briefly, we have already met Tommy Jameson, who had an attractive style and won the first two British amateur championships. He also played cricket for Hampshire and was Army rackets champion. Then there was Cazalet, who contested six successive finals (winning four) from 1926 to 1930 and thus set a record no one has surpassed. Amr and Ibrahim Amin, both Egyptians, played in six amateur championship finals, but these were not consecutive. One contemporary described Cazalet as 'a rough bruiser of a player, not an easy man to play'. Superficially, his resources were limited. His footwork and stroke-play did not inspire lyrical praise. But he was fit, he was a dogged and tireless retriever, and — as his record testifies — he was a great match-player with an iron will that refused to accept the possibility of defeat. He became a Member of Parliament in 1924, exercised his lungs for a year or so, and then won the amateur championship for the first time. He would make a speech in the House and then charge about a squash court like a lion released from a cage. Obviously a man who liked scoring points.

Kenneth Gandar Dower, another retriever with great powers of endurance, was one of the few amateurs who could hustle the great Abdel Fattah Amr. He was strong and adventurously unorthodox, with a penchant for half-volleys. Sport, in the broadest sense, was his thing — and he was good at it. Everything from billiards to big-game hunting. The quick-witted and tenacious Edward Snell was a fine competitor who used the heart-breaking drop and lob routine. Indeed, he developed the lob as far as it would go towards acquiring the status of an art form. He played three finals against Amr but never scored more than four points a game (which was about par for the course when any leading amateur played Amr). Snell would have been favourite for the 1934 championship, which Amr missed. But Snell was missing too — captaining the Jesters on a North American tour. The Amr-less amateur championship was won by Cyril Hamilton. Like Snell and most of our other heroes, he was an all-round sportsman. In those days, a man could reach the top in a game without the exclusive dedication that has since become necessary. Three other players we should notice were Peter Reiss, who played in three semi-finals, John Gillies, a delicate stroke-player, and John Stokes, who had a more limited range (no fancy stuff) but used his shots admirably.

But the outstanding stylist among the early British amateurs was Dugald Macpherson. Brian Phillips, who reached the open and amateur championship finals in 1948-9 (only Amr had previously contested both in the same season), considers that other than such professionals as Charles Read and Don Butcher, Macpherson was the best 'technician' until Amr came along. 'He was a beautiful squash player. A greyhound. With lovely touch shots.' Macpherson reached the amateur championship final three times and won it twice. Some sources suggest that he might have achieved even more but for a slight deficiency in terms of strength and ruthless efficiency. His volleying, they added, might have been more decisive. But it seems to have been agreed by the pundits of the day that he moved gracefully (the cliché 'poetry of motion' popped up in a reference to his footwork) and was an artistic stroke-player with superb ball control and an enviable variety of attacking shots. He was clever, too. His placing of the ball was exemplary. Even those critics who sought weaknesses in his game did it without conviction. What a joy Macpherson must have been. He was the only player to beat Amr after the Egyptian had leapt to supremacy, and he maintained a remarkable standard for almost a quarter of a century until he retired in 1948 at the age of forty-six. He had made a come-back in order to help Queen's Club in the Bath Club Cup competition. Gerald Pawle, an English international who became a distinguished writer on the game, did some homework on Macpherson and came up with the fact that he represented Queen's Club in a hundred matches between 1923 and 1948, and that his last appearance was in the first division challenge match. He played beautifully and Queen's won the championship. With that, Macpherson retired. In its consistently high quality, his career has few parallels.

According to Macpherson himself, it all began with a rather bizarre coincidence. When the 1923 British touring team arrived in America, one of the players was promptly detained to help the police with their enquiries, as the agents of the law so delicately tend to put it. Something to do with money, as Macpherson recalls. Anyway, the chap concerned had to go to the other kind of court and there was a vacancy in the team. Macpherson was handy because he happened to be spending a year at Harvard. He filled the gap, improved throughout the tour, and attained a level that — once he was back home — enabled him to beat almost everyone in sight.

Macpherson was a Harrovian, bursting into full flower about a hundred years after the game he adorned had thrust its first shoots up into the sunlight at his old school.

All the players we have discussed so far were amateurs. Their expertise on court was matched by their competence in giving the game an administrative coherence it had formerly lacked. But the first pre-eminent players, men of such character that they also had much to do with popularizing the game, were three London-based professional coaches. Inevitably known as 'the three musketeers', these were Charles Read, Charles Arnold, and 'Oke' Johnson (who presumably preferred to be reticent about such an assortment of christian names as Ariel William Bedwin). They were a class ahead of their contemporary professionals, and Read, the best of them, had reasonable claims to be regarded as the first great player. He was born too soon (1889), too early in the game's development, to merit genuine comparison with such successors as Amr, Mahmoud el Karim, and Hashim Khan. But the degree and duration of his suremacy stamp him as the first member of the game's élite. Every generation has its vanities and in those days there seemed little prospect that anyone else would play as well as Read for so long. At thirteen he had his first job, helping out at Queen's Club, London. But he spent three years coaching at Harrow — drinking, as it were, from the fountain of the game's youth — before returning to Queen's Club at the age of seventeen. He was there for thirty-five years and kept reminding visitors how effective the drop shot could be on a court that was a yard longer than most. Read was professional champion at lawn tennis (1921-7), rackets (1925-32), and squash (1920-30). Obviously this genial chap was never at a loss when it came to doing something constructive with a moving ball.

Even Read, though, could not quite cope with Johnson on the latter's own courts at the Royal Automobile Club, where Johnson, who was appointed RAC professional at the age of seventeen, could make the ball do everything except talk. Johnson was later to achieve enduring renown as the man who taught Amr how to play — which is to say that Johnson's guidance helped Amr to attain areas of excellence even Read had not explored. To RAC members Johnson was a friend and philosopher, as well as a coach. Even from the gallery he could kindle fresh fires of endeavour with his cry of '8-all . . . anybody's game'. Arnold, an inventive joker prone to play shots behind his back, was professional at the Bath Club (Palmer-Tomkinson country) from 1912 to 1937.

These were fine players and men of strong and pleasing personalities. The best of their immediate successors were Don Butcher (Conservative Club) — who deprived Read, sixteen years his senior, of the British open and professional championships — and Jim Dear (Prince's), who was born five years after Butcher, was also stronger and faster, and took over from him. These were the men — Butcher twice, Dear three times — who tackled Amr in the series of challenge matches from which the Egyptian amateur emerged with five consecutive British open championships in the 1930s. Six if we count 1933, when nobody bothered to challenge him. Butcher was champion until Amr beat him. Dear became champion when Amr retired.

Butcher, who emigrated to Melbourne in 1957, was a model for aspiring players — a facile and attractive stroke-player with a variety of shots and a smooth rhythm in playing them accurately. Words like 'grace' and 'beauty' came to mind when watching him in action. He had a delicate touch and a delayed, accurate drop shot. In many ways he was the Macpherson of the professional game. As a match-player, though, he had weaknesses. Like many lovely things, his squash tended to be fragile. He did not take the initiative often enough and his stamina was suspect. 'He was a player of shots,' says Macpherson. 'He had an incredible drop from any position in the court. But he wasn't very strong and would not compete with today's players. Amr was much fitter.'

Dear, born a month after Amr in 1910, was considered by many critics to be his equal in anticipation, speed, and volleying. In the first of their 1935 challenge matches, Dear volleyed with an irresistible splendour to lead 3-9, 9-6, 10-8. His touch often seemed magical, especially on half-volleys and drops. He repeatedly pushed Amr very close to the limit, without quite inspiring confidence that he could win the three games necessary to beat him — and for two seasons after the war (in which he served in the RAF) Dear was still good enough to take Karim to five games in the open championship. That is a measure of the relative ability of all three players.

These British professionals of the 1920s and 1930s played thrilling, arduously fast squash that contained a wealth of shots. They knew about training and practice. They knew about working their opponents this way and that. They also knew the value of deception. They knew how much it hurt to keep digging the ball out of the corners. But even these formidable players were, in a sense, merely the supporting cast. It is now time to meet the star of the show, the man whose name keeps coming back like a line from a well-remembered song.

Four

A Sudden Breeze from Egypt

The story of Abdel Fattah Amr reads more like fancy than fact. It has the qualities from which legends are born. This Egyptian aristocrat and sportsman was the friend of a king. He came into squash from nowhere, like a sudden breeze on a still day, and dominated it for six seasons. Then he retired, when still at his peak, and vanished into diplomacy and, ultimately, into the seclusion of rural England. Even his name acquired a vague air of mystery. We find him listed on the roll of champions as 'F.D.Amr Bey'. The 'Bey' and the grander 'Pasha' that replaced it were titles of rank. But where on earth did the 'D' come from? The obvious way to find out was to ask him. Far less obvious was a means of tracking down the hidden diplomat. But we pick up a few wrinkles (both kinds) in the newspaper trade. Amr told me that his nephew had the same name, so they had popped in a 'D' — David became the accepted extension — as a distinguishing mark. A brand image, you might say.

Amr's diplomatic career, first as an attaché and then as ambassador to the United Kingdom, coincided with the reign of King Farouk and his retirement in 1952 coincided with the military coup and the advent of General Neguib. There was a wind of change in the political climate of Egypt. Well, not exactly a wind. More like a Force 10 gale, which has consequences listed on the Beaufort scale as 'trees uprooted and considerable structural damage'. It cannot be wondered at that Amr — like many before him in similar situations, and many since — thought it prudent to recede from even the most modest prominence. So he buried himself deeply in the land that had become his home, and presumably cocked an ear for anything that went bump in the night. There were rumours of politically-inspired anxiety, increasing weight, a dash of hypochondria. Rumours. And silence.

The dramatic conventions would be neatly observed if I left the story there and allowed your imagination free play in devising an epilogue. But honesty impels me to add that Amr is fit enough to gad about a bit in his old age and that, a quarter of a century after the coup, the embassy of the new Egypt say that they 'have nothing against him, in any field, and regard him as a very fine sportsman and a pioneer of squash in Egypt'. In short, the old lion could roar again in the sunshine if he chose to.

But let us change the metaphor and go back a little. While our three musketeers — Read, Arnold, and Johnson — were laying about them, d'Artagnan was preparing to join the ranks — sharpening his sword and doing his exercises, so to speak. In Egypt, Amr was quite a horseman. He won a few races. He also played polo. But it was as a tennis player, attached to the Egyptian Davis Cup team, that he arrived in England in 1928. 'The first time I saw a game of squash was at the RAC. I was introduced to the club's professional, "Oke" Johnson, who took me in hand.' But Dan Maskell, who was then under contract to play lawn tennis, rackets, and squash at Queen's Club (shortly afterwards he moved to Wimbledon), recalls an introductory chapter to the story. The setting was Queen's Club.

'I was introduced to Amr, who wanted to play tennis but couldn't get a court. I suggested that if he wanted some exercise, why not play squash? He said he hadn't played before. I hit a ball up on the front wall and he hit it back. Then I played the ball to the front wall and the side wall and onto the floor. He hit it straight back. So I played it from the front wall to the side wall, the back wall, and the floor. He hit it straight back. By the end of the session I was hitting the most difficult shot — front wall, side wall, floor, back wall. But he still took it. Before we finished we were playing games. I couldn't believe he hadn't played before. I thought it was impossible, unless he was pulling my leg. I played two or three weeks with him. Then I told him he was so good at the game he should be playing with Charles Read, who was head squash "pro" and professional champion — which he did, a few times. Then he went to "Oke" Johnson.'

Predictably, Johnson found him an apt pupil. At first Amr's

match temperament was somewhat brittle. His opponents were mostly bigger and more assertive men. But Johnson taught him to suffer and fight through it — then suffer again, and fight through it again. And Amr became the perfect competitor. By the 1931-2 season he was ready to seize power. But his opponent in the final of the British amateur championship was Dugald Macpherson, who had already beaten him twice — at Roehampton and Queen's Club. Macpherson modestly points out that the first of these matches occurred when Amr was still new to squash ('it wasn't a proper match'), the second when he was still some way from the top. But the final of the amateur championship was obviously a severe test for Amr.

'I'd played Victor Cazalet for an hour and 50 minutes in the semi-final and Kenneth Gandar Dower for an hour and 45 in the quarter-final, and I was absolutely done,' says Macpherson. 'We didn't train (nobody trained until Amr came on the scene) and in those days I didn't know anything about glucose. I knew I wouldn't beat him. I was tired from the beginning. Amr won two games. Then I set about getting every single thing back. At the end of the fourth game I pulled this leg muscle and in the fifth I just stood there on court. I couldn't play. He agreed that it wasn't a fair match and he played me again. The RAC against Queen's Club. And I beat him. That was in my court — number four at Queen's, in which I was never beaten.'

Macpherson thus defeated Amr in three of their four important matches. 'But I wouldn't suggest I was better than he was. Amr became far better than any of us in the end, because he became a "professional" amateur.'

With that rather shaky start, Amr was on the way — and he did not lose a game in any of his five subsequent amateur championship finals. He missed the 1934-5 event: already diplomacy was interfering with the life-style of a man who clearly knew what was what in the way of recreation (like Macpherson he was a mountaineer as well as a squash player). But in the 1932-3 season Amr not only won the amateur championship. He also won his challenge matches with Don Butcher for the open title. It was to be thirty-four years before anyone else achieved that twin triumph. Coincidentally, that was another 'professional' amateur from a distinguished family, Jonah Barrington. Amr won the open championship five times (plus 1933, when he had no need to win it because no one challenged him) and the amateur championship six times. Barrington's ultimate tally was six and three. Neither was ever beaten in the final of either event. Nowadays there are so many professionals competing almost full-time, as distinct from coaching, that it seems unlikely that any amateur will challenge the feat of Amr and Barrington in holding both titles at the same time.

We have to remember, of course, that in Amr's day there was actually no 'final' in the open championship, which consisted merely of a best-of-three challenge series between the same two players. *The Squash Rackets Association Handbook* of 1930-1 contained the bald statement: 'An open championship has been instituted, and, for purposes of challenge, C.R. Read has been designated open champion.'

This system was discarded in 1947, but its details deserve recording. The holder had to accept one challenge every season, or forfeit his title. A challenger had to satisfy the SRA that he was good enough to have a reasonable chance of success. Receipts from the gate and from subscriptions on behalf of both players were pooled to form the purse, the winner taking two-thirds (£66.13s.4d. in the old coinage) and the loser one-third (£33.6s.8d.). The challenger or his supporters had to guarantee that if the purse did not amount to £100, they would make up the difference. But this provision did not apply if the holder was an amateur. If either player was an amateur, the professional took the entire purse. When the holder was both open champion and British professional champion, a professional of British nationality could challenge for both titles simultaneously, one financial guarantee covering both events (in the 1930s this practice of staking both championships on one challenge series was applied on three occasions). The first match was played on the holder's home court, the second match on the challenger's. In each case the home player could choose the time of play and the make of ball to be used, as long as it was of an approved type. Had a deciding third match ever been necessary, it would have been played on a neutral court. Like the time of play and the ball, this would have been chosen by the SRA after consultation with the players.

Whatever the system used, Amr was unquestionably top man. Macpherson says the secret of Amr's success ('like that of all the absolutely top players') was that he returned everything, he hardly ever hit the tin — and the longer the match, the greater his pace and accuracy. But it may surprise you, as it surprised me, that Macpherson should describe him as the first 'professional' amateur. Amr, it seems, was working to a Barrington-type schedule, playing four hours a day. 'He became mechanically accurate, and he got so fit, which is the only thing that really matters in the end at squash. He had this series of challenge matches with Jim Dear and he always put on the pace at the end and won. In some ways Amr was better than today's players. He was more accurate. He hit up and down the side walls to a length. He made the ball stick to the side wall and it never came off the back wall (now they hit harder and it does come off). That was why he always beat Jim Dear. The ball clung to the side wall and Jim was always diving into the corners.' Amr and Dear met six times in challenge matches for the open championship. Dear won two games on three occasions and one game in the other three matches. This evidence does indeed suggest that Amr outlasted Dear rather than outclassing him.

In addition to his uncommon fitness, the slightly built but athletic Amr was a perfectionist with an enviable gift for learning and remarkable powers of concentration. He was prepared to work, too. Thus he rose rapidly from nothing to everything. The parallels with Barrington become increasingly interesting. The social background. The fact that each was coached by foreigners (Amr by 'Oke' Johnson, Barrington by Nasrullah and Azam Khan). The dedication to perfection that made them submit to hours of court work every day. The fitness, precision and concentration that sprang from this. Their common habit of playing a long series of clinging drives to a length and then (with little or no adjustment of the stroke as a warning) making the alarm bells ring with a sudden drop. Their rapid rise from obscurity to supremacy. Their unique joint achievement of winning the amateur and open championship in the same season.

But we should not push those parallels too far. Barrington's revolutionary stature sprang largely from his intense analysis of the game's physical stresses, and his astonishing self-discipline in adapting his body to meet those stresses. Amr's revolutionary stature sprang largely from his — then unfashionable — willingness to practise for hours, make a thorough study of stroking technique, yet curb his talent with calculated tactical restrictions during competition. Barrington and others have done all this too: but the extent to which Amr did it made him a radical figure in his day.

As a competitive game, squash had taken huge strides forward during the decade before Amr came into it. But his greatness lay not only in the span of his pre-eminence. It also lay in his influence in pushing outwards what had been regarded as the limits of the possible. He made squash a better game. That was the legacy he left us. And once more, as with Charles Read a few years earlier, there were many who said: 'We shall never see his like again.' Obviously Don Butcher, Jim Dear, and (initially) Dugald Macpherson had the ability to play with him, though not stay with him. But Amr's dominance of the amateur game became slightly ridiculous. Hubert Winterbotham, the editor, suggested in the 1936-7 edition of *The Squash Rackets Annual* that, if really put to it, Amr could give a start of seven points to any amateur with the possible exception of Kenneth Gandar Dower. It was thought that no amateur had ever been that good at any game. And when Amr retired in 1938, he was only twenty-eight years old and still in his prime.

The sudden breeze vanished. But squash was now a different game: even in Egypt (Amr was on holiday there when he won the inaugural Egyptian amateur championship at the Gezira Sporting Club, in March, 1936).

Let us examine Amr's game more closely. We know of his fitness, stamina, and precision. His footwork was quick. So was his anticipation. When he wanted to, he could take the ball earlier and whip up the pace. He was a peerless match-player and his technique was as close to perfection as anyone could reasonably hope to get. He had some dazzling shots — a masked angle, a drop, a cross-court backhand volley played into the nick. His court manners were exemplary and he had the quality of mercy, though it sometimes struggled with the competitive instinct with which Johnson had imbued him. In the amateur championship of December, 1936, Roy McKelvie (who played for Scotland both before and after the war) had a good win over Victor Cazalet — then three weeks short of forty — but could make nothing of Amr, who conceded only thirty points in the six rounds of the championship.

'Amr was almost unplayable,' says McKelvie. 'He was so perfect, in a rather restricted way. He didn't use the court like Dear, Hughes, and Karim. But everything Amr did was meticulous, impeccable. His length was supreme. It was frightfully difficult to win a point . . . . When I played him in the amateur championship it was love, love and three. He said to me afterwards: "McKelvie, I give it to you on a plate and you can't take it." He had been trying to set them up. He would give it to you, but his perfection didn't allow you to have it. He did give you the chance, but it was remarkably difficult to take because of his instinctive response. You played a perfect drop or a perfect angle. But whatever you played, it was nothing to him. He was there. His instinct was to chase it. He gave it to you . . . then he took it away. But I don't think Amr would have had any answer to Hashim. What Amr could do, Hashim could do a little bit quicker.'

A picture is beginning to emerge. We will ask Brian Phillips to add some shading, a last touch of detail. Already it has been noted that Amr had much in common with Barrington. But at moments Phillips might almost be talking about 'The Little Master' of tennis, Ken Rosewall:

'Amr was tiny, about 5ft 5 in. He had a little wrist and a thin, pencil grip on his racket. It was like a wand. Very light. He had trim steps. He never seemed to be hustled. His style was drilled and precise and immaculate. He looked a model. He was probably the best attacking player I've ever seen. He was not so good in defence. Might be a bit lost at the back of the court. But he didn't have much retrieving to do. And when he was in front of you, you really were in trouble. In those days we used the Silvertown ball, the squashiest of all the balls ever used (Edward Snell called it "the poached egg"). With this, Amr used a slow, defensive lob down the wall. He could make it die, with that ball. Amr was so deceptive. He came in on the backhand and hit a diagonal, or an angle, or a drop, or this defensive lob. Dugald Macpherson, Peter Reiss, and Amr were the best amateurs of the day. It was by going ahead of the other two that Amr made his contribution. He was that much faster in his stroke-play than anyone else. He withered people with his speed. He used to win the "amateur" easily.'

McKelvie confirms that point about the ball: 'The Silvertown ball was much softer than the ball you play with now. It would lie down, on a drop shot or a length. A masked angle would work. It was the ideal stroke-player's ball.'

Playing conditions in general remained a provocative subject for debate. In those years before the Second World War there were two topical issues which should be recorded here. Canada and the United States were trying to standardize court floors — the Canadians insisting that the US should abandon white-painted flooring in favour of their own unpainted, unstained hardwood. And in Britain there was speculation about the possibilities of courts with transparent walls providing one-way vision: a huge 'fish tank' with spectators clustered around it. The game was becoming a joy to watch, thanks largely to a diminutive Egyptian aristocrat who, luckily for you and me, was not strong enough for lawn tennis.

The remarkable story of Abdel Fattah Amr, diplomat and squash player, would not be complete unless we noted one more extraordinary feature of his career. It says much for the kind of man he was that in December, 1935, he was unanimously invited to captain Britain against the United States at the Bath Club. He appreciated that. It was like a foreign decoration in recognition of distinguished service. Amr was to play only two more seasons. Then he concentrated his talents on the game called diplomacy. As we take a last look back at the peak in view between the wars, we see Read, Butcher, Dear, and one or two amateurs — gathered round a little man who liked climbing mountains.

Five

'You Never Hear His Feet On Floor'

Jim Dear beat Bert Biddle in the 1938-9 challenge series for the British open championship. Amr's abdication, Dear's regency, and the war amounted to an eight-year interregnum during a period of Egyptian rule that spanned a total of eighteen seasons. The new monarch was to be Mahmoud el Karim, professional at one of the most famous clubs in the world, the Gezira Sporting Club in Cairo. Amr was champion for six years. Then Dear popped in for a quick one (he had been working up quite a thirst) before Karim's four-year reign began. Karim was sorting out his gear in readiness for a trip to London when Hitler took one liberty too many and Britain suddenly had a bigger game to play. So Karim had to hang about for seven years before wading into Dear — who was then thirty-six years old.

We can imagine Dear's feelings. By this time the courtesy and charm of these wondrous Egyptians must have been impressing him the way birdsong impresses the badly hungover. First Amr. Then Karim. They were nice chaps and all that — but had no one told them that it was Britain, after all, who had invented the game they insisted on playing so well?

Karim came from a poor family. As a boy he played golf and lawn tennis at the Gezira Club. One day an American officer, short of a sparring partner, asked Karim to join him on the squash court. Karim, then fifteen, enjoyed the game so much that he was soon giving it all the time he could spare — either practising on the primitive, stone-floored, roofless courts (he was to find British conditions a sharp contrast), or watching others. The opportunities for sharpening his game by using better players as a hone were limited. But like Amr, his aristocratic predecessor, the young professional was prepared to suffer, to exert mind and muscle in the cause of improvement. In Karim's case there was an additional incentive in the prospect that success would be good for his pocket as well as his pride. It should not be assumed that these men had a natural genius that marked them out as born champions. Their talent was obviously exceptional. But it was nurtured by their dedication to the game; by their relentless practice; and by the fitness they sweated to achieve (because the best car in the world needs petrol in the tank). Effort is the most underrated component of the achievement that begins life as an aptitude. The loveliest flowers will wilt unless watered. Might as well leave the seeds in the packet.

Karim learned much from playing with Amr and was obviously in a similar class. But his first chance to measure his progress occurred when Victor Cazalet and Kenneth Gandar Dower turned up in Egypt. He discovered that he could beat them, which was an encouraging indication that he might be able to pluck even bigger apples from the tree. But he needed a ladder — or, to be mundane about it, a means of getting to England. The patronage of King Farouk solved the problem. Later, a subscription list was organized in London.

Technically, Brian Phillips was probably the best of Britain's post-war amateurs. 'Karim was a lost soul in London, looking around for someone to play,' he recalls. 'Amr was out of it. Too busy. I was playing Karim and I got to 6-0 in the first game. Then Karim slipped and banged a knee on the side wall. His world collapsed around him. He was crying. Tears rolling down his cheeks. He thought his chances had gone. He was taken to hospital. The knee was wrecked for six weeks. He had to play Jim Dear in the last open championship played under the challenge system — and this happened before their first match. But they did play, later in the season. And Karim got the championship.'

In the second of the 1947 challenge matches Dear led 9-5, 9-7, 8-4 and, at 8-all, boldly chose a one-point 'sudden death' finish. The gamble failed. Dear held on until 7-all in the fourth game. But he was tiring now. Karim was thrashing up the pace.

'Karim only beat Jim Dear in those challenges because Jim would never train for anything,' asserts Dugald Macpherson. 'He played for pleasure and always enjoyed himself. Smiling and laughing. Once, at game ball against Amr, Jim played the most ridiculous drop shot. I played with Karim quite a lot, because he wanted training. I made him give me, I think, six and two hands — and for about quarter of an hour we could play together.' What about the speculative view that Karim might have been able to beat Amr before the war?

'Not a hope,' said Macpherson.

Dear came within a point of beating Karim in two of their three matches. He never quite got that far against Amr. The collateral form thus tends to confirm the accepted view that Amr was the better of the Egyptians. It also suggests that these three players were more or less in the same class. When we look ahead and find that Karim could not take a game from Hashim Khan in either of their two open championship finals, the evidence that Hashim was in a higher class than any of them is almost conclusive. I say 'almost' because we cannot be sure how far Amr might have developed with the stimulus of Hashim's company on court. We must remember, too, that Hashim was playing squash before he was big enough to hold a racket properly, whereas Amr's entire playing career spanned only one decade. When Amr retired, Hashim was still picking up what money he could by stringing rackets and serving as a playing partner for British officers in Peshawar (he had yet to acquire his first post as a professional coach). Hashim was about five years the younger. Had the door of opportunity opened for him sooner, he might have played Amr often enough to settle all arguments. As it is, we must be satisfied with the inconclusive pleasures of conjecture.

Roy McKelvie tells me that if he had to rank the leading players of his era (the years immediately before and after the war) the order would be Hashim, Amr, Karim and Dear. But by the time Hashim came along, McKelvie was a critic rather than a competitor.

'Amr, Dear, and Karim were the outstanding players of my career. These three would leave anybody cold. Nobody could touch them. Dear was a great court games player. Very tough. He improvized all the time. He had none of the artistry or the beauty of Amr and Karim. But he had a wonderful flair for playing anything with a moving ball. Only Denis Hughes has had some of the shots Jim Dear had. Amr and Karim — one the aristocrat and one the professional — were both charming. Gentlemen — a hundred per cent — on court and off it. Karim was a joy. He was the most beautiful stroke-player, with a range of shots beyond anybody else. I found tremendous pleasure in playing Karim because he wasn't ruthless like Amr. If I had to play the eternal match, in heaven or hell, I would play Karim. Just for fun. Always exciting. Always interesting. After that, Butcher — he was wonderfully versatile, but hadn't got the hardness of these later players.'

Karim smoked cigarettes even while he was training, but said they did not affect him: that if the system was used to the habit, giving it up suddenly would do more harm than good. He had eyes like a hawk. His anticipation was sharp. At times he moved like lightning (but with a quiet, almost noiseless rhythm). He took the ball early without loss of accuracy and was imaginatively aggressive. Always looking for a kill, he had the virtuosity to achieve it one way or another. Karim did not mind hitting winners off the wrong foot: he was merely interested in hitting winners. Amr worked and waited for his openings and had a more delicate, caressing touch. Chessboard stuff. The taller Karim had a longer reach and his squash had a disciplined fury about it. His game was a smouldering fire that burst into flame whenever he spotted a chance to go for a winner.

Dick Hawkey, who was then among Britain's leading amateurs and subsequently became a prolific source of advice and instruction, refers to Karim as 'a graceful, stylish stroke-player, rather like a super-Amin'. Brian Phillips makes a similar comparison with Ibrahim Amin, who was to become the only Egyptian (other than Amr) to win the British amateur championship: 'Karim wasn't unbeatable. He was in a comparable class with Amr, but he was about 6ft 1in tall and had a sweeping style. He was very much like Amin — they were near to twins in their style of play, with Karim a little more severe. Both had the Egyptian touch. Asran and Safwat have kept it going.'

Roy Wilson contested five British amateur championship finals (winning two) and was once runner-up to Hashim for the open title. He has some vividly illuminating comments on the Amr-Dear-Karim era and that of the Khans:

'Karim was at the top when I was at the bottom, coming up. He was standing on the pinnacle in his long, white trousers. He used to stroll about. He made it look easy. He never struck the ball hard. He used to whip it like a kid whipping a top, and it always died second bounce. You were forever shovelling the perishing pill out of the crack. The ball was always close to the wall or the floor. In his era Jim Dear was, I suppose, the British counterpart. Again, the long, white trousers and a fairly effortless demonstration of where to put the ball. There was no mad scramble. The ball was just stroked hither and thither. One year, when I reached the amateur quarter-finals, I played him in the open. I ran like hell — I was very nearly ill — and I mustered three points.

'With Karim, I didn't see how I was ever going to get a proper hit at the ball. It was the same with Jim Dear. They were craftsmen. Controllers of the ball.

'For me that was the end of an era of precision and effortless hitting. Then there was a new dimension — a bludgeoner of the ball, a getter-back of balls previously classified as winners. His name was Hashim Khan. That was the new dimension he imparted — bludgeoning the ball harder than it had been bludgeoned before, and hitting balls that most others couldn't get back. Rosewall returned cannonball serves as winners. Hashim did that as a squash player — the "winner" was returned. Later he brought new shots. He aimed at the crack between the wall and the floor. He invented that shot and perfected it. The ball often rolled along the floor.

'But a lot of accuracy was lost in the process. Hashim didn't care if the ball was out of direction. With his pace he could retrieve. He could run up the wall and didn't mind if he had to. It was beneath Karim's dignity to hurry and he would never get himself in a situation where it was necessary. I played Karim and Hashim. Karim made me feel outclassed. Hashim made me feel worn out. I couldn't get rid of the ball. I never felt outclassed. But I never felt I was going to win — unless I could take a year off for training and set aside a day to play him.'

Karim won the British open championship at his first attempt. It was the last to be contested under the challenge system. Then he won the first three championships played to the modern knockout format, beating Dear, Phillips, and Abdul Bari in the finals. The scores suggest that it was getting easier all the time: five games with Dear, four with Phillips, three with Bari. Karim was assuming a stature to challenge Amr's. Then Hashim turned up and spoiled it all. In two successive finals he beat Karim in straight games, conceding only five points in their first match and only twelve in their second. But Karim's place in the history of the game was secure. Only Hashim, Amr, and Jonah Barrington won the British open championship more often. Only Hashim surpassed Karim's sequence of six successive open finals.

In Hashim's extraordinary and delightful book he gives us this picture of Karim: 'Never before do I see a man like this in squash racquets. He is higher than six feet, long arms and legs, and he moves about court like I see dancer in ballet, soft and smooth, you never hear his feet on floor, and how he turns and runs and strokes, you want to watch all day, it is wonderful. He is what one calls a stroke-player, his play has rhythm, no jerks. And he has many many different shots, some I see for first time anywhere.'

But Hashim took over and Karim (as if deciding it would be a good idea to put some distance between them) went to Montreal in 1953. A pleasing reminder of Karim's affable nature, his capacity for fitting in, cropped up at a New York restaurant one evening in 1976. I was dining with Stewart Brauns, of the USSRA, who always sees the game within an international context. 'Karim,' he said, 'went through Farouk, Neguib, and Nasser. Then he became very successful in Montreal.'

A long way for the struggling young professional who was dreaming his dreams in pre-war Cairo. He made a little history, and a lot of friends.

What of the other players, the courtiers of king Karim, who slipped their names into the roll of honour during the years between the war and the whirlwind called Hashim? We have noticed that — other than Dear initially and Hashim terminally — the men who had the distinction of sharing a court with Karim in open championship finals were Phillips and Bari. Phillips, an amateur, had a pleasantly unusual game which respected the basic long-and-short pattern. He hit hard, to a good length, and he had one or two technically idiosyncratic ways of going for a short nick. Bari could be described as a scout for the new regiment of squash players then being mustered in Peshawar (though before settling in England he worked at the Cricket Club of India in Bombay). His role in squash was similar to that of Leif Ericsson in the discovery of North America: neither made a lasting personal impact, but each had a precursory historical importance.

Bari and Hashim were related and knew each other as boys in the village of Nawakilla on the outskirts of Peshawar. Then Bari went to work in Bombay and later established himself as the best player in India (this, of course, was before partition). In 1944, his club promoted the inaugural championship of Western India, open to both professionals and amateurs. Hashim came down by train from Peshawar for his first experience of playing indoors on wood in front of a big gallery. In those days the courts at Peshawar were roofless and cement-floored and had only the most modest accommodation for spectators. Hashim therefore had to adapt his game and his temperament to an unfamiliar environment. He also discovered that his childhood acquaintance — they had not met since — had acquired the finest drop shot he had ever seen. But Hashim was too quick for the large and heavy Bari — and beat him in the final, for three successive years, until partition. After that, Bari was top man in India and Hashim top man in Pakistan. Bari was sent to London for the 1949-50 season and was beaten, but not disgraced, when he met Karim in the final of the open championship. It was suggested to him that he should go home to Pakistan and in future represent his native land, rather than India. He decided to stay in Bombay — and in the following season Hashim was sent to London. He was five or six years older than Bari but, on the other hand, had been beating him.

Bari was significant on four counts. He was the first opponent to provide a genuine measure of Hashim's potential, the first of his people to win the Australian open championship (1950), the first to travel to England and challenge Egypt's dominance of the game, and the first to settle in London as a professional coach (in 1953, at the Junior Carlton Club). He was thirty-three years old when a thrombosis of the brain killed him in December, 1954. Coincidentally, the open championship was in progress at the time.

That was the season in which the professional championship of the United Kingdom was first played. Jack Giles, who won it ten times and then retired, recalls that when Bari first arrived in England he knew no one and was taken along to Giles for a hit (this became the accepted thing for newcomers to do, and the affably helpful Giles was delighted with his new intramural responsibilities). The first time they shared a court, Giles was impressed by Bari's superb, deceptive combination of the drop and lob. 'He never used this to the same extent in match-play. He played a very good drop. But he didn't use that combination so much.' Giles remembers him as a big, solid, powerful man who hit hard — very hard — yet could switch off the machinery in that immense forearm and play the most gentle of drop shots. Bari was a gentle man, too: quietly spoken, diffident, and extremely popular.

The leading British professionals of the Karim era were Dear, Bert Biddle and Leslie Keeble. But after Dear's success in the last season before the war, it was to be twenty-eight seasons before another British player — Jonah Barrington — became open champion.

Nor could the best amateur, Norman Borrett, find a solution to the problem called Karim. But Borrett was perhaps the most interesting uninteresting player in the history of squash. He won the first five British amateur championships contested after the war (a sequence no one has matched). He had a different opponent in every final and did not lose a game to any of them. Therefore his efficiency as a match-player could not be questioned. But efficiency, as we know, is not necessarily attractive. Borrett was the first outstanding post-war exponent of a brand of squash that was soon to become fashionable (Hashim, in his early years, raised it to an even higher level). This consisted, essentially, of exerting maximum pressure at minimum risk. The avoidance of errors assumed more importance than the ability to hit winners. But pressure was maintained by taking the ball early and hitting it hard and low to a length, with an occasional drop or angle thrown in to vary the pattern.

'Borrett was superb in his co-ordination and his ability to hit a moving object,' says Roy Wilson. 'The side walls had no function — they were just there to hold the roof up. The drop shot wasn't played, except as a slight mis hit . . . He hit accurately close to and down the walls, and generated pace by stepping in to the ball early. But it was rather tedious. Nothing much happened, but unfortunately you didn't get many points.'

Borrett was a forceful and determined competitor. His game was based on sustained speed, sound ball control, and persistent retrieving. This kind of squash demands fitness and stamina — Borrett had both — because it is primarily a physical test, rather than a gauge of stroke-playing virtuosity. Since Borrett and Hashim came on stage, players have mostly found it expedient to suppress any tendency towards artistic flamboyance. Hughes, Taleb, Amin, and Zaman kept the heritage alive by occasionally playing from the heart rather than the head. But stroke-players now had less time for their shots, and hit fewer winners. Hunt and Mohibullah (Junior) are the most eminent modern graduates of a school opened by Borrett and Hashim a quarter of a century ago.

The purpose of this chapter was to discuss the relatively short period between the war and the advent of the greatest of squash players. In those few years the Egyptian empire ruled in turn by Amr and Karim had its last era of supremacy — an era dominated by a technical brilliance that honoured the legacy bequeathed to the game by Abdel Fattah Amr. At the same time the massively amiable Bari quietly reconnoitred the ground in readiness for the Mongol invasion. The Pathans were now to come charging and crashing among us.

Six

A Family of Champions

The extraordinary thing about the four champions who succeeded Karim — and held the British open title for thirteen consecutive seasons — was the bond between them. All were Moslems of Afghan descent. All were Pathans, the race who roam the heights between Afghanistan and what is now Pakistan. All were from the same tribe. Their roots lay not merely in the same province, but in the same town, Peshawar. Not merely in the same town, but in the same suburban village, Nawakilla. Not merely in the same village, but (except for Roshan) in the same family. They sprang from a tribe of Pathans who settled in the plains rather than the hills. This explains why the squash-playing Khans were not, superficially, true to type. A much more obvious example of a breed renowned for powerful physiques and strikingly good looks burst upon us in the 1970s in the shape of Hidayat Jahan of Quetta, who would look utterly in character with a horse between his legs, a sword between his teeth, and the dust-clouds of battle all around him. Indeed, Jahan creates his own echoing gunfire. In 1975, a few hours after he had played a match on a recently-built court at Leicester, I was hitting a few with a local professional on the same new court and noticed, with surprise, that there were dents in the tin.

My partner explained in two words: 'Jahan's forehand . . .'

By contrast, Hashim and Azam are small men. Is it entirely a coincidence that these two and Amr, three of the greatest players in the game's history, would all be invisible behind a 5ft 6in wall?

Before discussing the Khans in more detail, perhaps we should take a closer look at the environment that produced them. Our day out with Hashim at Peshawar taught us much. But a few additional facts will clarify the recipe and may even enhance the flavour of the dish. Take, for example, the word 'Pakistan'. This was coined in 1933 as a compendium of the land's components — P for the Punjab, A for the bit of Afghanistan that is now the North-West Frontier Province, K for Kashmir, S for Sind, and Tan for Baluchistan. Our primary concern here is the NWFP, which was born from a division of the Punjab in 1901.

The trading agencies of that massive mercantile enterprise, the East India Company, had to be defended. This meant troops, forts, territorial expansion, and (in 1858) the decision that the Crown should take over from the East India Company the responsibility for governing the country. Britain's first, chastening experience of Indian mountain warfare was against the Gurkhas, of Nepal, in 1814. But it was in the north-west, from 1838-42, that the first Afghan war taught the British how much trouble they could expect — and where they could expect it. That ruggedly mountainous frontier was to become incessantly irritating. Belligerent tribes of Afghans were always charging to and fro, and in the second half of the nineteenth century the area assumed additional importance because of Russian meddling in the affairs of central Asia. The Khyber Pass, which rises just outside Peshawar, had always been a hazardously lively theatre for invasions, migrations, trade, smuggling, and banditry. But for this continuing tradition, there would have been no need for the concentration of British garrisons in the North-West Frontier Province of what was then India. No likelihood of the squash courts on which off-duty officers sharpened their reactions. No possibility that local lads like the Khans would pick up the game and a few annas, even rupees, while doing chores for the sahibs in the recreational areas of the cantonments.

As late as 1931 the teenage Hashim found himself bobbing about in the fringe of a tumultuous fracas. A well-organized Islamic political movement tried to create an independent Pathan state and 47,000 troops were needed to restore order in the NWFP.

We can catch the flavour of this exciting history by re-reading our Kipling. He had a sensitive nose for what was going on around him while he was scribbling away on behalf of the *Civil and Military Gazette* in Lahore. When I passed them in 1976 (almost a century after Kipling's day) the offices of that once-renowned journal were just a tumbling heap of rubble populated by dusty little men — and donkeys loaded with bricks and trampling on memories. But Kipling's work lives on and, as Hashim showed us, the land he knew remains much as it was. The homes made of baked mud. Men with ginger-dyed hair. Public letter-writers. Dreamers sitting on their heels and looking at the day. The indifference to noise. The capacity for intrigue. The code of honour. The feuds — hot blood pumping through the veins and sometimes spilling out of them. The tribal areas that recognize no laws except their own. The smugglers' market, on the edge of Peshawar, where a strange assortment of modern merchandise turns up — goods that, to borrow the western cliché, 'fell off the backs of lorries'. One can still wander about that strange country and see it as Kim did. Happily, though, justice in the tribal areas is not what it was early in the nineteenth century, when the Governor of Peshawar, an Italian general called Avitabile, found it useful to take a portable gallows on his travels. Do not ask me how an Italian general came to be governor of Peshawar. The world made no more sense then than it does now.

The Pathans are a race of herdsmen, farmers, warriors. Mostly handsome and virile, they have unusually good eyesight and are among the best marksmen in the world. From an early age they learn how to use a rifle and a knife. They shoot straight because they must make the first bullet count — partly out of pride, partly because during the interval between shots they might be transferred from this world to the next. As mounted infantry, they have few peers, anywhere. People like that, living in the hills as they do, are — in the long term — unconquerable. The British could not subdue them. Nor, on the other hand, could the Pathans subdue the British. Thus was created a bond of sorts: a grudging, mutual respect.

All that is part of the Pathan tradition and its essence survives. This was sharply confirmed early one morning in October, 1976. Having accompanied our massively boisterous dogs on their dawn assault of inner Buckinghamshire, I settled down with coffee and the paper. Tribesmen in the NWFP, I read, had actively resented a government decision to take over some timber forests — and the fighting Pathans had joined in the fun. In short, lads were still at it.

But as we have noticed, the big fellows in the hills have little brothers who settled in the plains: and it was from this stock that the Khans were bred. Hashim established himself as the best player in India and then, after partition, as the best in Pakistan. But he was already in his thirties, expecting perhaps a few more years of competitive squash before concentrating exclusively on coaching for the Pakistan Air Force. Then the government and the PAF put their heads together and decided that, as the younger Abdul Bari had settled in Bombay, they needed someone else to represent them in London. Hashim was the obvious choice, but was he already too old? They decided to take a chance. So Hashim flew to London: and began to compose the most illustrious chapter in the history of squash.

'My first impression of Hashim,' says Roy Wilson, 'was of a short, dumpy little man with a barrel chest. Inside that chest was a pump that circulated blood with oxygen in it — and continued to circulate blood long after his opponent had gone home. And on top of that chest was a big, grinning head with very little hair on it. He had no bottom. I'm sure his plimsolls were three sizes too large. He started off, and the shoes followed. Then the shoes stopped and Hashim went on — inside the shoes. There was a squeal of shoes on the floor, then a squeal of feet in the shoes. I nearly had hysterics the first time I saw him.'

Brian Phillips makes a similar assessment: 'Hashim hadn't got the feather touch, but he was severe — essentially a speed and power player, with an almost indefinite capability of return. The rubber shrieked on the floor as Hashim turned. He could be wrong-footed, but it didn't make any difference. He had this barrel chest and a lot of his resistance came from exceptionally deep breaths.'

Jack Giles reminds us that, although the early Hashim concentrated on maintaining maximum pressure at minimum risk (with the proviso that he hit low even when playing safe), he later acquired a range of shots that made him less dependent on his astounding capacity for retrieving. There were angles, drops, and fierce drives buried in the side-wall nicks with more consistent accuracy than anyone else had achieved. 'He did all the things that anybody playing today does, but he did them quicker and in most cases better.'

Another interested spectator was Dugald Macpherson — still involved in the game that had meant so much to him, though his playing days were over. 'On the whole the Pakistanis are the quickest to see the ball,' he says. 'Hashim is the best player I've seen. An extraordinary man. When he started he held his racket halfway up.'

Hashim turned out to be better than even Hashim had suspected. 'From beginning, was little worried by Karim. They said he was the best. He play the shot and he finish the ball. But after I play him, that was easy. First tough match in England, fellow was from South Africa. Peter Hildick-Smith. He was tough man. Just like tiger. He was very good runner. After that was Azam and Roshan. Roshan's stamina weak. Otherwise very good stroke-player, good style. That time Michael Oddy and a few more was also playing very good.'

Hashim beat Karim in two finals, Wilson in a third, then Azam twice and Roshan once to make it six in succession. But in March, 1957, Roshan stopped him. Hashim won the first game. But in the second his shin muscles tightened up and that was the end of him. Hashim regained the title the following year, beating Azam in the final. Then Azam took over. As I said before, there is some uncertainty about Hashim's exact age. But it is commonly supposed that he was born in 1916 and this is confirmed by the evidence in his own book, which indicates that he was thirty-five when he won his first British open championship, forty-two when he won his last, and forty-three when, in his ultimate appearance, he twisted a knee playing Azam. 'Wind stays good, yes, but you push too hard and you have accidents with legs.'

As Macpherson said, an extraordinary man.

When Hashim flew home after winning the championship for the first time, they made a great fuss of him, first in Karachi and then in Peshawar — where the schools were closed for the day and everyone crowded into the streets while he was driven through the town in an open car. When he won the title again, the Pakistan Air Force made him a lieutenant-instructor at Risalpur, a job carrying more money and a pension too. When he won his third championship, against Wilson ('strong player'), Hashim decided it was time to train a younger man as travelling companion, practice partner, rival, and potential successor. So he began to wean from tennis his brother Azam, nine years his junior, who worked at the same club in Peshawar. As Hashim has told us, the conversion from tennis was initially distressing for Azam.

'It was very hard work,' says Azam. 'I couldn't finish one game. I have to walk out of the court. Chest, legs, body, everything . . . He make me work hard. I have to go for every ball. The second day I just managed to finish the first game. Third day, was little better. Gradually getting better. Playing two games, three games. Getting a bit longer the game, day by day. Could stand up and sometimes play for an hour, two hours. About three or four months before going to England, started serious training. To London, December 1952. First match I played was amateurs against professionals. Roy Wilson. Was very nervous. Lost in five. First match in England. First match anywhere. Mostly tennis before that. Squash for fun. Play Hashim in final British professional championship. Next is open championship. Played Brian Phillips in trial for open. Not nervous. Beat him in three.'

That 'trial' assumed more significance for Azam and Hashim than it did for Phillips: 'It was a pretty perfunctory one. Fixed up at the last minute. I happened to be at the Lansdowne, and Hashim was introducing his brother around. We played in a very hot court, the A court upstairs. There were just a few people around. There was not much needle, in the circumstances. But one was very impressed with his ability to get to everything and return it. It was a pleasant enough game and at the end of the day Azam was obviously a player. It became a "trial" and fitted quite neatly into Hashim's book. But it was just that I happened to be there, and was pleased to be introduced and get to know somebody new.'

That first season it was Azam's misfortune to be drawn in the same half of the open championship as Hashim. But in the nine subsequent championships he was runner-up three times and then won the title four years running. His competitive career ended early in 1962 when he ruined an Archilles tendon. But during the 1956-7 season he took over the New Grampians Club at Shepherd's Bush, London, where he later gave many fine players — Michael Oddy and Jonah Barrington among them — some usefully harsh lessons in match-play. But for Azam, neither Oddy nor Barrington would have fulfilled his potential.

'Azam was underrated,' says Oddy. 'For my money he was the greatest. He was certainly by far the greatest influence on me. I moved from Scotland to Leicester and then to London, in September, 1958, having got to the semi-finals of the "amateur" in March. Azam got down to the business of making me a squash player — not so much by coaching, but by putting me under so much pressure that I had to play. I couldn't lob: but he made me. Azam was the perfect orthodox squash player, if you wanted to study how squash should be played. Everything was absolutely right. He could play a volley-drop from anywhere, from anything the slightest bit loose. His accuracy of shot was quite phenomenal. He was a raw beginner when he began under Hashim, the elder brother. But I think he could have won the last two of Hashim's opens (towards the end he was "carrying" Hashim). He won four opens running and then bust his Achilles. I suspect he would have won Mohibullah's, Taleb's, and perhaps one or two of Jonah's.'

Of that argument, more in a moment. Before moving on to the next of the Khans to arrive in London, we should notice the reputation Azam acquired for never using new gear in a big match. Some thought he was superstitious about this, but Azam denies it. 'Not use in championship new shoes or new racket or new grip. New shoes could be slippery, or not used to them. Like to use racket two or three times before playing match. And use grip a couple of times before you go into championship. By the time you get used to grip, may be game down, two games down, maybe too far down.'

Wisdom worth remembering — at any level of competition.

Hashim and Azam were cast in the same mould. They began their careers at the Pakistan Air Force officers' club in Peshawar. They were physically of the same type. The elder brother trained the younger. It was hardly surprising that they played a similar type of game. But the next of this family of champions, in terms of seniority, came from different stock. Roshan was only a distant relative, by marriage, and his squash matured at Rawalpindi rather than Peshawar. He was taller than Hashim and Azam and, though less fit and perhaps less stable temperamentally, was a more elegant and attractive stroke-player. He won the British open championship once, was runner-up twice (to Hashim and Azam), won the United States championship three times, and also won titles in Canada and Egypt. He beat Hashim in four countries — Britain, Australia, Pakistan, and the United States.

But in 1957 he hurt his left knee ('very unfortunate I hurt my knee after I start beating him — otherwise I beat all of them') and failed to consolidate his supremacy. He also had a bad habit.

'I was a smoker and they were not. I start smoking at about fourteen, which is a very, very bad thing. Stamina was a weakness. If I was not smoking, I was more faster than Hashim.' His last appearance in the British open championship was in 1962, when Taleb beat him in a semi-final.

Unlike the three other Khan champions, Roshan stayed at home — in Karachi, as a petty officer in the Pakistan Navy — rather than accepting an overseas job when his playing days were over. 'I had many offers. Australia, Canada, America, England. I refused because of my children. Torsam and the other child were very young. I don't want to leave them alone. And the Navy support me. I think, inside my heart, if someone do a little thing for me, I don't want to forget him.'

One afternoon in 1976, Roshan climbed on his motor-scooter and joined me in a Karachi hotel for a chat that seemed necessary for my enlightenment and yours. Basically his story concerned the first three years of the 1950s. It sounded like a tear-jerking melodrama. Frustrated ambition. Poverty. Sleeping in the street. The door of opportunity suddenly opening, just as he was thinking of putting his dreams behind him and giving up the game. The tale acquired additional pathos from Roshan's occasional tendency to slip diffidently into the third person when talking about himself, as if discussing someone else — a young man he once knew. Jonah Barrington has the same habit.

When Hashim won his first British open championship, Roshan's father was a professional at Rawalpindi and Roshan himself had a job as assistant professional. In 1951 he won the Pakistan professional championship, at Kakul, and naturally wanted to measure his game against Hashim's. But he could not get to Hashim, and no one believed in Roshan's chances anyway. In desperation, he gave up his job and joined his elder brother, Nasrullah, in Karachi. In the words of his son, Torsam, Roshan 'wanted to improve his game and be the top player in the world'. The move was bold but hazardous. There was no prospect of financial security, no guarantee that he would get the chance he had been denied in Rawalpindi. But Roshan reasoned: 'Hashim is not taking part in any championship in Pakistan. How can I get chance to show my game? Karachi very big city. Maybe I get chance to go to England.'

In 1952, when Azam took up the game seriously, Roshan hoped that the brothers might compete in the Pakistan professional championship. But while Roshan was on his way from Karachi to Kakul, Hashim and Azam were on their way from Peshawar to Karachi and London. Very frustrating. Later some friends of Nasrullah offered to put up 5,000 rupees if Hashim would play an exhibition match with Roshan. But nothing came of that scheme either, in spite of the publicity it attracted. A further disappointment was the fact that Pakistan's professional champion was languishing at home while others — Azam from Peshawar, and Safirullah and Mohamed Amin from Karachi — were granted the trip to England that Roshan so ardently craved.

'I was still in Karachi. The champion. It was unfair.' But how on earth was he to get to England? He had a baby son, Torsam. Nasrullah had only a modest job, tennis and squash, and had two sons to support, Rehmatullah and Amanullah.

'I don't have a penny,' Roshan told me. 'I was lying on the street, with no house, no job, no racket, no shoes.' He even had difficulty playing in Karachi. 'All day I used to help Naz with the tennis, to get some money. They would not allow me to play squash. At night I used to go to open ground — polo ground, where Inter-Continental Hotel is now — to run around. The position was so bad I couldn't buy a racket to practise. And if I could, I couldn't play. There was that much politics against me. I told Naz, I don't think I get a chance. I better go to work, some job, to make money, because the situation day by day is getting worse.'

Thus, in 1953, Roshan almost gave up the game ('was a very near period').

But Naz had a friend who took Roshan to meet an officer in the Pakistan Navy, told him the story, and produced newspaper-cuttings as supporting evidence. 'Officer said, "I will put you in the Navy as messenger. This job is not suitable for you, but I am opening the way".' This officer, said Roshan, was a squash player himself and used to play with Mohamed Amin, professional at the Karachi Gymkhana Club. When Amin rejected a challenge from Roshan, the suspicion that other professionals might be 'ducking' Roshan inevitably gained a degree of substance. And the messenger was summoned by the chief of staff.

'He said, "Do you think you will beat Hashim?"

'I said, "No sir. I am not claiming I am going to beat him. But I want chance to play him. Request that you press him to play me in Pakistan, or send me to England."

'So they said, "Right. When is going to be Kakul championship? If you win for third year, we promise we will send you to England."'

Did Roshan win the Pakistan professional championship for the third consecutive year? You bet he did. No matter that Hashim and Azam did not compete. Roshan took the trophy back to Karachi for the Pakistan Navy. They scrapped the messenger's job, increased his pay, and told him he would just play tennis and squash. As for the trip to England, they did not have much foreign currency. How much did he need?

'I said, "Pay my ticket and give me little bit money and forget me". First trip was one pair trousers, one shirt, one pair tennis shoes. Snowing — and wearing tennis shoes. People laugh. And one long overcoat borrowed from the stores, to be returned. No squash gear at all. No racket. Got £5. People are saying "You will die hungry in England".'

For a time, that possibility did not seem unduly far-fetched. When Roshan had paid his landlady in advance ('23 Cranley Gardens — I still remember') and had taken a taxi to the Pakistan Embassy, he had little more than £1 left. He was handed over to Henry Hayman, then Secretary of the Squash Rackets Association, and they went to Lillywhites in Piccadilly Circus. 'They give me shoes, socks, shorts, shirts, two rackets. £15 or £16, something like that. But there was only £1 and some pennies in my pocket. So Mr Hayman said, "Roshan, you like to pay now or later on?" I said, "If you don't mind, I will pay later on." So Mr Hayman think Roshan has travellers' cheque or something, and he paid the money from his own pocket.' Hayman then bought Roshan lunch and took him on a taxi tour so that he could meet the professionals at the West End clubs. 'Abdul Bari was at the Junior Carlton. He was my cousin. He allowed me to play without paying anything. I used to play with the members.'

Roshan and Nasrullah, who had also come to England, then sought help in raising enough money to live on. Inevitably, Naz had a friend in Birmingham (he was one of the breed who seem to be born with friends everywhere). Then there was the Embassy and, of course, the Pakistan Navy. And Roshan got his expenses. 'Is about £4 a week: £2.10s to the landlady and £1.10s. tea and toast and one meal a day.

'First tournament was Dunlop championship. At that time was 500 guineas, very high championship. Winner would take 105 guineas. Slowly, slowly, I start winning. I reach the semi-finals. Beat Azam. The match was very tough. But because of my health and food situation, was worse. The next day both legs were sore, ankles swollen. I was not able to walk. Spent all day in my room. One day was rest. Next day I come to Lansdowne Club. I could not wear my shoes, because both ankles swollen. So I put shoes without laces, and press foot. In the changing-room journalists talking to Karim ask "You never see this boy before — what do you think about him?" Karim said, "This boy is very good, but I will beat him easy because I have more experience." Then they came to me. I said, "I heard what Karim said. He will get lots of trouble. Not very easy." Then we go to court. I beat him 9-6, 9-0, 9-1. The result is before everyone.'

'Now, position is very good. Lying in the street . . . Nobody allow you to play . . . You become sports officer Pakistan Navy . . . You become a champion . . .'

For Roshan, that was the end of the beginning. The rest we know — except for Roshan's reminder of his difficulties in trying to compete with Hashim, Azam, and their nephew Mohibullah. 'They were practising together, to beat me. They were very friendly to me. But on the court nobody was playing with me in practice. The championship to win was very tough to me. To beat all three to become world champion. I had three Geoff Hunts against me.' But in 1957, as we have noticed, Roshan beat Hashim in the final of the British open championship.

'I was trying to play by stamina. When I found he had lots of stamina, I played my strokes game. He couldn't get there. I took over by strokes.'

Roshan's story, here and there, is doubtless coloured and romanticized by his intensely personal reaction, his occasionally somewhat egoistic view, of the rivalry between a small group of struggling sportsmen in one country over one particular period. But its binding thread is sound: and it is a vividly extreme sample of the kind of tale many sportsmen could tell us. They may sometimes talk blandly of such things as pride and ambition. But champions also have something in common with criminals in that they can be powerfully motivated by hunger and resentment.

The youngest of this family of champions, Mohibullah, benefited from the avuncular encouragement Hashim and Azam gave him, from the coaching and practice they provided, and perhaps most of all, from the fact that they had marked the route to London. He was only seventeen when he joined Hashim, Azam, and Roshan in the semi-finals of the 1957 British open championship. During the next five seasons he was runner-up to Azam on three occasions. Then that Achilles tendon wrecked Azam's career and in December, 1962, during a championship punctuated by his twenty-third birthday, Mohibullah bounced back from match point down to beat Abou Taleb and thus win his only British open title. Whereupon Mohibullah joined Uncle Hashim in North America and began to carve himself a distinguished niche in the hardball game. He did return to Britain to defend the championship, but a year's absence had blunted the edge of his softball squash. Michael Oddy stopped him in the semi-finals, in straight games.

After thirteen years, the reign of the Khans was over — but they had brought an imperishable fame to a nondescript village called Nawakilla.

Imperishable, too, is the memory of Mohibullah's squash. Though he was the last and least of the line, he was supreme among the Khan champions in terms of entertainment value — an important commodity in those days, because the game was beginning to reach out and embrace a wider public. He played a squash match as though there was no tomorrow — as though all his living had to be crammed into one isolated segment of sporting endeavour. So he hit as hard as he could, ran as fast as he could, and exploded about the court like a jumping cracker. His acrobatic qualities were astonishing. Brian Phillips recalls one picture in a gallery of glittering miniatures:

'Hashim was playing Mohibullah at the Lansdowne once. They were both going great guns. Mohibullah rushed to the back. He did get the ball. But his momentum took him up the wall. A woman on the end of row E was so affected that she shrieked. She was so distressed that she had to leave the court.'

Connoisseurs could be mildly disparaging when making the inevitable comparison between Mohibullah and the elder Khans.

But they enjoyed Mohibullah. He excited them. And he had the same effect on spectators less well-versed in the vocabulary and grammar of the game. He showed them what fun it could be. Mohibullah quivered with vitality. He was a contortionist. He seemed to be made of rubber, especially at the wrist. And while his body and limbs were twisting about, he was pulling faces and sticking his tongue out and curling it this way and that. Disjointed, double-jointed, or whatever, he was dynamically ungainly, and left-handed, too. He was an extrovert, an actor: totally unabashed about the grotesque spectacle he often presented, and totally uninhibited. Even the draught he made sent out shock waves. He covered the court like a very angry octopus. The place reverberated with crashing and banging and thumping noises. When he hit the tin, there was such an echoing din that one had mental visions of sentries at Wellington Barracks peering apprehensively into the darkness, and ducks in St James's Park waking up in a dither.

As a general rule (Barrington in squash and Rod Laver in tennis have been notable exceptions) a man's game reflects his character. Mohibullah did not spend his spare time knitting. He lived. His dedication to fitness and training did not seriously challenge that of Hashim and Azam. Because of this, we may suspect that his dominance of the softball game would not have lasted long even had he stayed in it. Indeed, in the only British open championship Mohibullah did win, Taleb was match point up at 8-1 in the fourth game. Then Taleb, as Michael Oddy puts it, turned to the gallery as if to say 'What shot would you like me to finish it off with?' And he never did finish it off.

But in fairness to Mohibullah we may suggest that, had he wished, he could have won the championship earlier than he did. This is not to suggest that he was as good a player as Uncle Azam: merely that by the time Azam was in his middle thirties, Mohibullah had closed the gap sufficiently to beat him. Mohibullah was at his peak then, beating players like Roshan, Taleb, and Mohamed Dardir in straight games. But Azam beat him in five games in the 1960 and 1961 finals. The second match, in particular, aroused suspicions that family seniority might have had some bearing on the result. Even the *Squash Rackets Association Handbook*, which is not a publication prone to controversy, stated that the final 'had an air of unreality about it and there were many who thought that the younger player could have won had he been so minded'. When I tackled Mohibullah on the subject he would not commit himself beyond the vaguely significant comment: 'I was waiting for my turn'. Roshan was more forthright: 'Mohibullah was a very good player. He spoil his life with that politics. "You not beat us — you have lots of time".'

But we must also be fair to Azam. Oddy, remember, suggested that Azam, too, might have become British champion sooner than he did — that towards the end he was 'carrying' Hashim.

'There was so much of the elder brother business,' says Dick Hawkey. But Jack Giles — and we have to respect his judgement while suspecting that he may be unduly if admirably eager to believe that the great Khans were always making a totally genuine effort — has no tolerance for these suspicions. 'In my view there was absolutely no truth that Azam had to let Hashim win, in the same way as later they thought that Mohibullah had to let Azam win. One only had to play them to see who was winning and who wasn't.'

And where, in any case, does the speculation lead us? Just before the war another Pathan, Samiullah, who never had a chance to play in Britain, was in the habit of beating the pants off Hashim. But by the end of the war Hashim was probably good enough to have won some, if not all, of the championships Karim won. We may suspect that at times Azam deferred to Hashim and Mohibullah to Azam. But there is no reason to question Giles's belief that the top men were Hashim, Azam, and Roshan, in that order.

'Mohibullah was nowhere near the same class,' says Hawkey. 'Hashim, Azam, and Roshan were a street ahead of anything else there was, or ever will be. They were crushing. There was just no way you got a point off them, unless they gave you one or took a risk. I'd give anything to see Roshan play again, but I couldn't care less about Hashim and Azam. Sheer speed. Very fast. A smell of burning rubber. Finished up at the other side of the court. Fantastic! But if only Roshan could have been fit . . .'

Oddy, though, is in no doubt that Azam was a better player than Roshan: 'After coming back from winning the Australian "amateur" in 1959 I beat Mohibullah on the Friday night in the quarter-finals of the open, and played Roshan at 2.30 p.m. on the Saturday afternoon. I was one-love and 6-3 up before he ran me into the ground. Had I had a day's rest . . . But there was no way I could have taken a game from Azam. I was 2-2 with Mohibullah and had a match point in one I lost. He was not in the same class as Hashim and Azam, and not as good as Roshan and Taleb — a vastly better squash player than Mohibullah.'

Roy Wilson has told us that in his view the 'bludgeoning' Khans introduced a new era after an old one had ended with the effortless precision of Dear and Karim. The vivid clash of styles affected Brian Phillips, too, and it is from him that we will take a last impression of the family of champions.

'There was this complete contrast between artistry and efficiency. The Khans were like jet-propelled frogs, with rubber shoes shrieking as they tore about the court. Hashim had this barrel-chest that filled him up with oxygen, and a powerful forehand and backhand. They didn't play anything subtle in the early stages of a match. Just flailing away. Flogging the ball around. An occasional angle. Later on, they used more strokes. Roshan was far more volatile than Azam, who was a much better workman at the game. Roshan was a funny man, very temperamental, the least stable of them all. Azam always delivered the goods. Mohibullah was very fast — and cocky. Taleb was cocky, too. It was fascinating to see them fighting each other.'

We will get to Taleb soon. First, a closing note about the enduring stature of the once-great but now ageing Khans. In 1976, Pakistan International Airlines brought the four champions together again to attend an open tournament at the new PIA Squash Complex in Karachi. Such distinguished successors as Jonah Barrington and Geoff Hunt were among the players taking part. But the clouds of glory mostly trailed behind an elderly little spectator, quiet and dignified, who was coolly appraising them. It was as if the twenty years between had never happened. There could be no king but Hashim. One evening a bunch of us left all the bubbling banter, gossip and reminiscence that pervades every major tournament, and went back to the hotel for one of those midnight winding-down sessions that separate an evening's squash from a night's sleep. Barrington, carefully puncturing his Chicken Kiev, mused about the aura of supremacy surrounding the man from Nawakilla:

'You know, it's as though Hashim was still champion . . .'

Seven

Sparks in the Shadows

It is provocatively controversial, almost futile, to compare one generation with any other. But the evidence suggests that Hashim, Azam and Roshan raised the game to a level attained at no other time before or since the lads from Peshawar advanced from chores to championships. There is enough collateral form to indicate that Abou Taleb and Jonah Barrington fell short of that level, and it would be uselessly hypothetic to speculate how good Barrington might have been but for the fact that his squash education did not begin until he was twenty-three. As I write, it seems possible that Geoff Hunt and Mohibullah Junior, alleged to be almost nine years younger, may be climbing to peaks unsurpassed even during the Khan era. But we must leave that judgement to future historians.

Between them the Khans demonstrated every virtue of squash: speed and stamina, power and touch, the ability to put the ball away, and (particularly in the case of the sensitive Roshan) facile, unfussy stroking, wrist-work, and court craft. These Khan champions cast long shadows. But there were sparks in those shadows, glittering gems partly eclipsed by the greatness around them. The most obscure of them all were the Pakistani professionals who never achieved prominence in London, which was the only place that mattered in those days. We have no satisfactory measure of the potential ability of such men as Hashim's boyhood friend and subsequent brother-in-law, Safirullah, or Safirullah's brother, Samiullah, though we know he was too good for the young Hashim. Or the renowned Said Ali, who was still flowing about the courts — and trailing a long white beard — when he had long exceeded the biblical span of three score years and ten. Nor must we forget Mohamed Amin, self-styled 'number one tricky player', who still delights in demonstrating the shots that justify the tag. Amin also gave the game five squash-playing sons, including such competent craftsmen as Yasin, Saleem, and Maqsood, who are all familiar with the route from Karachi to London.

You have to go to Pakistan to catch the flavour of such men as Safirullah, Samiullah, Said Ali, Amin, and other fine players who have made, at most, only fleeting appearances on the international stage. Some of their countrymen became well-known and respected in Britain, but were doomed to play the roles of understudies. One was Nasrullah, Roshan's elder brother. These two, incidentally, are grandsons of Abdul Majeed, who worked at the Peshawar Club for sixty-five years and inspired the development of squash among a small section of the indigenous population.

Nasrullah became a professional at the age of sixteen and had a succession of jobs in India and Pakistan. Tennis was his main sport, as competitor and coach. He was already in his thirties when he first visited England — with Roshan in 1953 — and three years later his belated challenge to the oligarchy of squash was further handicapped by cartilage trouble. But Naz had begun an illustrious career as a British-based coach. By a quirk of fate it was the death of Abdul Bari (the first man to beat him in a major British tournament) that created a vacancy for Naz at the Junior Carlton Club. He stayed there for nine years and then spent five at the Lansdowne and Royal Aero Clubs, which occupy the same premises off Berkeley Square. Between 1964 and 1969 Naz and the equally congenial men around him — plus the renowned Bruce court — made the Lansdowne the game's spiritual home. His most famous pupil, who came to regard him as a mixture of mentor and father-figure, was Jonah Barrington. In those days the Lansdowne bubbled with enthusiasm for squash. Everyone who worked downstairs at squash level wanted to play. If they could not play well, they wanted to play anyway. And if they could not play, they wanted to talk about it. Visitors were caught up by the tide and swept along by it. When Jonah won the open championship and Naz the veterans' it seemed totally appropriate. They were good for each other.

Naz was a stern coach. But he was, nevertheless, a charming man. His playing style was a joy and his appreciation of elegance, even beauty, was almost Latin in its intensity. He was not the fittest and toughest of match-players, but he always looked good. He was a composer, an arranger, rather than an outstanding soloist. To explore the musical analogy in a different direction, had Naz been a ballad singer he would have been a Jack Jones rather than a Tom Jones. He would have achieved his effects by subtlety of phrasing rather than by 'socking it to them'.

Our club ladder league at Beaconsfield used to feature a large and energetic American called Tom Jones. His job was associated with marketing bandages, and both knees were heavily encased in his company's products. This was puzzling because, otherwise, he exuded health and strength. On court, the puzzle was soon solved: he played like a goalkeeper, repeatedly flinging himself full length and bouncing on his bandages. One ran over him, rather than round him. His wife, he said, attracted a good deal of envy among her sex because she was married to 'Tom Jones'.

Naz's successor as the dominant figure in the British open veterans' championship was a close friend of Azam's, Jamal Din. 'Jamal was not fit enough,' says Michael Oddy, 'but for sheer skill he was superb — one of the best stroke-players who ever stepped on a squash court.' Jamal played drop shots so easily and accurately that he might have been shelling peas. Most of the leading Pakistanis were descendants of two connected families. But Jamal and his younger brother Khan Din were outsiders, though both came from Peshawar. Others who had no connection with the two prominent families were Amin, his brother Zain Khan, and Yusuf Khan, one of that select group of professionals whose coaching career has spanned three continents. Yusuf comes from Nowshera, which is not far from Peshawar. He had a pleasing style and his forehand volley lingers in the memory. He came upon us during the great Khan era and, would you believe it, popped up again when playing for the United States against Pakistan during the open team tournament played in Karachi in 1976. The forehand volley was still there. But, inevitably, the pace of the game was now too much for Yusuf's ageing legs. Oddy rated him as a better player than Jamal, but was grateful to both. The Scot was coached by Jamal at Edinburgh, by Yusuf at Leicester, and by Azam in London.

Did they, one wonders, have the faintest suspicion that Oddy would be the man to depose their race from the British championship?

For a time the most obvious threat was posed by the foxy and enviably talented Mohamed Dardir. He was seventeen before he took up the game seriously but he was Egyptian professional champion the next season. In the same year, 1951, he was chosen to tour England as a cricketer but decided to concentrate on squash. Dardir was in the same league as Hashim, Azam and Roshan, if not quite in the same class. Had he been granted similar opportunities for intensive preparatory practice, he would doubtless have worried them even more than he did. As it was, the Khan clan were rather relieved when Dardir was spirited away to Australia in 1962. This was another of those strange episodes that have tended to punctuate the careers of leading Egyptian and Pakistani professionals. The Australians wanted Dardir and he was ready to go. But he suspected that if the news leaked out he might be hustled back to Egypt. So the Australians whisked him away quickly and quietly. His expertize and his capacity for passing it on had a great deal to do with the development of playing standards in Australia and, later, New Zealand. In 1976 I heard that he had settled down happily, had a sports shop, was building a house on Waiheke Island in the Hauraki Gulf (off Auckland), and was savouring the prospect of fishing contentedly from a small boat. No more competition. Little or no coaching. Just sea and sky and reveries.

Dardir's one-time protégé and eventual successor as Egyptian champion, Abou Taleb, was luckier in his timing. Dardir's chance of fame had been destroyed by the storm that the Khans blew up. But that storm was abating by the time Taleb arrived on the scene. His remarkable flair for the game, nourished by the inevitably long hours of training and practice, enabled Taleb to burst from the obscurity of a poor background and dominate the game much as Amr, Karim, and Hashim had done before him. The Khans had the final of the British open championship to themselves for nine consecutive seasons. But in 1962 Taleb beat Roshan in a semi-final and had a match point against Mohibullah in the final. A year later Oddy knocked Mohibullah out of the running and Taleb won the first of three successive championships.

Taleb's supremacy occurred during a lean period for the professional game. The men he had to beat were mostly leading amateurs — players like Ibrahim Amin, Aftab Jawaid, Tewfik Shafik, and Michael Oddy (there was not much to choose between them). The only professionals to challenge Taleb in 1963, 1964, and 1965 were Mohibullah, Mohamed Yasin, Khan Din, Gul Rehman (once each), Samir Nadim (twice) and Arthur Catherine (three times). Taleb's opponents, in short, were not in the class of those Dardir had to tackle. He had a relatively untroubled reign.

Taleb unquestionably had a great talent, but it was marred by the effects of its fulfilment. His self-discipline declined once the Khans had ceased to stimulate it. Casual and cocky, he began to assume that natural ability was enough for his purposes, that such things as fitness preparation and a discreet diet (he ate too much) were for less gifted players. He got away with it because his natural ability was exceptional and his opponents, when judged by the highest standards, were not. He was physically ill-prepared for the hard labour to which Jonah Barrington was to sentence him in 1966 — and mentally ill-prepared to resist or accept the eclipse that was to follow. Taleb lacked the strength of character to change his life-style in the cause of fitness. Nor, at times, had he the dignity to lose without subjecting his opponent to a rough physical challenge — barging into his man, or turning on the ball and hitting him with it. So he became a rather sad figure on court, the victim of his inability to control his gifts and the status that they had earned him. He retained his skill with the racket, his assumption of superiority, his desperate inner need to win. He *was* superior. But he never seemed to swallow the fact that squash, like most games, is 50 per cent talent and 50 per cent effort — and that the effort had to go into preparation as well as match-play. So the artist, surpassed by mere craftsmen who took the trouble to be fitter, often became sullen and petulant.

We could appreciate the emotional pressure under which Taleb was labouring. But this explained his behaviour without excusing it. His background was modest and he had little education. Suddenly he was a well-to-do celebrity. He was in the Air Force and every time he won the British open championship he moved up a rank, and had a new car. He began to take it all for granted, living the happy-go-lucky life that suited his nature. Had he been a less cheerful, gregarious, and popular man, the temptations might have been easier to withstand. But Taleb had this zest for life and all the good things it offered him — a zest reflected in his joyously adventurous squash. Towards the end of his marvellously exciting competitive career, one often thought of the circus clown — crying a little inside, while laughter swelled around him.

It would be well to remember the best of Taleb: the pleasure he gave by his exhilarating, magical skills and his ebullient personality. Like Ilie Nastase in tennis, he was a child of nature — often at the mercy of his mood — and an entertainer whose virtuosity could be breath-taking. Years after his prime, Taleb's matches were still attracting the attention of every other player on the premises (a considerable tribute) because they knew he would be fun to watch, if not to play. He was always trying some fancy trickery, and grinning up at the gallery to make sure they were relishing it as much as he was. Squash was usually a happy game when Taleb was playing it. His tolerance for the more tedious components of technique and tactics was limited.

Taleb's game was cast in the same mould as Karim's and Dardir's. His eyes, wrist, and racket-work were superb. His touch — especially on the volleyed drop shot, the backhand reverse-angle, and his use of the side walls in general — was so sure as to seem inhuman. His footwork was far from exemplary, but his arm, wrist, and racket did all the right things. He was bursting with imaginative ideas and it was almost impossible to read his intentions in advance. He tended to leave his shots late and then do something daring and totally unexpected. He was such a master of deception that even the best of his opponents could be utterly wrong-footed, committing themselves in one direction while Taleb was committing the ball in another. Then the tubby little chap would look up and smile broadly, as if it were Christmas Day and he had collared all the presents. He could make a man look a fool, and often did. There was no profit for any opponent who found the key to Taleb's treasure house. Mind you, the artful improvisations would have been less effective without a solid basis of drives and lobs to a length. Taleb could play a hard-hitting game when he thought it necessary. He could pin a man back and he could make a clean kill, as well as confounding opponents with his wristy cunning. But when he was playing straight, sparring, imposing pressure without taking chances, one always felt that he was performing a rather boring chore that had to be got out of the way before he could start enjoying himself again. Laying the table in readiness for another feast, as it were.

When under pressure, Taleb could produce shots of controlled boldness. In attack he was a sorcerer. Like Nastase (the similarities are often in mind) he seemed to have not only the right shot for every occasion, but two or three shots. And like Nastase he had the exciting habit — in lesser players it would have been a folly — of playing shots dictated by the heart rather than the head. Taleb was not a percentage player. He was impulsive, governed by mood and instinct. A decade later another British open champion, Qamar Zaman, was to produce a similarly thrilling sample of audacious artistry.

Playing Taleb was like trying to run through a maze that was doubly baffling because the structural pattern of the thing was continually shifting. The Heliopolis professional was twenty-four when he restored the Egyptian line. He turned the open championship into little more than an exhibition series in the midst of a dress-rehearsal for the amateur championship, which in those days was played a month later. The professional game took several years to recover from the Khans and the void they left behind them. The game drifted into the limbo of 'shamateurism' and remained there until Jonah Barrington turned professional in 1969. During the ensuing six years, all the leading players turned professional, much of the hypocrisy was stripped from the game, and in terms of playing standards squash achieved a depth of expertise unparalleled since the Khans twenty years earlier.

For the moment, though, we are still concerned with the sparks in the shadows, the contemporaries of the four Khan champions. For example, the outstanding British professional, Jack Giles. Wartime service with the RAF prevented his career from taking off as it might have done. Then came Karim and the men from Peshawar. But in 1954 a new event was inaugurated for the benefit of British professionals who spent most of their time coaching and were hardly geared to cope with the annual invasion of Pakistanis and Egyptians. The professional championship of the United Kingdom was restricted to SRA members who were born in the United Kingdom and worked there. Giles won it for ten consecutive seasons, an agreeably round figure, and then withdrew from competition. Bill Moss and Dennis Harman made him sweat, but although they could pick up a game or two it was always Giles who picked up the three that mattered. His game was stylishly orthodox. In the best professional tradition he did all the basic things with a smooth facility that made him pleasantly instructive to watch.

One more professional we should notice at this stage, because he was already an accomplished player before the Khans receded from prominence, is Mohamed Yasin. He has three claims to attention. First, Yasin and his amateur relative, Aftab Jawaid, formed a tenuous bridge that stretched from the Khans across the span dominated by Taleb, Barrington and Hunt, and finally served as a basis for a new Pakistani invasion — that of Alauddin, Jahan and Muneer, with Mohibullah and Zaman close behind them. Second, when all the Pakistanis were working themselves into a sweat of patriotic fervour because Barrington was on the way to a seventh British open championship (which would have equalled Hashim's record), it was Yasin — not the youngsters — who stopped him. Third, Ken Hiscoe of Australia was the only contemporary who could match the astonishingly long duration of Yasin's career in the game's élite. Yasin was already twenty-three when he arrived in Britain for the first time, in 1963, and reached the last eight of the open championship. In 1974 he confounded Barrington and Zaman in turn to reach the final. In 1976 he was still good enough — hitting the nick with all sorts of shots from all sorts of places — to concede only eleven points to Cam Nancarrow in the Pakistan Masters. Watching Yasin's dynamic, magical performance that evening, I found it hard to believe that it was thirteen years since I had first seen him play — and that he had been a match-hardened competitor long before that.

Yasin is a springy little chap with bushy eyebrows and a solemn mien — a Victor Borge without the humour. During his early years he had a moustache like a hyphen. His English was limited, and Jawaid, with his charming gentility, was the dominant personality. At times Yasin, a shadowy figure in the background, seemed almost cowed in his presence. Yasin was clearly short of self-confidence and his relationship with Jawaid did nothing to dispel this. During this period Jawaid always beat him, though Yasin was a more exciting, technically more positive player. Throughout his career Yasin seemed to have no depth of belief in himself. When he beat Taleb in the 1969 open championship, Yasin had only Barrington ahead of him in the struggle for professional supremacy. But there was no sign of the strength of character that transforms a contender into a champion. Yasin had everything else. There was an echo of Hashim in his short grip, and he bounced about the court with remarkable speed, though in later years his stamina was vulnerable to sustained pressure. He was a shot-maker, always eager to bury the ball in the nick, and on the forehand in particular he needed watching closely because of his enviable capacity for deception. Yasin was a bustler with a good touch. One writes of him in the past tense only because he is past his prime. On his day he can still dazzle and delight us. What a pity that a sprained ankle prevented him from contesting the 1974 open championship final with Geoff Hunt. Even in defeat, the little man might have enjoyed a fleeting glimpse of glory.

Jawaid was born at Gurdaspur in the east Punjab, but was brought up at Quetta, where his father was a squash professional. He was another of the Khan clan and the family home was — almost inevitably —Peshawar. Between 1964 and 1970 he was British amateur champion three times (in successive seasons) and was three times runner-up for the open championship, once to Taleb and twice to Barrington. That is an impressive record. But his historic significance rests in two areas directly connected with his achievements. He was among the first leading squash players to be employed by Pakistan International Airlines, a job that gave him free flights and financial security and did not unduly inhibit his dedication to squash. Because of this convenient arrangement he had more opportunities than Yasin — and but for the encouragement of PIA it is doubtful if he would have become the first Pakistani to reach the final of the British amateur championship. In 1964, at the age of twenty-five, he won that title only a month after the Khans had lost their hold on the open championship. As one chapter ended, another began.

Jawaid was personable and clever. He was also a valetudinarian, seldom free of anxiety about his health in spite of his capacity for staying on court for hours without visible signs of fatigue. Physically, he was rather like the hybrid offspring of a standard lamp and a coat-hanger. He was 5ft 10½in tall but weighed between 9st and 10st, depending on how much he had been worrying and eating. His clothes hung about him in folds, as if searching for something to cling to. When he was jostled, one half-expected him to break. Instead, he merely became puffed and, with just the slightest shift of his gaunt features, indicated his displeasure at such caddish behaviour. Not that Jawaid himself was exemplary company on court. Prudent opponents left him ample room for a full swing. When he played Tewfik Shafik, who arrogated similar claims to air space, there was always a possibility that chunks of squash player would soon be flying about the court. Their matches tended to consist of a series of lets and penalty points punctuated by squash. Jawaid's arms and legs seemed to be telescopic. In spite of his apparent languor, he was effortlessly omnipresent.

Jawaid, you will gather, was interesting. But his squash was not — unless one had a taste for water torture, or driving along interminable motorways. He was like a ball machine with a brain. When he played Jeremy Lyon of Britain in the 1964 British open championship, I wrote in *The Times:*

> 'Jawaid is always far, far better than he looks. He does the basic things almost flawlessly well and keeps his man on the move all the time. Like so many before him, Lyon was continually hurtling from corner to corner. There was no end to all the chasing and turning. Lyon must have felt like a man spending his life digging holes and filling them up again, with the spade getting heavier all the time. He would no sooner settle down to the process of excavation in the back corners than a drop shot would set the alarm bells ringing for a dash to the front wall.'

Jawaid played squash the way Jane Austen wrote novels — almost faultlessly, but within a deliberately limited range. The impressive thing about him was that, unless Yasin happened to be around, he was always scratching about for practice partners. Conversely, the leading Australian and Egyptian amateurs (Carter, Hiscoe, Hunt, Parmenter, Amin, Shafik, and Zaghloul) arrived in bunches and could always practise under pressure. When Jawaid was alone in London, my wife and I sometimes invited him to spend a day with us in Buckinghamshire. He liked to do this when the amateur championship had been reduced to eight or four men. We would wander about our bit of England — perhaps to Windsor, perhaps to some out-of-the-way inn with low beams and large dogs — and talk of anything but squash. Jawaid knew this was good for him. He was clearing his mind. I can remember delivering him to his London hotel some time between midnight and one o'clock, and teasing him about the fact that those rugged, highly trained Australians had probably been in bed since ten. 'Yes,' he said, 'but I think perhaps they are not sleeping.'

Jawaid knew how to prepare body and mind for sleep and match-play. He also knew the kind of food that suited him. He and his wife once prepared us a chicken curry that burned an imperishable memory on English palates and saucepans.

The best of the Egyptian amateurs was that delightful chap, Ibrahim Amin, who has often been compared with Karim. He contested the final of the British amateur championship six times (winning it twice), a record matched only by Amr and Cazalet. And in 1964 — nine seasons after first winning the amateur title — he joined Taleb in the only all-Egyptian final the British open championship has ever produced. In the previous round Amin had beaten Jawaid, already amateur champion. Poised like a vulture hovering over its prey, Amin dominated the middle of the court and shifted Jawaid about with wondrous facility. The Egyptian used the side walls admirably and, with that remarkable wrist of his, repeatedly caught Jawaid on the wrong foot with a masked drop shot. 'Sometimes I tried a double-fake,' said Amin later, 'but it needed very good timing. I had to make him move first.' In the last of their five games, Amin even played a shot behind his back. With a flair such as his, there were no conventional limits. Not that he insulted the textbooks. It was just that he played more shots more often and more easily than most players. Angles, reverse angles, boasts, drops, nicks, good length hitting down the walls — he made it all look child's play. And because of his wrist, his capacity for nudging the ball in an unexpected direction, he could be bewilderingly deceptive. 'Once you gave Amin the middle of the court he was fantastic,' said Michael Oddy once. 'At the front of the court he was probably the most talented amateur I've seen. But he was beatable — by getting him to the back of the court and not letting him out. And he had a slightly suspect temperament. He let things rattle him.'

Watching Amin play squash was to think in terms of chess-masters, goemetricians, and conjurors. But in those days he was an agronomist by profession. He knew about crop production. As he swayed this way and that — lithe and graceful in his movements, with a slight stoop — it was easy to imagine him roaming the open country and bending to pick up a handful of earth to see what it had to say to him. One wondered what recondite, labyrinthine conversations he had with another wristy Egyptian international, Sherif Afifi, an entomologist who gave me a rudimentary education in the activities of the mealy-bug. Afifi studied at London University for so long that they began to think he was on the staff. He was one of the most agreeable adornments of the English squash scene. Then he suddenly fled to Virginia to expand his zoological wisdom. Nine years later the phone rang — and we had lunch together, with wives and dogs and little Omar, at a roadside pub in the Chilterns. The friendships made at the Lansdowne during the Barrington-Nasrullah era were the kind that lasted.

Tewfik Shafik was far more popular off court than on it. 'Everybody said what a nice chap he was off the court,' says Oddy, 'but we were certainly not good friends. I had a healthy respect for him, but playing Shafik was a hard, hard business. He had an enormous backswing on the backhand, and a pretty big swing on the forehand. I just didn't get on with him, on the court.' Shafik was not tall. But he was strongly built and could have looked after himself in the front row of a rugby scrum. He was a tough, bustling player who enjoyed belting the daylights out of the ball. His powerfully robust game could rip gaping holes in the defences of all but the very best opponents. Shafik's matches with Jawaid were memorably unpleasant. In the first game of the 1964 amateur championship final, Shafik went off court to have an eyebrow plastered after he had run across Jawaid's stroke, which was never a good thing to do.

Shafik was runner-up for the amateur championship three times. Then he nipped off to Algeria to exercise his professional talents as an architect. He wanted to build a squash court there. I hope this ambition had a more successful outcome than his boisterous labours at the Lansdowne.

Apart from Amin and Shafik, the Arabian amateur to look out for was Kamal Zaghloul, who had a degree in political science but never quite graduated at squash because he was more effective at keeping the rallies going than he was in finishing them. As Benjamin Disraeli put it, finality is not the language of politics. But Zaghloul came close to the top. He twice reached the last four of the British open championship. In the same tournament he had the unusual distinction, in consecutive seasons, of beating the reigning British amateur champion in the first round — Michael Oddy in 1962 and Ken Hiscoe in 1963. Zaghloul's boyish face usually wore a somewhat puzzled look. He was shrewd, strong, and nimble, and watched the ball so closely that he was difficult to deceive. He hit to a teasing length, had a useful forehand drop, and was a bonny fighter. But he lacked the severity of shot to take charge of a big match. His method was to scamper about and play sensibly and soundly until he had drawn his opponent's sting.

If you want it in a nutshell, Amin was a nudger, Shafik a thumper, and Zaghloul a runner.

These Egyptian amateurs were fine players and good company. But sportsmen cannot always break down the barriers with which politicians confront them. Diplomatic dissension temporarily checked the flow of Egyptian talent to London. When the next generation turned up, the best of them became professionals and settled in Europe. And the Egyptian game suffered because the top men were not around to bring the youngsters along.

It was during this period (the Khan era and the years that linked it to the Barrington era) that Australia emerged as a major force in world squash. We will discuss that exciting development in the next chapter. South Africa made an earlier impact on the international amateur game. Bill Whiteley was their national champion eight times between 1930 and 1948. Then the names that kept popping up were those of Gavin Hildick-Smith (always known as 'Peter') and the Callaghan brothers, Brian and Denis. Hildick-Smith contested the final of the British amateur championship in two consecutive seasons, first losing to Norman Borrett and then beating Brian Phillips. Five seasons later Denis Callaghan — fit, fast and a hard hitter — was beaten 7-9, 8-10, 9-1, 9-4, 9-6 by Roy Wilson in a final as memorably thrilling as the statistical evidence suggests. Hildick-Smith was interesting on two counts. First, he was coached by 'Oke' Johnson, the man who twenty years earlier had shown Abdel Fattah Amr what it was all about. Second, Hildick-Smith went to Haileybury and had British parents. The South African connection arose when his father took a job managing a mine out there. Hildick-Smith had a solid all-round game. He knew how to use the side walls, and he could raise the pace when he wanted to.

'Peter was no stylist,' says Phillips, 'but he was a strong, gritty player and had a knack of "mishitting" winners. After he'd done it six or seven times you began to suspect it was no fluke.'

Between Hildick-Smith's title and the first of Amin's, Alan Fairbairn and Roy Wilson contested three successive all-British finals. Fairbairn won the first two. He was already well-known as a cricketer. In 1947 he scored centuries in the second innings of his first two matches for Middlesex in first-class cricket: 108 against Somerset at Taunton and 110 not out against Nottinghamshire at Nottingham. As a squash player, he reflected the pattern set by Borrett and the early Hashim — a pattern that consisted, essentially, of imposing maximum pressure at minimum risk. 'He was a sportsman with remarkable co-ordination of muscle and eye,' says Wilson. 'He was in the same mould as Borrett. Persistent and accurate returns. But he also played a straight drop down the backhand-wall, from the back of the court, which was very annoying when you were tired. I played him for an hour and forty minutes in one final, which was a record for some years. I found it extraordinarily tedious, particularly since I lost.'

In the 1952-3 season Wilson was runner-up to Hashim for the open championship and reached the first of five consecutive finals in the amateur event — a feat matched only by Cazalet, Borrett and Amin. His last two finals both went to five games. As we know, he was just good enough to shake off Callaghan. But the previous season he lost to Amin after leading 8-0 in the fifth game. 'I was grossly unfit that season. It was a lean year and no one had taken more than a game from me. I drank too much. I thought I'd beaten him, but I was completely blown. He matured into a beautiful stroke-player.' Wilson himself was always bursting with vitality and was a brisk, aggressive player. He had guts too. 'A very hard man and a clever tactician,' says Michael Oddy. 'He would have been hard to beat in any era.'

In 1959 Wilson captained the first British team to tour Australia and New Zealand. When his competitive prime was behind him he poured his enthusiasm and energy into committee work and refereeing. To this day he remains a restless, boisterously inspirational character — the kind who lights fires in others.

Oddy, who won the Australian and New Zealand amateur championships on that 1959 tour, collected the South African title three years later. He thus made a comprehensively resounding impact on the developing overseas game. He won the British amateur championship twice. And as we have already noted, it was Oddy who rang down the curtain on the long-running Khan show by beating Mohibullah before a sold-out gallery in a 1963 semi-final of the open championship. He was beaten by Taleb in the final. But reaching the final was itself a considerable achievement for a British player: Oddy was the first since Wilson lost to Hashim eleven years earlier. As we have noticed, Oddy was also the first leading British player to be coached by Pathans: Jamal, Yusuf and Azam. That tuning up — plus his powerfully effective game, his strength of character, and the iron in his competitive nature — enabled him to withstand the rising tide from overseas that was threatening to engulf the British game. 'I was left to fend off the Egyptians and Australians. When I quit, I did think to myself — maybe I was a bit blasé — that in view of the attitude of the players at the time, it was very unlikely that a British player would win the amateur championship again. I was not to know that a Barrington would emerge. Jonah was underrated. At his best he was a phenomenally good player.'

Oddy was large and strong and maintained a blistering attack. He played like a whirlwind that knew exactly what it was up to. His violence was always calculated. He found the nick when it mattered. He cut his winners to an instant death. The year he beat Mohibullah 9-1, 9-6, 9-2 in thirty-five minutes, Oddy was not even seeded. But he out-hit the reigning champion — in terms of accuracy, at least — and gradually destroyed his confidence. There were a few delectable rallies as they swapped subtleties in probing for an opening. But essentially this was squash by machine-gunners. Oddy's last three winners (he was never a player to depend on the other chap's mistakes) were a drop shot, a clinging drive down the backhand-wall, and a backhand so brutal and so heavily cut that it was not merely killed. It was interred — probably in slices.

Oddy was only twenty-six at the time but, sadly, he was playing his last season of major championships. In 1964 he was persistently plagued by ill-health and was advised to rest. In the following year he formally retired. But in the 1971-2 season he returned to the game at club and county level and soon demonstrated that, whatever he might have lost, it was not his eagerness to score twenty-seven points before his opponent got off the mark. He was a ruthless competitor.

A contemporary of Oddy's who withdrew from the front rank even sooner, because he had chosen a career in the Army, was Nigel Broomfield. His flair for the game was precocious and prodigious. Three times in four seasons he won the junior tournament for the Drysdale Cup. Three years after the last of those successes, at the age of twenty, he beat Amin 9-1, 9-7, 9-4 in the final of the British amateur championship. The following year, 1959, he did it again, though this time Amin managed to take a game. In between, Broomfield became amateur champion of South Africa, too. Geoff Hunt and Gogi Alauddin were to match the rapidity of his rise through the ranks and Mohibullah Junior was to surpass it. All three became professionals. But Broomfield's potential excellence was never fully explored. For him, the Army was work and squash was play. Run down the list of Army champions and you find him labelled first as Officer/Cadet, then Captain, then Major: during a period when Azam, Mohibullah Senior, Taleb, and Barrington were winning the British open championship and Broomfield was still in his twenties. He kept popping up, often as a member of the Haileybury team in the old boys' competition for the Londonderry Cup. His game still had a beautiful simplicity about it. He was a 'pressure' player with a good wrist. He struck the ball cleanly and he struck it hard.

'He was brutally good as a boy,' says Oddy. 'Completely outstanding. Superbly talented.' Unfortunately, the talent was confined to barracks soon after it flowered. Broomfield was born exactly ten years before Hunt. But already he seems more like a dream than a memory.

A player with marked similarities to Broomfield and Oddy — in terms of age and background, build and method — was Jeremy Lyon, who reached the semi-finals of the amateur championship on three occasions. The first was in January, 1965. Shafik had been blasting his way through the tournament with his inimitable blend of rugged violence and sudden subtlety (he had a delicate forehand angle). But Lyon beat him in straight games in thirty-five minutes. Shafik had eaten hamburgers on the eve of battle and suspected these were the cause of stomach trouble that made him feel slightly dizzy. Lyon was no help. At the crux of the match he assaulted Shafik's morale with some winning backhand drops from deep in the court. Then Lyon pounced for the kill. As usual, straight, hard hitting was the basis of his game. But his timing of drops and angles was exemplary. Lyon was a farmer and in 1968 he became a stockbroker, too. The two jobs did not leave him much time for squash and in any case he was now in his thirties.

So he retired. By that time he had played more international matches than any other English player.

The most exciting ornament of the British game in those days was a Welshman whose name has been cropping up throughout our story. Denis Hughes, a wizard with flat feet, was among the greatest shot-makers in the history of squash: and he was imaginative and daring in exploiting his remarkable aptitude for the game. Hughes had the wit to devise the most absurd ideas — and the skill to make most of them work. He refused to recognize the frontier between the probable and the improbable, between the bold and the reckless. He thought percentages were strictly for statisticians. Such shots as the reverse angle and the corkscrew lob might be luxuries to others, but to Hughes they were bread and butter. He read the geometry of squash as fluently as he read a balance sheet. He made nonsense of the conventions. He was so joyously unpredictable that, half the time, one suspected even Hughes himself had no notion of what he was going to do next. Inevitably, he often hit down when going for a shot too literally based on the Tertullian philosophy 'It is certain because it is impossible'. And he was no devotee of training and practice. Like Taleb, he was an artist with a taste for social pleasures and an allergy to drudgery. Hughes found hot courts — notably the Bruce court at the Lansdowne Club — inimical. He lacked the physical and mental endurance to enjoy an attritional five-game slugfest that drained all the laughter out of the game. A notable exception occurred in the 1958 British open championship when he came from behind to subdue Yusuf in the fifth game of an attractive and thrilling match.

Like Taleb, Hughes saw himself as an entertainer. At the end of a rally he would often adjust his spectacles and look up at the gallery to make sure they were having fun: if there seemed any reason for doubt, he would promptly dispel it with some sample of his flamboyant ingenuity. This frequently happened when he was obviously puffed and temporarily in no condition for a lot of running. He went for quick winners then, making racket and ball do the work. Hughes was a fine tennis player, too. He and Gerry Oakley took Ham Richardson and Vic Seixas to five sets at Wimbledon in 1957.

In January, 1968, Hughes was seeded for the tenth time in fourteen seasons in the amateur championship. A month later he had a severe stroke, precariously won the struggle for survival, but emerged from it partially paralysed. He had won the biggest match he had ever played. But his career was over.

The strength of British squash in the early 1960s lay in Oddy, Lyon and Hughes, in Richard Boddington and Gerald Massy, and in Tony Gathercole and John Skinner (whose combined hip measurements were such that, whenever they played each other, squash became an unusually interesting study in circumnavigation). All were suffering from a degree of shock because of a sudden realization that Britain no longer dominated the Anglo-Saxon amateur game. A better trained breed of rugged and aggressive competitors were displaying more consistent ball control under prolonged pressure. They came from the other side of the world, spoke a strange kind of English, and blew into the West End social clubs like a breeze fresh from the Blue Mountains.

The Australians had arrived.

Eight

The Big Island

The first Australians I ever swapped shots with were Helen Gourlay, who played tennis for a living, and Barry Court, whose wife did. Barry assesses himself thus: 'Good reach. Not too fast on the feet. But a squash player of great potential.' The second assertion falls short of the truth. The third exceeds it. He knows this, but his sense of humour is irrepressible. Margaret, who watched us for a while one day and then quietly slipped away (perhaps she resented the terrible things we were doing to a beautiful game), achieved more than any other woman in the history of tennis. In 1967, during a fourteen-month retirement, she also became Western Australia's No. 2 squash player. The No. 1, a friend with whom she went into business at Perth, was Helen Plaisted, who in 1964 represented Australia in their first women's international match with Britain. She won. So did Australia.

Squash is booming in Perth these days. But the Australian game's oldest and strongest roots are buried at the other end of the island. The first court was probably that built at a physical culture institute in Sydney about 1918. The same company built a court (with rounded corners!) at Melbourne in 1929. One sportsman who used to train there was Harry Hopman, a Davis Cup tennis player who was to acquire even greater renown as captain of Australian tennis teams. He took up squash at the end of his career as a Davis Cup player, won the Australian amateur championship at his first attempt, and between 1933 and 1937 appeared in five successive finals, winning three.

An intervening development at Melbourne, which was to

become the hub of the Australian game, was the construction of a court at the Royal Melbourne Tennis Club in 1927. Courts were gradually introduced at other Melbourne tennis clubs. But squash was still regarded primarily as a means of fitness training for more popular sports, notably tennis and cricket. Don Bradman, the 1939 South Australian champion, recognized its value in maintaining and improving ball sense, footwork, balance, and suppleness of the wrist and legs. He also considered squash 'one of the most exhilarating of all games.' But in this judgement he was ahead of his time: it was to be twenty years before squash became widely accepted among Australians as a game worth playing for its own sake, and not merely as an adjunct to others. The Australian amateur championship was inaugurated in 1931. A national association was formed in 1935. But growth was slow. Australians tend to be paradoxical: a conservative breed of gamblers. Like most successful pioneers they advance carefully, consolidating every gain before pushing on. Their squash players were also using a faster ball than the type prevalent in Britain — and the Australian game was presumably less attractive in its variety.

In the early years squash quickly spread from Victoria to New South Wales. There were scattered outbreaks elsewhere, but no sign of an epidemic. As in Britain, the game was mostly played in private clubs that also catered for other recreational activities. But a sharply contrasting development — public courts built exclusively for squash — was to have a revolutionary impact on the game as a whole and the Australian game in particular. Shortly after the war, a few speculators took the temperature of the water and decided to plunge. The public were interested. Then, suddenly, very interested. By the middle 1950s public courts were springing up all over the country. The national champion, Brian Boys (who was to become a respected coach), went on a scouting mission to Britain during the 1955-6 season, was beaten in the third round of the amateur championship by Ibrahim Amin — who won the tournament — and went home to talk about it. The capital cities of the Australian states were soon more densely populated with squash courts than those of any other country in the world. These new courts, built by private enterprise, were open to anyone. So Australian squash swiftly swept through every segment of society. Granted this broad basis of recruitment, the huge numbers involved, and the Australian's intense eagerness to compete, it was inevitable that playing standards should rise rapidly.

'Australia is the only country where the game is opened up and available to the average person in the street,' says Geoff Hunt. 'See an article about an average Australian and you find that he plays squash. That's an indication of how squash is, in Australia. That's the reason Ken Hiscoe and I started. Cam Nancarrow. Bill Reedman. We've all come from an average working family and have got through. Sydney's first, Melbourne second. Then the capital cities of the other states. Almost all the country towns with maybe over 50,000 people have a set of squash courts — one centre, perhaps, with at least three or four courts. I estimate there are about 1,000 courts in Melbourne. The most interesting thing is a six-court centre built in 1960 near the middle of Melbourne. It's a pay-as-you-play centre run by the Victorian SRA for a profit, like all the other commercial centres in Australia. They have revenue coming in from their own squash centre. It also has the biggest gallery, though there's no glass back wall. The last time Jonah and I played, there were 550 people in.'

One of Nasrullah's sons, Rehmatullah, who had his first trip to Australia in 1972, gives an outsider's view that is no less enthusiastic: 'I like the idea of squash in Australia because anyone can walk in and play, which is good for squash and good for the people. You can hire any equipment you need. Another thing I like is that every court owner makes sure his courts are very clean. And these pennant matches — league matches. If you stop anyone in the street and ask if he's played his pennant match this week, he will tell you "Yes" or "No". Everybody plays squash. Go to a public centre and every night somebody is playing a competition. Even Geoff plays pennant matches. That's good. It improves standards.'

Jonah Barrington often makes the point that squash must thrive whenever it becomes established in a society with a large and prosperous middle class. The speed and the extent of the game's expansion in Australia confirm his opinion. The public nature of that expansion, together with a zest for competition, had a healthy effect on the level of skill. There may be something, too, in Mohamed Dardir's assertion that Australians move and react faster than players from countries that enjoy less sunshine.

But Australia's first genuine experience of international competition was chastening. In 1959 Roy Wilson captained a British team — the other players were Michael Oddy, Nigel Broomfield, Denis Hughes, and Jeremy Lyon — who spent two months touring Australia and New Zealand. Britain played three international matches against each country, won the lot, and lost only one of the twenty-four individual matches played. In the respective national amateur championships, all four semi-finalists were British (Oddy beat Broomfield in both finals). Six years earlier Gerald Pawle had committed himself to the view: 'It is doubtful whether a fully representative English team of amateurs will be defeated by any nation in the foreseeable future in a match played under standard SRA conditions.' Well, that 1959 team was reinforced by a Scot and a Welshman. But Pawle was still making sense. The challengers — Australia, Egypt, New Zealand, Pakistan, and South Africa — were on the way but had yet to arrive.

Nevertheless, that all-conquering British team of 1959 were impressed by what they saw. Wilson was to write later of the fitness and stamina of the 'intensely competitive' Australians, of their capacity for work and their eagerness to improve. And by 1963 — only four years after being rocked back on their heels — the amateurs from 'down under' were on top of the heap.

In January, 1962, Ken Hiscoe reached the semi-finals of the British amateur championship at the first attempt. The man who stopped him, after Hiscoe had won the first two games, was Amin — the man who had stopped Boys six years earlier. That was also the year in which Dardir went to Australia. 'He would play four of us top amateurs one after the other,' says Hiscoe, 'and we wouldn't win a handful of points between us.' Most of the Australians had never seen anyone play the game as well as Dardir played it. He taught them to keep their wrist up and the face of the racket open. He taught them about footwork and shot-making. And the Australians watched, listened, and learned.

At the end of 1962 Britain was swept by blizzards (the worst since 1881) and had seventy-three consecutive nights of frost — and the Australians began the first of two tours that, within twelve months, inflicted an equally severe frost on British amateur squash. Between 18th December and 21st January, Australia beat Wales 5-0, England 4-1, Britain 4-1, South Africa 4-1, and Scotland 4-1. The players were Hiscoe, Owen Parmenter, Dick Carter, Kenny Binns, Doug Stephenson, and John Cheadle. In the middle of that tour, a week before his twenty-fifth birthday, Hiscoe became the first Australian to win the British amateur championship. He was one of four Australians who achieved more than the seedings suggested they would. The others were Carter, who beat Amin to reach the last four, and Parmenter and Binns, who reached the last eight. The Australians had tasted blood and before 1963 was over they had returned to the assault. There followed an extraordinary *tour de force*. Within eight days Hiscoe, Carter, and Parmenter beat Pakistan, England, and Britain in turn: all by the maximum 3-0 margin. Australia lost only four games in nine matches. Their British opponents could not find much of an excuse in the fact that Oddy and Lyon were both out of action, because of influenza, and Michael Corby was gadding about India playing hockey. Those eight days — indeed, those twelve months — provided astonishing evidence of Australia's advance. And Hiscoe, Carter, and Parmenter again reached the quarter-finals of the amateur championship. Aftab Jawaid deprived Hiscoe of the title. But the Australians had made their point.

Australia's reserve on that tour was their junior champion, Hunt, then sixteen years old. It seemed unfair that anyone so young should be so good. Hunt beat John Skinner in straight games in each of their two reserve matches during the international series. In the amateur championship he lost in five to Tewfik Shafik. 'I learnt how tough international competition is,' wrote Hunt later. 'My narrow defeat blooded me to the tactics of the big swingers I was to meet in later years.'

So 1962 and 1963 were the years in which Australian squash 'came good' and Hunt, a boy among men, had his first trip from the big island to Europe.

At this phase of our story we move into a period still so close to us that there is some danger of the historic perspective becoming blurred. The critic cannot adequately fulfil his function until the cast have cleared the stage. Of the triumvirate who dominated those 1962-3 tours, Hiscoe is still hammering away as an itinerant professional and looking around for antiques that, in his view and Beryl's, would be better off in Australia. But Carter and Parmenter receded from international competition years ago. Carter was only 5ft 5½in tall, but always busy. We called him 'The Ant'. He burst upon us in 1963, when he beat Kamal Zaghloul and Amin in successive matches and reached the semi-finals of the British amateur championship unseeded, at his first attempt. But his big achievement was in reaching the final in two successive seasons. In 1966 he met Hunt for the first time, beat him in five in a semi-final, but then lost in five to Jawaid. In 1967 he handled Jawaid in straight games in a semi-final but then came off worst in a five-game match with Barrington.

By Australian standards Carter was lukewarm in his appreciation of the volley and the cross-court nick. But he used his other strokes with flowing facility and was a cute tactician. He trained hard and was a quick, bustling retriever with deep reserves of stamina and resolution. He was very much a 'croucher', and never let the ball out of his sight. Carter was more at ease buffeting the soft English ball around the warm Bruce court at the Lansdowne Club than he was in Australian conditions. He played well in London and was always good company. He was a cheerful little chap — the kind who wakes up wearing a smile and seldom takes it off. He exuded boyishness. Parmenter, by contrast, prematurely accumulated enough grey hair to give him a dignified, academic air. He always looked slightly puzzled, even worried, as if he had opened the wrong door and walked into the squash court instead of the library. He was a good tennis player and, consequently, volleyed well. From mid-court he hit low and could put the ball away in the corners. He had a formidable straight kill and his backhand always commanded respect. A well equipped player, but not quite in the top class. In later years the dapper Parmenter kept turning up at Wimbledon and talked about squash in Japan. He was working there. Something to do with mustard and things like that.

Hiscoe, too, was a competent tennis player. But at fifteen he took to surfing — which, at Bondi, is difficult to avoid — and for a decade he was also a life-guard. 'I'd followed all sports pretty closely, but had never heard of squash. That's how small a game it was.' He was already twenty when he discovered squash at a commercial centre in Bondi. That was in April, 1958. Two years later he was Australian amateur champion, and except for one interruption by Hunt he was to hold that title until 1968. No other Australian had achieved a comparable dominance. Internationally, Hiscoe's historic significance lay in the fact that during 1962 and 1963, as we have seen, he became the first Australian to win the British amateur championship — and played first string for two touring teams who lifted Australian amateur squash from a promising obscurity to an overwhelming supremacy. Hiscoe not only saw the break-through happen. To a great extent, he made it happen.

He reached the last four of the amateur championship in six consecutive seasons (three times in a row, he failed to get past Jawaid). In the 1968-9 season the open championship was shifted from London and December to Sheffield and January — and Hiscoe shifted his attention to the open. He advanced to the last eight. He was to figure in the semi-finals on three occasions. And in 1976, when the British open championship incorporated the inaugural world championship, Hiscoe was still good enough to bustle into the last eight. A fortnight earlier, he had celebrated his thirty-eighth birthday. In short, this remarkable man was still close to the top — fourteen years after blasting his way to the semi-finals of the amateur championship at his first attempt. By this time, too, he had become a figure of considerable influence as president of the International Squash Players' Association (Hiscoe and Hunt became professionals in 1971).

All this by a man who took up the game late, in a country with no squash tradition.

Hiscoe is 5ft 10½in. tall, weighs 12st 7lb and is a formidably burly chap known in the trade as 'The Bear'. His voice has an unexpectedly high pitch. His hair has run the gamut of fashions from crew-cut to glossy abundance. On court, he favours a massively watchful crouch and, in the intensity of his concentration on the more delicate shots, plays with his mouth open as if only half-suppressing an urge to give the ball verbal instructions. His relentlessly aggressive game is based on exerting pressure by interceptive use of the volley. At his peak he played as though the back wall did not exist (it was easy to imagine him crouching at cover point rather than the middle of a squash court). Against all but the fastest opponents, he retains the capacity to put away anything loose that reaches him shoulder-high. He hits hard and low, keeps the ball close to the walls, and pounces eagerly on the slightest chance of a kill. Cross-court nicks are a speciality — usually hit with blazing brutality but sometimes, from high on the backhand, caressed to the slim and distant target as if drawn there by invisible elastic. His drop-shots are always placed with care and often with disguise. Any opponent who grants Hiscoe an opening in the forecourt cannot be sure what will happen next, except that it will be unpleasant to deal with. He also makes fluently positive use of the side walls. Those with experience of dashing, bending and stretching to retrieve it never need to ask why Australians sometimes call this shot the 'gut-ripper'.

The earliest memories are often the most vividly implanted in the mind. Let me select two from a fortnight in which 1963 became 1964. With England playing Australia at the Royal Automobile Club, Richard Boddington kept Hiscoe on court for sixty-eight minutes and four games. Boddington was left-handed, quick and wily. He was a player who encouraged error — with the drop, angle and lob — rather than enforcing it. On this occasion his touch was superb and Hiscoe was teased and hurt by drop shots that drifted to the floor as softly as snowflakes. A game slipped away before the violently erratic Hiscoe realized the futility of hunting a fox with a cannon. He took the lesson to heart, discreetly adjusted his tactics, and a superb match ensued. It ended with a winning drop — from Hiscoe, not Boddington. Two days later, when Australia played Britain, Hiscoe beat Boddington in straight games. This time Hiscoe knew what he was up against, and wasted neither energy nor points by unreasonable ferocity. Disciplined from the start, he picked his punches carefully and gave an admirably mature performance for a man who had been playing for less than five years.

That first match with Boddington was a beauty. But it was to be surpassed when Hiscoe met Ibrahim Amin in the amateur championship. I can recall the sense of inadequacy with which I settled down at a table, overlooking the swimming pool at the Lansdowne Club, and hurriedly tried the capture the flavour of the spectacle for *The Times*:

> 'These two had the packed gallery bubbling with the excitement of a match that stirred the pulse from first to last. It was like some art exhibit in which the detail was every bit as satisfying as the whole. But the phase that will stay longest in the memory was the beginning of the second game, when Amin, masking his intentions with wonderful wrist-work, had the baffled and bewildered Hiscoe dashing to and fro in ineffectively eager attempts to read the subtle structure of Amin's game. Both were adept at the volleyed drop shot, and Amin's angles

were always a joy. Yet it was Hiscoe who played the unexpected winners when they mattered most. Always his was red-blooded squash rackets, whereas Amin's strokes were a mixture of purple and grey. Finally Hiscoe, tight-lipped and dedicated, took charge remorselessly. The party was over.'

Those matches happened in the course of two weeks. Matches like them have been happening to Hiscoe for fifteen years.

We have discussed Hiscoe's achievements, his leadership of the Australian charge to amateur primacy, and latterly his influence on the expanding professional game. There is one further service for which we should be grateful to him — the example and inspiration he provided for Geoff Hunt. Hiscoe's bold shot-making, particularly his use of the volley, kindled a fire in Hunt and taught him how to keep it burning. Seldom has Sydney done Melbourne such a favour. Hiscoe dispatched Hunt on the road to greatness — and went along with him, just to keep the lad up to scratch. Later, Jonah Barrington was to teach Hunt a thing or two about physical conditioning: and they trod the heights together, their enduring rivalry in squash reflecting that of Rod Laver and Ken Rosewall in tennis. It is a moot point, incidentally, whether Barrington is more English than Hunt. Though Hunt neglected to be born in England, both his parents were English. Barrington, by contrast, had a Welsh mother and an Irish father — and he was born in Cornwall, which is almost an island (the necessity for a watershed narrowly prevents the Tamar from making both ends meet) and is reluctant to regard itself as English. This geneological aside is titillating, but not strictly relevant to the point I set out to make: which is that Hiscoe and Barrington in turn, in different ways, helped to drive Hunt towards the dominance he achieved in the world game. The drovers are now getting a little long in the tooth. But there is no danger of Hunt losing his momentum: four Pakistanis are using the whip on him.

Hunt's disposition invited that analogy. Like many great sportsmen, he seems listless, even languid, in his movements off court, as if the effort of getting out of bed had weakened him. Half the time, he looks about two beers below par. His easy-going composure is almost sleepy in its serenity. It is entirely in character that he has always enjoyed fishing for snapper in Port Philip Bay — with his father and, nowadays, with his son Benjamin too.

'There's a lot of snapper: a good fighting fish and a good eating fish. This is one of the reasons we get a lot of sharks. They follow the fish into the bay. There's nothing like bringing home a big fish, a 10 lb snapper. But I don't like this five o'clock business . . .' Off court, Hunt mixes easily but unobtrusively, with a self-effacing reserve that could be misconstrued as diffidence. He has nothing to prove, no desire to advertise the steel that lies just below the surface. Like all champions, he has more acquaintainces than he needs, and must choose his friends with discretion. But when there is no necessity to be on guard against those who want to make use of him, he can be congenially relaxed and relaxing, a fluent talker with an inimitably Australian line in banter. Essentially, though, he remains a quiet, private man.

Hunt and Barrington have something in common in that when they go into a dressing-room they change characters as well as clothes. The Hunt who emerges is boisterously aggressive, whereas Barrington discards his vivacity with his mufti and emerges as a player of calculated restraint. Hunt took up tennis when he was nine, had regular coaching, and played in junior competition. But when Geoff was twelve, his father, Vic, began to play squash for the good of his health — and Geoff, together with his brother and sister, Bill and Tricia (both were to play for Victoria), joined in the fun. He liked the game so much that at fourteen he dropped tennis. In his formative years he owed a great deal to four men: his father (who became an accomplished player and a shrewd student of the game), two former Australian amateur champions, Allan McCausland and Brian Boys, and finally Hiscoe. At fifteen, Hunt won the Victorian junior championship and a year later he won the Australian junior title and his first senior title: the Victorian. In 1965, at the age of seventeen, he became the youngest player to contest the final of the British amateur championship (at his second attempt) and, after his eighteenth birthday, the youngest to win the Australian title.

In 1970 Hunt beat Aftab Jawaid — the man who had stopped him five years earlier — at the cost of only nine points in the final of the British amateur championship. But by that time the British event had lost its traditional stature as an unofficial world championship: partly because of the quality of its Australian counterpart, but primarily because the birth of the International Squash Rackets Federation had led, in 1967, to the inauguration of official world amateur championships for individuals and teams. Hunt and Australia won all three of the series contested before he turned professional in 1971.

But the biggest event in the game, though Australians were sometimes reluctant to admit it, remained the British open championship: and in this tournament Hunt had lasting difficulty in proving beyond doubt that he was the best squash player in the world. He was certainly the most consistently successful. But the ultimate test was the British open: and it was to prove an elusive prize. The crucial years were those from 1969 to 1974 inclusive — a period in which the Hunt-Barrington rivalry had maximum validity because, with Hunt six years younger but considerably more experienced, each man was close to his peak. In that time there were five British open championships in which both competed. Barrington won three of them, beating Hunt in the only two matches in which they met. Hunt won the title twice. But on each occasion Barrington had conveniently been removed from his path: first by Cam Nancarrow, then by Mohamed Yasin. It is true that Hunt was an Australian playing with a British ball on British courts. But by now he was adjusted to this, and was thumping his opponents to oblivion in almost every tournament except the big one. When the British open came along, Barrington precariously managed to exert a slight physical and psychological ascendancy over a better squash player. And in the same tournament Hunt was beaten by Gogi Alauddin in 1973 and Qamar Zaman in 1975. In short, Hunt's record in the British open championship poses a small question mark against his standing among the all-time great players.

In passing, we should note that Barrington and Hunt share one distinction with Hashim Khan: they are the only men to win back the open championship. It is a further indication of the character and competitive class of Barrington and Hunt that each was to play the finest squash of his career *after* the disconcerting experience of being knocked off the pedestal.

Comparisons between Barrington and Hunt are inevitable and there are three things to be said in the Australian's favour. First, he won both the world amateur championships which Barrington ardently wanted. They did not meet in the 1967 series, in which Barrington was beaten by Hiscoe in the team event and by Nancarrow in the individual championship. But in 1969 they met twice,

Barrington winning the team match and Hunt the individual. Second, Hunt had a far more consistent record of success against everyone (Barrington included) than the Cornishman, who tended to be at his best when he had prepared himself — physically and psychologically — for one supreme test. Third, the Hunt of 1976 and 1977 was a better player than the man whose thrilling duels with Barrington were already a receding memory. In April of 1976 Barrington relaxed beside the swimming pool of a Karachi hotel and told me: 'The greatest player of my day has been Geoff Hunt, who has a prodigious record. The remarkable predictability with which he produces, under all kinds of conditions, the same extraordinary, precision-like squash. He's been doing this since about 1967 and has just completed a British season no one will ever emulate. He lost only one match — the last. He never stops thinking about his game, other people's games, how he's going to improve. When I'm no longer competing, one of my great pleasures will be to recall the battles I have had with him over the years. The beauty of my life is that I will not bore people with what might have happened. I will tell them what actually did happen.'

In addition to his astonishing overall record in that British season, Hunt will cherish 1976 for two mighty achievements. In February, eight years and six months after winning the inaugural world amateur championship, he won the inaugural world open championship. In December (eight months after Alauddin and the heat and humidity of Karachi had reduced him to exhaustion and defeat) he went back to Karachi and won the Pakistan Masters without losing a game. The field included all his leading challengers — Pakistanis playing in their own country. 'There was nothing I wanted more than to come here and beat them on their own ground,' said Hunt in the dressing-room, after the final. 'I'm very pleased with my game at the moment — and that encourages me to work harder.' While Hunt was talking and towelling down, my mind went back to another dressing-room — that at the Lansdowne Club in January, 1967, when Barrington had just become the only player except Abdel Fattah Amr to win Britain's open and amateur championships in the same season. 'At the moment the gap between me and these fellows is marginal,' said Barrington. 'I want to make it a gulf as big as the Grand Canyon.'

Those were the words of genuine champions. No thought of

resting on their laurels. Triumph was not a terminus. Just a stop on the road.

The final of that 1976 world open championship was one of the outstanding performances of Hunt's career. After almost an hour and a half of relentlessly arduous squash he had lost two of the first three games to the younger Mohibullah. But Hunt conceded only four more points, winning 7-9, 9-4, 8-10, 9-2, 9-2 after two hours and two minutes on court. The retrieving of both players was amazing in its speed and agility. Neither would admit that the other had hit a winner. In the third game Mohibullah was catching Hunt with the second or third drop in a series of gruelling rallies in which neither player knew whether he would have to rush forwards or backwards — but was aware, with a terrible certainty, that he would have to do one or the other very fast indeed. Hunt was hurt. But he was aware that if he lost the fourth game, too, his name would appear in the records of this first world championship only as runner-up. His competitive resilience has seldom been more severely tested or more gloriously demonstrated. In that game he had no mercy for himself and none for Mohibullah. Hunt played some of the tidiest, most disciplined squash of his career. He gave Mohibullah nothing to hit. He chased everything. And for all the thrilling, hotly-contested rallies that ensued in that game and the last, it gradually became apparent that the younger man was beginning to wilt — whereas Hunt had somehow burst through the pain barrier.

In squash, as in boxing and many other sports, one of the hallmarks of a champion is his ability to absorb heavy punishment and then bounce back to his best form. That is what Hunt did in the final of the first world open championship.

When Hunt returned to Karchi at the end of November, the climate was more benign that it had been in April, especially on court, where an air-conditioning system imported from Minneapolis had an enriching effect on the quality of the squash. The Pakistan Masters had four particularly interesting features. One was the regularity with which the game's most thrilling virtues were demonstrated. Another was the fact that, in spite of the depth of talent in the draw, twenty-six of the thirty matches (there was one walkover) were decided in straight games and only one went the distance. A third was Hidayat Jahan's 9-1, 9-3, 9-4 win over Qamar Zaman in only twenty-nine minutes — the most explosively exciting *tour de force* I have ever seen on a squash court. A fourth was Hunt's beautifully measured excellence. In match after match he demonstrated the wisdom of a comment Hashim made on flight 326: 'Must be able to play faster, change gear, every game if necessary.'

That, for me, was the basic pattern of Hunt's improvement during his first thirteen years of international squash. Initially he depended almost exclusively on what Barrington accurately and vividly described as a 'Blitzkrieg' — a rapid and sustained violence. He had a short game of sorts, but one felt it was little more than a concession to the tactical conventions: that its *raison d'etre* lay in the head rather than the heart. During his second phase he was extending and improving his repertory of strokes as a means of bringing more variety to the tactics and tempo of his game. During the third and final phase (preceded and sustained by interval sprinting over a quarter-mile or half-mile, the most arduous off-court training of his career) he has put it all together. Now he can smoothly adjust the nature of his squash not only from game to game, but from rally to rally. It would be understating the range of his mastery to suggest that whereas the phase-one Hunt took a breather when he had to, the phase-three Hunt takes one when he wants to. That is only part of it: but it is a part that reflects the general maturity of his game in 1976. It must be doubted if even Hunt, with his restless persuit of perfection, can improve much on his form that year.

Hunt's game is not as overtly attractive and entertaining as that of, for example, Qamar Zaman, Hidayat Jahan, or Ahmed Safwat. He is a player's player, a connoisseur's player, a crisply efficient match-winning craftsman. His game is a fierce cocktail mixed from speed, power, and precision. The quickness of his reactions and his footwork is astounding. When he has to change direction, he does so with such facility that it is like watching a willow quiver for a second on the suspicion of a breeze. He maintains pressure by taking the ball early and whacking the volleys exactly where he wants them to go. He seeks to bury the ball to a length, or into the cross-court nick. Or he forces his opponent to scramble about in a back corner — then hustles him up the court with a drop or a 'gut-ripper' angled off a side wall. There are sudden, small shifts in the structure of his game. At first he tends to play himself in: to find his range and his timing, to make sure that his shots are working, and hurt his opponent without taking undue risks. Then, perhaps, he launches a refined version of the old 'Blitzkrieg', with the drives harder, lower, and more punishing, the drops shorter, the angles tailored to hug the tin and the nick more closely. Next he may indulge in a less violent, more teasing assault, taking the ball later, playing fewer volleys, hitting slower drives that cling to the walls, yet repeatedly changing the pace. Whereupon his opponent (tempted to taste the poisoned fruit exposed by the abating storm) usually hits a few shots down. When the poor chap has adjusted his game to the new design, Hunt goes through the gears again: perhaps another burst of agile interceptions and flashing nicks.

Playing Hunt, 1976-7 model, was like playing two or three different men in the course of one match. There was no rest for the body or the mind, no constant feature except for the speed and the difficulty and the suffering. Running against Emil Zatopek must have been like that.

Hunt is 5ft 8½in. tall and usually on the lighter side of 11 st. In 1969 he won his first British open championship in January, married in May, and became a Bachelor (of Science) in December, graduating in chemistry. It was a good year. 'Teresa's been a great help and support. She never gets upset when watching me play. The only thing that would upset her would be if I tried to cheat, as some players do. When Gogi beat me in the British open, she didn't give me a kiss and say it was all right. Nor was she angry. She just said, "You didn't play well enough today, did you?"' About 1970 Hunt did some fencing with a mate, for pocket money and kicks when not playing squash. They worked hard all day, putting up paling fences. He enjoyed it: and that labour, like the fishing in Port Phillip Bay, doubtless increased his natural stock of patience. So you can put Hunt down as squash player, industrial chemist, fisherman, and fencer. A useful man to have around.

Barrington reckons that the Australian game will have no depth until they put their weight behind the movement for open squash — the abolition of distinctions between professionals and amateurs. In squash, as in tennis, the level of performance must rise throughout the world once all players are free to accept the money they are good enough to earn. Whether or not they have another job is irrelevant. Would you deny an industrial chemist the right to supplement his income by putting up fences? Barrington's point, though, was a comment on the fact that Australia's upper stratum of squash players had been unchanged for a decade — that there were no youngsters on the point of breaking through. Hunt, Nancarrow, and Hiscoe were still the top men. Rainer Ratinac had defected to the hardball game and become a professional at Salt Lake City. Bill Reedman and Kevin Shawcross were both in their late twenties and seemed unlikely to help Hunt check the Pakistani advance. Only Hunt's ability to hang in there was protecting squash from dominance by one nation: an unhealthy situation hardly likely to enhance the game's international popularity.

Nancarrow, younger than Hiscoe and older than Hunt, was somewhat overshadowed by each in turn. But he popped some impressive feats into the record books. Not the least of these was the fact that in 1972 he adapted his game so successfully to hardball squash that he won the Canadian amateur championship. Nancarrow reached the 1969 and 1977 finals of the British open championship. Hunt beat him each time. Twice South African amateur champion, he also won the 1972 Australian and British titles, the 1973 world championship (he had been runner-up to Hunt in two previous series), and then joined Hiscoe and Hunt in the professional ranks. Nancarrow represented Australia in the first four world amateur team championships, all of which they won. This was particularly satisfying in 1973, because by that time Hiscoe and Hunt were no longer eligible and the Australians were consequently vulnerable.

During the late 1960s Nancarrow also became pleasantly accustomed to finding himself described in the press as 'Jonah's Jinx', 'Barrington's Bogy', or even 'Jonah's Jonah'. Barrington in particular always found him difficult to play. Both are left-handed and Nancarrow is a raw-boned and rather ungainly six-footer. His long reach compensates for the fact that his feet tend to be more firmly planted that most. He also has a deceptive style. It is difficult to know what he is up to when he moves in on the ball. Half the time, Barrington could not read his game and anxiously had to make a rapid choice between going round the front of him, round the back of him, or asking for a let. There was no question of Barrington striking his usual rhythm and for a long time he was psychologically intimidated by the combined problems of Nancarrow's build, movement, and playing method. Nancarrow beat him in straight games on two big occasions: the 1967 world amateur championship and the 1969 British open championship. After that 1969 match at Sheffield, he led Barrington 5-2 in their personal series. But a month later Barrington sorted him out in straight games in a semi-final of the world amateur championship — in spite of an ominous awareness that, before going on court, Nancarrow had hit the jackpot twice on the Lansdowne Club's 'fruit' machine.

That win buried the bogy.

It should not be assumed from all this that the frustrations Nancarrow heaped on Barrington were exclusively mental in their origins. Nancarrow may look a little awkward and slow and casual, but he is a fine player: and more disconcerting than most opponents in that he is unorthodox and unpredictable. Essentially, he has the usual Australian approach in that he is always looking for means of ending a rally, rather than waiting for the other chap's mistakes. He is a superb nick player. The difference between Nancarrow and most of his breed — in addition to the physical characteristics we have already noticed — lies in his enviably flexible wrist-work and the kind of winners he produces. He uses a lot of drops, angles, and reverse angles and flicks the ball on and off the side walls in a way that tampers with the conventional geometry of such shots. His touch is so good that he is always dangerous when allowed to drift to the front of the court. For most of his career Nancarrow tended to be a sluggish and erratic starter, though he could always tighten up his game in adversity and swing a match his way with a sudden burst of winners. Since there has been a baby around his house, he has been waking up earlier: both on and off court.

His genial serenity perfectly complements the breezy vitality of his wife Mavis, a former Australian international. In her playing days she was so restlessly energetic that she used to bounce up and down, on the spot, when there was nothing more constructive to do.

Reedman, who benefited from Hiscoe's example and advice at the Bondi Waverley club, worked on his physique, his stamina, and his squash with such immense dedication that they called him the Australian Barrington. He won the 1967 Australian junior championship and made his break-through by beating Nancarrow and Ratinac at Parramatta two years later. In 1970 — having raised the fare by selling his bread round, playing exhibitions with Nancarrow, and receiving additional help from his club — he made his first trip to Britain. Ratinac stopped him in the third round of the open championship. But in the amateur event Reedman reached the final unseeded. In successive matches he fought back to beat the top seed, Aftab Jawaid (who led 9-1, 9-5, and 7-4), and the eighth seed, Mohamed Asran (who won two of the first three games and then led 7-0 in the fourth and 4-0 in the fifth). Gogi Alauddin beat Reedman in the final. Two years later Reedman returned to the assault and again reached the final unseeded. In the semi-final he won a thrilling match with Qamar Zaman, Jawaid's nephew, who was playing in Britain for the first time. Zaman had three match points, Reedman six. The contrast between them was exciting. Zaman had the artistry and touch, especially on his drop shots. Reedman demonstrated the Australian virtues: taking the ball early, hitting it hard, and going for a kill at every opportunity. Reedman led 9-3, 9-5, and 7-5. Then Zaman won nineteen points out of twenty-two to win the third game 9-7, the fourth 9-1, and lead 6-2 in the fifth. A backhand follow-through cut Reedman's nose. The streaming blood spattered his clothes and the court. But his response to the final crisis was magnificent. At the end both men showed firm nerves, unyielding determination, and an astonishing capacity to absorb punishment and come back for more. Neither would submit. The finish was an anticlimax: Zaman played a backhand drop, retreated on Reedman's line of approach, and conceded a penalty point. 'I've never been as tired,' said Reedman later. 'I didn't know where I was.'

The final presented a more familiar problem, but Reedman was beaten by Nancarrow. At the time these two lived at opposite ends of the famous Sydney Harbour Bridge. Theirs was the first all-Australian final. At that time Reedman was twenty-three and the future looked rosy. But the following year, 1973, was to be disconcerting. He missed the Australian team for the world amateur championship series but paid his own way to South Africa — because that was where it was all happening and, in the cause of improvement, he wanted all the tournament competition he could get. He decided to stay around and play in the open events. But his national association told him that if he did so they would declare him a professional. So Reedman became a professional before setting foot on the usual stepping stone: a major amateur title. And in November of that same year he had an operation to split the sheath holding the muscle on his painful right shin. That was a bad year. But Reedman came back and, as I write, is snapping at the heels of the leading professionals.

The next Australian to leap into international prominence was Kevin Shawcross, who won the British amateur championship in December, 1975, and the world amateur title — on the same Wembley court — five months later. Whereupon the professional circuit acquired almost two hundredweights of meat and bone lubricated by vast quantities of beer.

Shawcross won Australia's junior and under twenty-three championships but then decided to concentrate on Rugby League football, which was a reasonable thing to do because Nature designed him for it. He was thus engaged when, by a coincidence, he found himself contemplating the implications of a damaged knee at a time when Nancarrow and Reedman were joining Hunt and Hiscoe in that select group of men playing competitive squash for a living. There was a gap to be filled in Australian amateur squash: and Shawcross doubtless considered, like Brutus, that there is a tide in the affairs of men which, taken at the flood, leads on to fortune. If not fortune, at least a modest fame — and the chance to taste some foreign brews. So he settled down to squash and at the advanced age of twenty-seven emerged as the biggest fish in the shrinking amateur pool. He also confirmed all the gossip that had been seeping out of Australia about his class as a player and the boisterous excesses of what we may loosely describe as his social activities. Even by Australian standards, the lusty, hard-drinking Shawcross is something special. 'I'm a country larrikin,' he confessed to me once, when cold sober.

Well, Shawcross said it: and *Brewer's Dictionary* defines a larrikin as 'a young ruffian or rowdy given to acts of hooliganism.' He is an engaging chap, though: massively genial and spreading laughter around him. Rather like a friendly whale. He comes from Lithgow, a coal-mining town in New South Wales, and looks as if he could tear the black stuff out of the confining strata with his bare hands. The family business embraces such diverse ventures as a squash centre and the farming of such things as blackberries and mushrooms. If you can imagine a hybrid of coalminer and farmer — and stretch the result upwards and outwards — then you have the beginnings of a picture of Shawcross. That ruggedly friendly face suggests that, when he was born, the usual reproductive processes were suspended so that he might be chiselled out of granite. He rises to 6ft 2in. and is anchored by size 12 shoes. In his Rugby League days he weighed 16st 7lb. But by the time he became world amateur champion he was 2st lighter ('In the past three weeks I've been down to four schooners a day') and was using a sprinting schedule passed on to him by Geoff Hunt. On court, he moves well. This is a relief for his opponents, who would otherwise need the agility of a gadfly — or risk a collision that could have incurable consequences. But for all his massive strength Shawcross, a left-hander with a long reach, has the sure and gentle touch of many big men. He also has a shrewd tactical sense and enjoys some fun. In the forecourt, for example, he often goes through the initial motions of a shot he has no intention of playing. As if to say, 'Pick a card, mate'. He has an odd way of tilting his head back and looking down his nose at the ball as though he had caught a whiff from a bad egg. In short, an interesting man and a fine player. In the 1976 Pakistan Masters he played an absorbing match with the wispy Gogi Alauddin. It had the quaintly entertaining qualities of a mastiff romping with a cat, and the squash was beautiful. The 'country larrikin' was a professional and looked it.

A moment that was pure Australia occurred when Shawcross was beating a compatriot, Mike Donnelly, in a semi-final of the 1976 world amateur championship. Donnelly was deep in trouble and deep in the backhand corner. He returned the ball somehow. But honesty instantly provoked the admission: '"Dabble" hit'. After a brief but perceptible pause for further reflection, Donnelly spat out his gut reaction: '"Bagger" it ...'

Men from the big island are like that.

By the time Shawcross won the British amateur championship (formerly an unofficial 'world' title) its prestige had been badly eroded. An official world amateur championship was introduced in 1967. And between 1969 and 1976 all the leading players — more than thirty of them — turned professional. The first of those developments was evolutionary and inevitable. Squash was expanding as a world-wide sport. During the 1960s international competition increased, in its range and in its intensity. Every season groups of tough, capable, well-trained players came to Britain for the big tournaments. With only a few exceptions, British players were inadequately prepared for such a challenge. The Australian and Egyptian amateurs (plus Jawaid from Pakistan) took command. And the overseas nations naturally began to ask a few questions. It was no longer necessary to submit to the trouble and expense of a trip to Britain in order to compete with the leading players. So why not circulate the big events around the world? There could thus be a fair deal for everyone — and a chance for aspiring players everywhere to watch (even compete against) the top men. And why should Britain continue to govern a game that had become too big for any one nation to control adequately?

The logic was unquestionably sound. The children had grown up and were insisting on the right to shape their own destinies.

This was a hazardous period and could have had a damaging effect on the game. Fortunately the parties concerned kept their heads and discussed the problem instead of fighting over it. And the right man was in the hot seat. John Horry, secretary of Britain's SRA from 1955 until he retired in 1972, had an unrivalled grasp of what was happening in world squash. In spite of his respect for tradition and his innate conservatism, he recognized the tide of change and — with his colleagues on the SRA — discreetly channelled that tide rather than attempting to resist it.

Once the ball was in play, the International Squash Rackets Federation happened fast. In April, 1964, Akram Khan, who was then Secretary of the Pakistan SRA, broached the idea in letters to Australia and Egypt. In December of that year the proposal received wider publicity when I reported, in *The Times*, an interview with Hussein Chaworby, manager of the Egyptian team then in London. The essential aim was the formation of an international federation to organize world championships in all the leading squash-playing countries in turn. The following month, Akram flew to London and met Horry: and the president of the SRA of Australia wrote to Britain, Egypt, New Zealand, Pakistan, South Africa, and the United States making six suggestions as a basis for the formation of the ISRF. Consultations went on throughout 1965. In January, 1966, a London conference — attended by representatives of Australia, Britain, Canada, Egypt, India, New Zealand, Pakistan, South Africa, and the United States — decided to go ahead. That year, they drew up a constitution: and in January, 1967, the inaugural meeting of the ISRF took place in London.

The new body assumed responsibility for organizing international championships, and took over from Britain the task of making and maintaining the rules of the game. For the sake of convenience, the three permanent officers from 1967 to 1975 were all British: Peter Phillips as chairman (a Harrovian, a coincidental link with the game's origins), Horry as secretary, and Chris Campbell as treasurer. For the sake of inconvenience — one could, at least, be forgiven for thinking so — the bunch of officers appointed in 1975 were New Zealanders. Governing a world game from islands in the Tasman Sea is tantamount to governing the United States from Hawaii. Possible, but difficult. Murray Day and his chums deserve our sympathy.

The ISRF resolved at their inaugural meeting that the qualifications for competing in the world championships would be the same as those for the Davis Cup competition in tennis — which meant, among other things, that only amateurs would be eligible. Five years later the Davis Cup nations discarded that restriction because it was turning the event into a second-rate embarrassment. The ISRF were confronted by a similar situation in that their best players, too, were moving over to the professional ranks. But they persisted in their discrimination against the game's finest exponents — barring professionals from an event that could, and should, be a shop window for the game. And the ISRF championships in turn became a second-rate embarrassment.

Nor did the ISRF honour their undertaking to add an open championship to the second international series. It was not until 1976 that official world open championships — and these were individual rather than team events — were organized for men (in conjunction with the British open championship in London) and for women (in Brisbane). In the same year the prototype of a world open team tournament was promoted in Karachi on the initiative of Nur Khan, chairman of Pakistan International Airlines. He wanted squash to have its own 'Davis Cup'. This was the original objective of the ISRF, though it had become somewhat obscured as the years went by. Nur Khan, incidentally, has an interesting approach to the difficulties posed by the fact that some countries will not allow their sportsmen to compete with South

Africans. He suggests an itinerant world open championship for which all nations would be eligible *except for those unacceptable to the host country.* By no means a satisfactory solution. But it could be as practicable as any.

In 1973 there were two more administrative developments. In April the European SRF was formed. This sprang from the expansion of the European game, just as the ISRF sprang from the expansion of the international game. The European SRF organized their own amateur team championship. But the professionals needed no further reminders that it was futile to rely on the ISRF or the national associations to protect and advance the interests of professional competitors. In February, 1973, the International Squash Players' Association was formed. They hoped for an amicable liaison with existing administrative bodies. But their primary aims were to organize and control the professional game, to stimulate competition (and its rewards) with an international fixture list, and to influence the future development of the game for the benefit of ISPA members. Their president was the first player to emerge from the big island and win a major international championship: Ken Hiscoe.

Like the ISRF, the ISPA was an inevitable link in an evolutionary process. But its inception was accelerated by the initiative of a far-sighted pioneer who had already done much of the ground work: Jonah Barrington, chairman.

Nine

A Soldier's Son

It was a hot day in the summer of 1975. Having exhausted the alternatives with a reluctantly thorough survey of every other byway in the Cornish parish of Morwenstow, my wife and I drove down the lane that leads to the house where Jonah Barrington was born. His elder sister, Geraldine, had suggested that we take over the premises for a week should the spirit move us in that direction. It did. Whether she had cause to regret the invitation is a matter for conjecture. She would be too polite to say so. But her visible amusement must have been moderated by a small cloud of apprehension when she saw about 14 stone of assorted dogs flood out of the car like a tidal wave. The English Setter, who looks before he leaps, examined the lawns and shrubbery and planned his explorations while sitting — massively thoughtful — on a hydrangea. The Gordon Setter, who does not look before he leaps, joyously discovered the cooling recreational possibilities of an ornamental pool. Thus did Scotch and Soda begin their assault of the Barrington family home. While the staid, elderly Shetland Sheepdog merely sniffed the air, looked at the day, and decided that we had opened a bottle of the right stuff. And Geraldine, smiling as she rode the punches, realized that this invasion was a considerably greater hazard than the measured calm of her preceding guest, a dignitary of the Church. But she put a brave face on it and, fingers crossed, set off for London — perhaps consoling herself with the reflection that although she was leaving the place, she was certainly not vacating it.

That charming and often hilarious holiday would make a book in itself. But its present relevance lies in the fact that those days in

Morwenstow painted in the background to a picture of the Barringtons that had been forming in my mind during the ten years I had known Jonah.

He is one of the most remarkable men I have ever met. A man commanding affection — as well as respect for his self-discipline and his inspiring, invigorating capacity for opening windows in the mind (unless those windows are firmly nailed down by bigotry). Geraldine, Jonah and Nicholas — whose birth intervened between theirs — have much in common. All three combine strength of character (combustible, when ignited) with intellectual agility, a stimulating flair for self-expression, the gift of laughter, and a host of other engaging qualities that I will not embarrass them by listing. Though they are mellowing with the years, all like to have their own way. In their youth the Barrington household must, at times, have been a hotly competitive environment.

Even in 1975, with a quarter of a century gone like a dream and the family scattered, it was easy to imagine the excited children's voices as, fresh back from some adventure, they clattered noisily through the hall with a Kerry Blue romping at their heels — the lot of them, no doubt, making straight for the kitchen to see what was cooking. The presence of the Barringtons still permeated every inch of that book-lined house. And every personality emerged distinctively through the books and knick-knacks in this room and that. One could browse through a volume, or merely look at the cover, and realize that — for one of the young, maturing Barringtons — it represented an intense yet passing passion. Because of this, one came to know them a little better. Equally powerful was the surviving aura of the family as a unit. It was as if we were just looking after the place for an hour while they popped down to the village. They would be back soon.

You know how a good fire casts a smouldering, comforting glow around it long after the flames have died. That was the effect this Cornish home had. A family had lived there for so long that, in a sense, they lived there still.

Morwenstow is perched above hostile cliffs once notorious for shipwrecks — and for the vultures who swooped on the consequences for personal profit. When taking a break from the stresses of squash and London, Barrington used to run along those cliffs in the cause of fitness. The man and the setting remind us of the mountaineer's song, 'To rest is not to conquer'. He has an affinity for high, lonely places. Kenya ('a country warm by nature and full of delightful surprises') has always meant much more to him than a location for altitude training. Cornwall and Kenya provided an emotional refuge for that rare commodity, a British sportsman who was world champion. Such wild, remote areas breed a hardy race of philosophers: strong-minded, even eccentric. An example was Morwenstow's famous parson-poet, Robert Stephen Hawker, who incorporated the refrain of a Cornish ballad ('And shall Trelawny die?') in his 'Song of the Western Men' and also gave the harvest festival its modern form.

Morwenstow looks out across the Atlantic towards the homelands of Barrington's Irish father and his Welsh mother. His father fought in the First World War and the Irish Civil War and had a few scars to show for it. Nick and Jonah inherited his refusal to tolerate the prospect of defeat. But Major Charles Barrington was not just a fighting man. He was also voluble, and an omnivorous reader. The shelves in the drawing-room are packed with books — predominantly about history, politics, and the Services — that tell us much about the range and depth of his interests.

'His great love was history,' says Jonah. 'Had he wanted to, he could have been a first-class historian, because he had a formidable mind and read voraciously. He was also one of the world's great talkers, and never happier than when doing it in a public bar — as in the Bush Inn at Morwenstow. My father was a very well-organized man. He was sartorially immaculate, always careful about his person. Punctilious. He loved to have a routine. In other words, he was a professional soldier. He had a tremendous determination in whatever he decided to do, even though it might seem trivial to others. If it mattered to him, he would do the job properly. He was thorough. But he never conceived that sport could be played in a professional manner. There was no status attached to it — and my father was very aware of status. He had no special ability at hitting a ball or kicking a ball. His athletic abilities related to firing a rifle, riding a horse. And he was a good schoolboy fencer.

'On the Irish side of my family there was a fairly heavy nobility and, over the centuries, a string of men with distinguished records academically and, frequently, at the Bar and in the political field. And tracing the course of the family one always finds the professional soldier cropping up — a sprinkling of generals and whatever. A lot of members of the family would come into the category of Chiefs and not Indians.'

Barrington's brother was an important influence during his formative years. 'Nick was pretty talented as a boy. Big, athletic, infatuated with sport. He was two years older than me and had a tremendous physical advantage and a bit of a mental advantage — he was a smart kid and wily beyond his years. The dominant factor in our lives was sport. We competed directly with each other in any game, individual or team (even when we were on the same side). We both had an intense competitive instinct. Neither of us would accept being beaten. I could appreciate the danger in my winning and his losing. He would try to take it out of me. But I always tried to beat him — and succeeded in a number of areas. It was a love-hate relationship: and that kind of relationship forges a terrific bond.'

Nick's best sport, incidentally, was squash. He was Cornish champion ten times in eighteen years and in the 1968-9 season he played for Ireland and was Jonah's first round opponent in the British amateur championship.

Jonah went to Kells, in County Meath, Ireland, to spend almost five years at a preparatory school which had a squash court — an unlikely facility, because squash courts were rather thin on the ground in those days. He was a success at Kells and for a long time was to look back on this period as the happiest and most satisfying of his young life. His world collapsed around him when he followed Nick to Cheltenham College. Suddenly Jonah was a nothing, an also-ran. His ego was hurt. He became anxious, difficult, rebellious. Moreover, at fourteen he was becoming short-sighted. The weight of his frustrations drove him to a nervous breakdown. But later he made the first team at tennis and squash. The local professional was Ted Millman, whose son Paul was to join Barrington in Britain's amateur international team (Millman won the plate event at the inaugural world championships and promptly claimed that he was 'the world's best worst player').

At seventeen Barrington moved on to university: Trinity College, Dublin, where many of the family had trained their minds. His record there was somewhat distinctive, but not distinguished. Instead of studying law, he drank Guinness. He did study history for a while, but failed his examination. The fact that he graduated to the tennis and squash teams was not regarded as adequate compensation for his academic negligence and a variety of misdemeanours. He was accused of being 'infrequently sober'. After two years he was banned from the premises. He had nothing to show for his career at Trinity other than a hangover and affectionate memories — and a £10 conviction for petty larceny. According to Barrington's own book, this arose from a drunken evening when he was on vacation in London. Though innocent of larcenous intent, Barrington and a friend were nabbed while trundling 'borrowed' wheelbarrows down Earl's Court Road. It seemed a good idea at the time.

For more than eight years (until he became a professional) Barrington drifted in and out of an extraordinary range of jobs. Over the first half of that period he had no sense of purpose and over the second half he would do anything to make ends meet while he concentrated on squash. He was often a schoolmaster — and occasionally groundsman, coalman, house-painter, carpet-cleaner, assistant secretary to the SRA, milk roundsman, dishwasher and nude model for art students. It reached the point where anyone who wanted anything doing no longer bothered to advertise in the 'situations vacant' column. They just sent for Barrington.

In 1964, at the age of twenty-three, he was back in Cornwall — out of a job and convalescing from an operation for a lumbar hernia. Life was a bed of thorns rather than roses. But one day John Mocatta, a squash player on holiday at Bude, called Nick for a game. Nick was out so Jonah played instead. Mocatta told him that there was a clerical vacancy at the SRA. In September, Barrington moved to London. In November, he discarded his glasses in favour of contact lenses. In January, 1965, he played in the British amateur championship for the first time and was beaten in straight games by Sherif Afifi (in the next round Afifi lost to Geoff Hunt, who was already good enough to be seeded fourth and in fact reached the final). Afifi was far too clever for Barrington. But the amiable entomologist was giving him a good deal of help and encouragement during practice at Paddington.

'At first Jonah wore thick glasses and had no idea about squash,' says Afifi. 'But he began knocking with me and Samir Nadim and other friends. Then he got interested. He wanted to prove to himself that he was capable of doing something — until then, he hadn't convinced himself that he could do anything. The match that put the flame in his determination was against Jeremy Lyon. He beat Lyon: and since then hardly a player in the British Isles has been able to get near him. An excellent example of determination. He gave up everything.'

At the end of that 1964-5 season Barrington made a total commitment to squash: specifically, to the harsh regimen imposed on him by Nasrullah Khan. Naz coached him and made him practise for hours every day. Off court, there was running to do and a weight-training course. Nor did Naz's demands end there. He insisted that Barrington should change his entire life-style and become an ascetic. All this was a far cry from the dissipation of Trinity and the years of drifting. It is a measure of Barrington's character that he was willing to stake everything on the gamble for success. There have been many more talented sportsmen whose progress was arrested half-way up the ladder — men who did not become champions but cushioned their disappointment with the argument that they would have achieved more had it been convenient for them to give more. But the only rung on the ladder that interested Barrington was the top one. 'There's only room for specialists at the top these days. You can't dabble. When I'm forty, I don't want to look back and say I could have been the champion if I had trained a bit harder. I want to look back and say I *was* the champion.' So he sacrificed what the rest of us would regard as a normal life and, no matter how much it hurt, subjected himself to the painful austerities of a relentless, single-minded climb to the summit.

It takes a special kind of man to embrace an obsession so frankly. There must have lurked, deep within him, an awareness that the ultimate limit of his powers might not suffice for his purpose — and that if he fell, there would be no psychological safety-net to catch him. No excuses.

Barrington had reached a relatively advanced age before taking a serious interest in the game. He had no outstanding advantages as an athlete or as a ball-player. But he had exceptional qualities of heart and mind. He dissected squash: its technique, its tactics, the special stresses it imposed on the body and the intellect. He studied the mechanics of the game and its players. The depth of his analysis of the game's physical effects — and his appraisal of the way in which he must adapt his body to meet them — was unparalleled. That is why he became the most comprehensively trained squash player there had ever been. And that is why he was eventually consumed by the fire he kindled. Because he talked freely about his methods, proved their validity, and then discovered that a younger generation of players — including Hunt — had taken the lessons to heart. They stiffened their own training schedules until, like Barrington, they were too familiar with the pain barrier to be intimidated by it. When that happened, his precarious authority (always physical and psychic in its roots) was steadily eroded. He was almost thirty-three when he was engulfed by the new wave. By that time there was a slight but worrying decline in his powers of acceleration from a standing start. That is something sportsmen in their thirties must reluctantly accept — with such obvious exceptions as Stanley Matthews in football and Ken Rosewall in tennis.

But Barrington proved everything he set out to prove. He was a practical visionary, a rare breed. His horizons were wide, but he was perceptive in identifying barriers and imaginatively tenacious in breaking through them. He was a successful radical in an area of sport largely populated by reactionaries. He showed Brtish sportsmen how to beat the world: and he told them exactly what it cost.

In the early years, though, he was often regarded as a fanatic, a voice crying in the wilderness. He had not been in the game long, yet he was boldly flinging open the windows of convention and letting in the fresh air of new ideas. His was a lonely road and there were dark valleys to tread before he reached the foothills of achievement. He must often have been beset by self-doubt. But he had an iron will. He remembered his Kipling ('If you can trust yourself when all men doubt you . . .'). And around him were Naz, Nick, Geraldine, and a few friends who believed in him: partly because what he was doing made sense and partly because they cared, and knew how much failure would hurt him.

Barrington, his own guinea-pig, trained and practised through the summer of 1965. He was now twenty-four. In his first big championship he had been beaten by Afifi. In his second he was to be submerged by another tributary of the sparkling stream of Egyptian talent. Tewfik Shafik beat him in straight games in the second round of the 1965 British open championship. A month later, in the amateur event, Barrington could take only ten points from Richard Boddington. But in those early months of 1966 Barrington was chosen as Britain's reserve against Australia — he beat Cam Nancarrow in the reserves' match — and made his first appearances for Ireland (he was also qualified for England, but allowed his Irish father to make the choice for him). Off court, he gave up his clerical job with the SRA and at Easter, the end of the season, he sought the help of Azam Khan, the man who had knocked Michael Oddy's game into shape.

In those days Barrington was a wildly indiscreet shot-maker who often seemed eager to perforate the tin. His squash was noisy, exciting, erratic. Azam's morning lessons in match-play were crushing, sobering. Barrington scored one point in their first match: and that, more or less, was how it went on during the summer of 1966. But Barrington's squash was acquiring discipline ('I thought Azam must be a good model, and he never played a flashy shot'). The Cornishman's game lost its fancy trimmings and became less spectacular, less fun. But it also became more efficient. He was learning how to win. And he was learning fast.

This was the second phase of Barrington's development as a squash player. In later years there were to be two more. He was to rescue from the scrapheap a few of his early shots and practise them until they could be used safely: in a way that respected the percentages instead of defying them. Thus he began to exploit the side walls for tactical purposes, to hit occasional nicked kills, and to use his wrist for deception. All this gave his game more variety. During the final phase (after organizing a man-to-man challenge series with Geoff Hunt and taking a hiding) he emulated Hunt and Ken Hiscoe by seeking more pace — a greater capacity to impose pressure — through taking the ball earlier and volleying more often. It was ironic that by the time he had done all this (and thus become a superb player) his rivals and the years were catching up with him.

At the beginning of the 1966-7 season Barrington's game was immature. Naz and Azam had done what they could. Barrington himself was trained to such a pitch ('fitness means you don't take risks in order to finish a rally quickly') that no one could challenge his physical and mental stamina. His strategy and tactics were based on that advantage. The years of self-indulgence were over. It was discipline all the way: 'clingers' down the walls, lobs, a remorselessly tight length punctuated by drops, usually on the backhand. His aim was to tease and tempt his opponents to impatience and self-destruction, or simply wait until their knees buckled. It was very effective, too. In October, he had an inspiriting win over Jeremy Lyon. The fruit was ripening. But it would be unfair, we reasoned, to expect anything remarkable. After all, Barrington had played in the British open championship only once, the amateur twice, and had won merely one match in each event. He needed more experience of the big occasion. Moreover his concentration on squash was, at the time, less than total. A personal tragedy was imminent. For six months of that year his father was dying from cancer. Barrington was continually travelling between London and Morwenstow. In an effort to compensate, he increased the severity of his training and practice. In every way, he was under awful stress.

Charles Barrington died in November, having taken pride in the fact that his formerly fickle younger son had at last achieved a sense of purpose and a promising degree of success. In December, Jonah became the first British player since Oddy to reach the final of the open championship, the first since Jim Dear to win it, and the only amateur to do so except for Abdel Fattah Amr. His last match, with Aftab Jawaid, was the first all-amateur final. In January he won the amateur championship and thus became the only player except Amr to win both titles in the same season. He was three months short of his twenty-sixth birthday.

This was an astounding performance. It transformed the 'fanatic' into a national hero and an international sporting celebrity. But many, including Barrington himself, were aware of the hazards attendant on such a sudden and startling advance from nothing to everything. It can make a man complacent or, conversely, shatter his morale because of the realization that in future he will have everything to lose and nothing to gain — instead of the other way round. And leading sportsmen learn more from defeat than victory. In this case Barrington's rivals were beginning to understand his game and work out means of frustrating it. They would be more difficult to beat, next time around.

Barrington dodged the hazards by making constructive efforts to improve his game — and by setting himself targets. The most comprehensive of these was to win eight big championships between December, 1967, and February, 1969. He ticked off six: the British open, the British amateur, the Egyptian open, and the South African, Australian, and British amateur championships.

But in 1969 the Australians arrested him on the last lap. Cam Nancarrow beat him in the British open championship and Geoff Hunt beat him in the world amateur series. Barrington would have turned professional eighteen months earlier had he won the inaugural world amateur event. This time, though bitterly disappointed to be thwarted once again, he took the plunge with two symbolic gestures: he 'coached' Naz for a guinea and sold me a racket for a shilling. With that, the revolutionary had found a new cause: earning a living as the game's first full-time itinerant professional. He told us that since January, 1966, when he gave up his SRA position, he had done no work except for occasional part-time jobs. 'Over the past four years I've built up debts of £1,000. I shall be going hard for ten years. The dominating part of my plan is to become world open champion. I shall work for an open championship. Squash is going to become a big sport. The game should be made open at this stage.'

As it turned out, the official world open championship did not happen soon enough for Barrington to have much chance of winning it. He was to be balked in that ambition, as he had been in seeking the corresponding amateur title. Nor did he have the satisfaction of leading Britain to the team prize. But between the ages of twenty-five and thirty-one he won the British open championship — regarded until 1976 as the *de facto* world championship — no fewer than six times in seven seasons. Only Hashim, with seven out of eight, surpassed that record. Amr was champion for six seasons. But that was in the days of the challenge system (one year there was no challenge, and it is no disparagement of the players concerned to point out that in the other five seasons Don Butcher and Jim Dear were the only men Amr had to beat). Professionals won the open title for twenty-one consecutive seasons until Barrington broke their hold. Then he turned professional and restored it. He was British amateur champion for three consecutive seasons, a feat matched only by Amr, Norman Borrett, and Aftab Jawaid. He broke through to the top during the formative years of the ISRF, which was conceived at a time when Australia, Egypt and Pakistan were beginning to dominate the game. He did so not because he was a throwback to a great British tradition, but because in many ways he founded a tradition of his own.

Barrington's mighty record demanded many great match-winning performances. In its context, none transcended his 9-4, 9-1,

8-10, 9-5 win over Abou Taleb, the holder and top seed, in a quarter-final of the 1966 open championship. Taleb, apprehensive when he realized what a tough competitor Barrington had become, made a belated effort to reduce his rotundity. In the first round he beat Tony Gathercole. Barrington had a usefully testing match with Michael Corby, who was to succeed Lyon as his closest domestic rival. So to the night of December 16th. Richard Boddington ('the time before you play is worse than playing') took Barrington away from the Lansdowne Club for an hour and half before the match. They drank tea, chatted about this and that, and drove round the West End viewing the Christmas lights. That excursion left Barrington relaxed and ready. None of his nervous energy had been wasted. When Barrington and Taleb stepped through the door of the famous Bruce court, the gallery was packed. Already Barrington had inspired the respect of the *cognoscenti* and fired the public's imagination. Now for the supreme test: the ambitious newcomer against the reigning champion. Taleb had a lot to lose. He did his best to look confident and cheerful. But there was fear in his eyes.

What happened, briefly, was that Barrington first proved he could beat Taleb at squash — and then proved that his courage and concentration could withstand a multitude of distractions, not the least of them physical intimidation. The soldier's son finished the match with four bloody bruises, three on the back and one on the jaw. He was struck so often by shoulder, ball, or racket that he must have wondered where sport ended and war began. He had to take everything except punches. There were other, more farcical digressions from the main theme of the drama. Taleb was glowering with fury one minute, grinning the next. Three times he was granted permission to leave the court: twice to change his trousers, once to fetch a handkerchief. But nothing disturbed Barrington's composure. He was there to win — and he knew the perils of impatience, or bad temper, or trying to 'mix it' with a stronger, more experienced player who was turning the match into a roughhouse. Barrington kept his head and played his game: and it was too good for Taleb. It was too good because of Barrington's ball control and tactical discipline. Because he refused to join Taleb in the reckless stroke-play that is born from desperation. Because he was witty enough to read Taleb's wizardry and fast enough to frustrate it. Because he could deceive the deceiver. Because he could win the play for position and then hit a winner — usually a backhand drop — that was measured to an inch. Because he blended the long and short games astutely and accurately.

Barrington did lose his rhythm for a spell and hit a few down. Taleb took the third game on his fifth game ball. The crux of the match came in the fourth game when Taleb, in hand at 5-6, hit what momentarily looked to be a perfect length down Barrington's backhand. But as the ball was dipping into the corner — it was no more than a foot from the floor — Barrington played a winning volleyed drop straight down the wall. It was the sort of shot that makes champions — and breaks them. It broke Taleb. He had turned on the heat in every conceivable way, but it had done him no good. This was an ugly match. But it was beautiful, too. It had the gallery in the grip of an emotional tension with few, if any, parallels. Because it was so much more than a squash match.

Barrington made a telephone call to Morwenstow and then relaxed for a few hours. Although he had won a match, he still had to win a championship — and there was an obvious danger of an adverse mental reaction after a triumph such as that over Taleb. Apart from anything else, he was now *expected* to win.

Ibrahim Amin won a point more than Taleb. By 1966 the youth had gone from his legs. But he still had a marvellous wrist and a vast store of craft and cunning. He tried to play at his own pace rather than Barrington's. But the loping agronomist, stooping solemnly over the ball as if examining an indifferent crop, could allow no margin for error when he went for winners. Barrington's quickness preyed on Amin's mind and forced him to take risks. He did win ten consecutive points — two in succession with backhand reverse angles that flickered and died like the last flames of a spent fire. But Barrington knew that speed and fitness would see him through if he could sap Amin's stamina by keeping him on the move and giving him little to hit. And Barrington did exactly that. But this was a delightful match: the squash of the chessboard.

The final, like Barrington's three other matches, went to four games. But most of it was one-sided. Only in the second game could Aftab Jawaid seduce Barrington into the hypnotically monotonous driving to a length at which the Pathan always

The three Egyptians who, between them, held the British open championship for 13 years.
Right Abdel Fattah Amr, open champion from 1932 to 1937, and six times amateur champion.
Below Two professionals.
Left Mahmoud el Karim won four open championships from 1947 to 1950 before Hashim introduced the reign of the Khans.
Right Abou Taleb, three times champion (1963–65) when the Khans were deposed.

The three British winners of their national open title: the *de facto* world championship.
Above left Jonah Barrington (with the author) won six of the seven championships played from 1966 to 1973. *Below left* Don Butcher won the first two challenge series, in 1930 and 1931. *Below right* Jim Dear, in 1938, interrupted the supremacy of the two Egyptians, Amr and Karim.

The three most persistent winners of consecutive British women's championships.
Right Margot Lumb (five titles, 1934 to 1939). *Below* Heather McKay (*left*), sixteen times champion since 1962 and still competing, with Janet Shardlow, who won ten championships—as Miss Morgan—from 1950 to 1958.

Above Seven winners of the British open championship.
Left to right Azam Khan, Geoff Hunt, Hashim Khan, Jonah Barrington, Roshan Khan, Mohibullah Khan Senior, and Qamar Zaman.

Below Geoff Hunt (*left*) and Qamar Zaman, who contested the final of the 1977 world open championship.

Right Heather McKay in action against Sue Cogswell.

Pakistani courts, ancient and modern. *Left* One of the open-air Peshawar courts on which Hashim Khan learned to play. *Below* The main court at the Pakistan International Airlines squash complex in Karachi, opened in 1976.

The three players from Lahore who initiated a resurgence of Pakistani squash in the 1970s.
Above left Gogi Alauddin in action at Karachi. *Above right* Sajjad Muneer.
Below Hidayat Jahan at Ziarat, a mountain resort near Quetta.

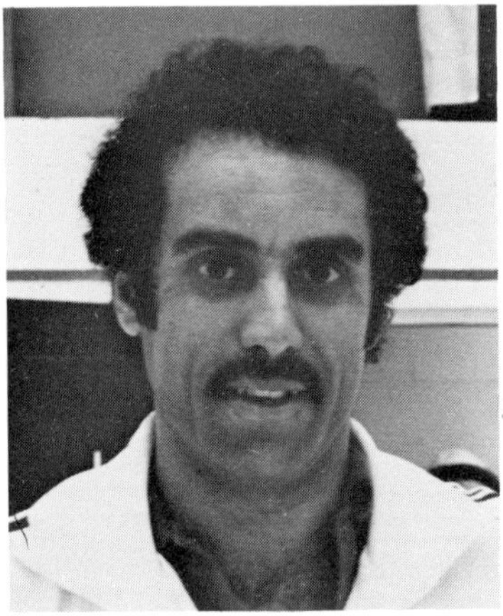

Above left Hashim Khan's son, Sharif, North American champion eight times in nine years, 1969–77.

Above right Mohibullah Khan Junior, runner-up to Geoff Hunt in the first official world open championship (1976).

Below Ken Hiscoe, whose example and inspiration fired Australia's rapid advance in the game during the 1960s.

excelled. In the rest of the match Barrington's tactical authority was seldom in question. He varied his short game, used the side walls effectively, and produced some teasing 'clingers' when he wanted to keep Jawaid quiet. Jawaid had been suffering from a feverish cold. John Ward took him to five games in the first round. Ahmed Nadi took him to four in the quarters (whereupon Jawaid collapsed in the dressing-room and the club's conventions were waived so that his wife could go and comfort him). But Jawaid looked fit enough in his semi-final, in which Mohamed Yasin, a busy little chap, had a match point at 8-6 in the fifth game: but put a backhand down after a total of 146 shots, punctuated by three lets.

After the final Barrington did some press-ups, discussed his plans for Christmas training runs along the Cornish cliffs, and passed round the champagne. He assumed the status of world champion so easily and naturally that he might have been slipping on a well-worn coat — or, more likely, a training suit. He had been giving squash his serious attention for little more than two years. But he had made up for lost time by the intensity of his physical and mental effort. Nasrullah and Azam had helped a great deal. But they could not play his matches for him. They could not guarantee the consistent maturity of his squash, or the guts with which he confounded Taleb. It took a man to 'win big' the way Barrington did in 1966.

That championship was significant in another sense, too. The semi-finals and final were filmed, with the aid of a glass panel in the back door and a platform perched high above the front wall. Squash had become so important that the publicity media could neglect it no longer.

Barrington's tactical assurance and ball control were less impressive when he won the amateur championship a month later. But like all true champions he had the capacity to win even when his game was not at its peak. That was a gauge of his strength of character and the thoroughness of his preparation. He won four matches in straight games and then ran into Ken Hiscoe and Dick Carter. Each in turn had him on the hook. But neither could keep him there. Hiscoe led 9-5, 9-2 and was still playing well when in hand at 4-5 in the third game. He was hitting some glorious winners, especially with his cross-court backhand volley. For two games Barrington was ominiously subdued and untidy, feeding Hiscoe's volley with loose shots that floated off the walls towards the middle of the court. But in the third game Barrington began to hit the ball instead of pushing it. His game became more positive and more accurate. At last he was doing what he wanted to do — weaken Hiscoe's legs by mixing the long and short games at speed. The crisis was tense. But Barrington won that third game and, surging with confidence, took the fourth from 0-3 down. Hiscoe's backhand angles (or boasts as the Australians call them) were strokes of delectable purity. But his legs could no longer cope with the wearying task of bustling up and down the court. Soon Hiscoe was getting stranded by yards. The court seemed to be getting larger every minute. In the fifth game he was leaden-footed, and Barrington destroyed him in eight minutes with a string of drops.

Hiscoe's analysis of the final phase of the match was terse: 'I was rooted, mate.'

In the final Carter led Barrington 9-1, 6-9, 9-7, 7-4 (and Geraldine and Nick could no longer bear to watch). Then Carter drew Barrington out of position and tried to pull the ball away, to a length, with a backhand volley. But instead of taking him to match point the shot went into the tin. He did not score again. Barrington drew level at two games all (after ninety-three minutes) and went through the fifth in one hand and less than four minutes.

It was an amazing volte-face. The genial little Australian was not winning easily. But he was playing better squash and there seemed to be no reason why this should not produce the obvious result. He was much more consistent. He varied the pace astutely and used the wide walls neatly to draw Barrington to the front of the court. The virtues of Barrington's length were nullified by the fact that his trusted ally, the drop shot, deserted him. Repeatedly it went into the tin — the bottom of it, like as not — instead of winning him points. But in the crisis of the fourth game he played such tight squash that Carter had to win points rather than waiting for Barrington to give them to him. One startling error gave Barrington a chance: and he did not need another. Carter was overwhelmed by frustration, fatigue, and remorseless pressure. We were sorry for him. The prize within his grasp had been snatched away with a terrible finality. But we were proud to share the same kind of passport as Barrington, who in two successive matches had come from behind to crush tough Australians who could not stay the course with him. Barrington had learned something, too. He could not afford to spend an hour reducing such players as Hiscoe and Carter to exhaustion: because in that hour they might be good enough to beat him.

But for the second time in twenty-seven days the champagne was flowing in Berkeley Square. We drank the cup to its dregs and we kept a restaurant open until a late hour. Our beds could wait. Because we had seen history made, we knew we would never see its like again, and we were reluctant to let today's glory become tomorrow's memory.

For similar reasons — a wish to capture for the benefit of posterity the flavour of those crowded, exciting days in which Barrington lifted himself from the shadows to the summit — I have discussed in some detail the first of his two open and amateur 'doubles'. He was to mature considerably as a squash player and go on to win many great matches. But any mountaineer will tell you that there is nothing to equal the exhilaration of that first sweating, straining heave to the topmost point of the highest crag in reach. He may master the same climb again. But this will only tell him that he is still the man he used to be: and that the view is still the same, although the shifting sunlight may illuminate different details. The joy of such a hard-won discovery can only happen once.

Whereas Hunt had his first trip to Europe at the age of sixteen Barrington was twenty-six before he travelled in the opposite direction — for the 1967 world amateur championship series. That was an educational if disappointing experience. In those days the Australian and British balls had contrasting qualities and the players of both nations tended to be less effective — Carter was an exception — with the alien ball. (Barrington's advocacy of an Australian-type ball had much to do with its introduction to British courts in 1970.)

Barrington, though, soon made his mark overseas. A particularly satisfying early example was his 9-4, 9-2, 9-7 win over Taleb in the final of the 1968 Egyptian open championship: played in April on Taleb's home court at the Heliopolis Sporting Club in Cairo. By some telephonic miracle Barrington was able to tell me after the match that this was his most thrilling win apart from his first British open championship. 'It was a very hot day and there was a packed gallery. There was tremendous tension, even before we got on court, and we were both very nervous at the beginning. I got away, but it was a tough struggle. I could never relax. In the third Taleb went to 7-1, playing beautifully, and the crowd was very excited. I had to pull myself out then. They gave me a wonderful reception and said it was one of the best matches they'd ever seen here.' In August of that same year, at Perth, Barrington had a triumph even more remarkable. He adapted his game to Australian conditions so effectively that he beat Carter, Hunt and Hiscoe in successive matches to win the Australian amateur championship. Two years later, in Australia's revived open championship at Melbourne, he was afflicted for the first time by an alarming, mysterious respiratory ailment. But he survived that match, against Doug Stephenson, and went on to beat Hunt in the final. Towards the end of the third game Hunt was struck near an eye by Barrington's backswing. After that, Hunt's face was a spectacularly bloody mess because for some reason he would not clean up. In the fifth game he was also attacked by cramp, which sometimes reduced him to one leg and a swinger. What with all this, and losing too, it was not the kind of match that Hunt needed in his home town — or, for that matter, anywhere else.

Barrington's big battles with Hunt (as distinct from those in less important events) produced impressive evidence of the Cornishman's fighting qualities, his physical and mental stamina, and his ability to play tidy, shock-proof squash in a crisis. Hunt, too, became increasingly resilient as the years went by and his training methods acquired more severity. As Barrington puts it, 'He tires again and again — and still comes back.' But Barrington, and later Gogi Alauddin, tended to give Hunt a lot of bother through their retrieving ability, their tactical discipline, and their knack of slowing the pace and tossing the ball high to his backhand: especially when a warm court was making it difficult for Hunt to put the ball away.

Two memorable Barrington recoveries occurred within three days during the 1969 world amateur team championship in Britain. In the fifth game of a 90-minute match at Nottingham, Aftab Jawaid led Barrington 8-3, match point, but hit three forehands down and lost the match in one arduously dramatic hand. This was one of Barrington's finest performances because, once again, his backhand drop was letting him down — which meant that he had to slog it out and play Jawaid at his own game. Two days later, at Birmingham, Barrington beat Hunt 2-9, 9-4, 8-10, 9-4, 9-7 in an epic struggle lasting an hour and fifty-five minutes. The squash was fast, positive, punishing. Both men absorbed a lot of pressure and pain. But the quickness of their retrieving and the soundness of their ball control seldom faltered. At the end of that year they met at Birmingham again, this time in the final of the British open championship. Hunt went into that match with the heartening knowledge that he had beaten Barrington on five successive occasions. But Barrington beat him 9-7, 3-9, 3-9, 9-4, 9-4 in two hours and thirteen minutes. That was the most cruelly exhausting squash match I have ever seen. The last two games took an hour and towards the end Hunt had twinges of cramp. Both men were driven very close to the limits of their resources. In the dressing-room afterwards, their eyes were glazed and their voices mere murmurs issuing from the frontier of collapse. They were drained, crumpled, almost helpless. Neither looked strong enough to fight his way out of a paper bag. What a poignant contrast there is between the public drama of sport and the private suffering that is often the cost of it. No match, said Barrington faintly (between great gulps of tea), had hurt him more. 'It was ruthlessly hard. The mental side of that battle was horrifying.'

The last major contest between them was the final of the 1972 British open championship at Abbeydale Park — a congenial club conveniently placed between modern Sheffield and the 'Morton' of *Jane Eyre*, the 'Pemberley' of *Pride and Prejudice*, Little John's grave, the notorious plague village of Eyam, and some of the finest walking and climbing country in England. There is also an isolated pub branded on the memory because it contains the only bar in the world where I have ever ordered milk! (Barrington had been exercising on the windswept moors.) A rest day during an Abbeydale tournament is a ticket to adventure. Go west — and taste the air and the history.

Early in 1972, though, our gallant Cornishman was feeling anything but chipper. His wisdom teeth had caused a painful infection, his gums were swollen, and he had picked up a stomach bug. Hunt and Hiscoe had turned professional but seemed to be giving him the cold shoulder. His mother's health was declining, and his association with Madeline Ibbotson — whose marriage with Derek was breaking up — was attracting some embarrassing publicity and causing scattered outbreaks of social friction. Madeline and Jonah married as soon as they could. They took in a third partner when an eccentric dog called Basa firmly attached himself to the team (changing packs as it were) while they were on a training run at Mombasa. And a fourth when Nicholas was born. As Barrington goes slowly over the hill as a contender for the big championships, there are rich compensations in the fact that, for the first time since his childhood, he is part of a settled family unit with a well-organized life-style. Even in those dark early weeks of 1972, Madeline's vivacious company was a comfort. She was also bringing order to his *modus vivendi* — and her experience as a runner was a constructive stimulus to his own training.

Barrington beat Hunt 0-9, 9-7, 10-8, 6-9, 9-7 in an hour and fifty-five minutes. Hunt led 6-0 and 7-4 in the fifth game. But he was cooked. The rallies were lasting too long. Barrington read all the signs (he knew them well) and aggressively seized the chance for a successful surge to the tape. When playing Barrington on such occasions, Hunt must have felt like Sisyphus in hell — rolling his boulder to the top of the hill and watching it roll back down again. He could never make the damned thing stay up there.

Two old friends, Mohibullah Khan (senior) and Yusuf Khan, popped over from America that year. Mohibullah tested the concentration and temper of Clive Francis. Both were asked to moderate their language. Mohibullah was accused of stalling. After winning in the fifth, he roared with joy and went dancing and whooping to the dressing-room as if it was the first match he had ever won. He had not changed: still full of beans (although that year they came in a slightly larger tin). Yusuf's first and last opponent was Hunt. So he had time for a close look at the new generation. 'People are so fit now. But I am very disappointed. The game has so changed. Everybody just hitting hard. Power. Stamina. Not so intelligent. No one take risk, because no one making strokes.'

Well, maybe some of the laughter had gone out of the game. Speed is the enemy of subtlety. The artist may survive in a climate of haste, but he cannot thrive in it.

Mohibullah and Yusuf were the past. Abbeydale's revolutionary new court was the future. Designed in consultation with television technicians, it had a free-standing glass back wall, a camera pit behind a glass panel in the tin, an electric scoreboard, sloping lateral galleries providing standing-room just above the out-of-court line, and further galleries higher up the outer wall. It thus managed to pack spectators around and above the court so that proximity created an intimate, exciting rapport between players and public. The club were imaginative and bold in devising such an arena and raising the money to build it. The only basic improvement one could envisage was a fanwise extension of the main gallery behind the court, with each row wider than the one below it. As it was, the Abbeydale designers were so much ahead of their time that the squash 'theatres' constructed at Wembley in 1974 and Karachi in 1976 seemed conventional and old-fashioned by comparison: notably in their failure to capture the intimate quality of Abbeydale's earlier initiative.

It was appropriate that Barrington, himself an innovator, should win the first major championship to be played in this stimulating environment.

He was always bursting with ideas. It was in 1966 that he decided to earn a living as a professional squash player. But in 1969, when he began to do so, it was difficult to work out how to set about it ('I was really the only competitive "pro" at that time'). But he recalled a daunting experience during a short exhibition tour of South Africa after his 1967 trip to Australia. 'The South African side, who had been to Australia, had reported to their association that Jonah Barrington had verbal diarrhoea and should give a talk on the game. I had some gall. I'd only been playing seriously for three years. But I fronted up at the Wanderers Club at thirty-six hours' notice before a substantial gallery. To talk and demonstrate — never having done so before. I remember thinking "What the hell am I going to tell these people? How many ways are there to tell them to hit the ball down the wall?" In detail, squash is a very boring game. But I thought: "You practise on your own, to certain patterns. So show them that. Tell them about the Khans, and anything else that comes to mind. And see how it goes." I'd been a teacher. And squash was my subject.'

Thus began the Barrington clinics. They are the perfect medium for a fast-talking Celt with a sense of fun — for a famous player who is also an irresistibly enthusiastic advocate of the game's virtues. He is a sporting evangelist, firing everyone around him with a zest for the cause. And in addition to suiting his personality and his abilities, the clinics have a practical advantage over individual coaching in that they enable him to punch the message across to more people more quickly (with a proportionate increase in his earning rate).

There was money to be made, too, through contracts to endorse the merits of this product or that with the weight of his name and reputation.

But although such things as clinics, endorsement, and instruction disseminated via books and tapes were all very well, there remained the essential task of organizing — from scratch — a rewarding competitive programme. The existing professional and open tournaments were lamentably inadequate for any professional who wanted to compete throughout the year. Barrington's first experiment was to invite Geoff Hunt to join him in Britain for a 15-match series during the 1969-70 season. Hunt won it 13-2. But there was obviously a market for this kind of thing: especially if more players and more countries could be included. The necessary sponsorship arose from a chance meeting between Barrington and Shakir-Ulla Durrani, who was then Managing Director of Pakistan International Airlines. In August, 1970, Barrington set off on a tour of the Far and Middle East with Aftab Jawaid (a PIA employee), Rainer Ratinac, Sharif Khan, and Abou Taleb. That tour achieved three things: it helped to popularize squash in countries that had little or no knowledge of the game, it laid a foundation for today's thriving professional circuit, and it marked the debut of PIA as sponsors of international squash.

Barrington 'sold' squash to the publicity media, too. Throughout the world, it began to attract a wider interest. He had the guts and the brains to take hold of the game, shake the cobwebs out of it, and lead it to a brighter future. His achievements, character, and methods have had an immense influence. His achievements demand respect. His character attracts attention. His methods inspire confidence because he has proved their efficiency. He taught squash players that in order to reach the top they had to work off the court as well as on it. To train as well as practise. Even on court, his systematic drills have had a dash of originality. One day I turned up at the West Warwickshire Club, Solihull, and heard beat music issuing from the squash courts. This track-suited figure was down there, his 5ft 10in. and 10st 8lb crouching to challenge the most exacting of all opponents, himself.

'I went through a spell where I started to find practice on my own increasingly difficult. There comes a stage when the improvement is only marginal. After the world amateur championship in 1969, I was very depressed because Geoff had beaten me by a clear margin in the final. I found it that much more difficult to go on the court, with that demise behind me, and keep playing the strokes that had failed me. I had to con myself a little bit and one day I decided to take the radio down. From then on, I've never had a problem. It's company and it also fits in to some extent with the movement and flow of practice. I once had a Mozart piano concerto on. That took me very nicely through a controlled drop shot session. But essentially squash is an animal game. It's very primitive in its movement — crouching, jumping, stamping, lunging. That's not like a normal human being. It's more akin to an animal. It takes one, a little bit, back into the jungle — but with the disciplined patterns of our everyday life. Beat music is our answer to tribal music, which works the African up to a frenzy.'

Well, Joe Frazier trained to similar music for similar reasons.

Barrington was a born fighter. But he was not a born champion. His squash has never been marked by the severity of his winning shots. But his pride and burning ambition were never satisfied with one outstanding performance in a tournament. He had to keep on winning until there was no one left to play. So he made himself a champion. Because of his intelligent approach to the task, his intensity of effort, his loathing for failure, he became a rare winner in a nation of good losers.

He had the nerve to believe it was possible.

Ten

The Barrington Breed

One morning in 1975, while driving to a Davis Cup tie at Eastbourne, I passed a sign advertising the proximity of 'Runnymede Squash & Tennis Club'. A decade earlier, such an order of precedence would have been startling enough to provoke a double-take. But many tennis clubs who used to regard squash as little more than a winter diversion now depend on their busier, more prosperous squash sections for financial security. Squash is outgrowing its distant relative. What happened to tennis in the United States — comfortable indoor facilities attracting the entire family all the year round — is happening to squash in Britain. As we move towards the 1980s there can be little doubt that the British people are playing more squash than tennis, that squash has become one of the nation's most popular participant sports (as distinct from spectator sports), and that Britain has more squash players than any other country in the world.

In passing, we may note that the priorities of the publicity media tend to be influenced by the number of people who watch a sport rather than the number who play it. It can be argued that squash and a few other sports consequently receive less attention than they deserve in the press and on television and radio.

The British game is thriving at club level. In 1976 Philip Ayton, Stuart Courtney, Jonathan Leslie, and Ian Robinson managed to break Australia's hold on the world amateur team championship, though this achievement meant a good deal less than it would have done in those earlier years when all the leading players except Abou Taleb were amateurs. The European amateur team championship seems likely to remain an English empire for some time. But Sweden are overtaking Ireland and Wales, and challenging Scotland. When we consider the élite, rather than the part-timers, the prospect is disquieting for Britain. The last sixteen of the inaugural world open championship, played at Wembley early in 1976, provided a sound guide to the international pecking order. Those players included six Pakistanis (three of them joined Geoff Hunt in the semi-finals), four Australians, three Egyptians, two South Africans — and Jonah Barrington, who was fast approaching his thirty-fifth birthday. In spite of Barrington's example during the previous decade, there was not another British player in sight.

This sits rather oddly with the fact that the British game is, as a whole, healthier than most. Playing standards are probably as good as they ever were. But that is no longer enough. Because in squash, as in many other sports of British origin, several overseas nations have pushed their levels of performance beyond ours. There is no reason why the leaders and the led should not change places again. It is equally possible that newcomers may take over: perhaps Japan or some other country where the game is currently being played only by a small minority and in a primitive manner. In short, it will become more and more difficult for Britain to reassert their traditional supremacy. For the moment, though, the most constructive thing we can do is to work out why Britain have already lost ground.

The cynical may suggest that in recent years there has been a growing tolerance of the quitter — the man whose effort declines as his difficulties increase — in almost every segment of our life as a nation. Plus an increasing willingness to condone second-class levels of performance. There may be something in this. But the generalizations are too sweeping and in any case are probably less true of sport than many other activities. It is possible, though, that the broad mass of British sportsmen have taken the Olympic creed — the important thing is not to win, but to take part — too much to heart. As far as squash is concerned, winning is certainly less important to British players than it is to those of, for example, Pakistan and Egypt — countries in which sporting renown is often the key to a considerable improvement in social and financial status. (The incentive to endure the hardship of time-consuming training and practice is correspondingly greater). Overseas players have often pointed out that their British rivals, though talented, are usually vulnerable in terms of fitness and stamina. Compared with the Australian game, Britain's is less intensely competitive and has much too high a proportion of private as opposed to public courts. Players who can afford to pay club fees cannot reasonably be classified as 'hungry fighters' and most of them, in any case, are over thirty and regard squash primarily as good exercise for people more responsibly committed to a family and a job.

The British game would benefit enormously if every city had a public squash centre serving as a competitive and social rendezvous for local and transient enthusiasts. The Wembley Squash Centre, opened in 1974, set an example of sorts. But it is not particularly convenient in its location or heart-warming in its character (overseas players in London are just as likely to make for such friendly private clubs as the Lambton in North Kensington).

An equally important cause of Britain's relative decline (and this one would be easy for administrators to remedy) is the outdated distinction between professionals and amateurs. During the 1960s it became almost impossible to distinguish leading amateurs from professionals. Players could no longer afford to reach the top and stay there without some form of support — for example, free or cut-price equipment and enough 'expenses' to cover the cost of travelling to and from tournaments. Throughout the world, the game's good name was tarnished by 'shamateurism'. Before the war, the definition of amateur status required only five lines in the *Squash Rackets Association Handbook*. Less than forty years later it required 156 lines, in much smaller type. Why bother? It is impossible to devise amateur rules that can be interpreted and enforced in a uniform way in countries with conflicting attitudes towards the question of subsidies for sportsmen. Between 1969 and 1976 the expansion of competitive squash for players who frankly embraced professionalism did something to clear up the mess. But the canker remained, spreading confusion and cynicism, creating divisions within the game, and inhibiting the advance of playing standards. The cure for all this is simple: bury the distinction. Give players on the way up more chances to meet those at the top and more incentive to beat them. Let all players compete together openly and earn as much as their abilities allow.

Open squash would benefit all nations. But at present Britain would probably benefit more than most because the popularity of the game has given them a numerical advantage in playing resources. Failing the abolition of distinctions, the SRA should follow the example of the women and make British tournaments open to everyone.

It does credit to Barrington — but is an embarrassing comment on his leading rivals — that no British player has beaten him since Jeremy Lyon did so in 1966. For a long time his main challenger was the dashing and handsome Michael Corby, whom he beat twice in the final of the British amateur championship (they were the last British players to reach the final until Jonathan Leslie did so eight years later). Because of a rearrangement of the fixture list, Corby had the quaint distinction of reaching the amateur final twice in the same year, 1968, and was twice in the last eight of the open championship in 1969. His career spanned two generations of British squash. He first played for England in 1963 — alongside Lyon, Richard Boddington, Tony Gathercole, and John Skinner — and twelve years later, to the very month, he was still good enough to feature in the semi-finals of Britain's first exclusively national amateur championship. The odd thing about the 1975 line-up was that Courtney was the only competitor who was born in Britain. Through circumstances over which they had no control, Leslie was born in Tanzania, Corby and John Richardson in India.

Exclusive though it was, that tournament certainly had a cosmopolitan flavour.

Corby had something in common with Pancho Gonzales, the tennis player, in that he stayed near the top for an unusually long time because he was so talented as an athlete and games-player that he could play well while living in a manner that stayed well clear of asceticism. His squash was true to his nature: brisk and busy, restless and fidgety, attractive and exciting, but volatile and sometimes infuriating. He had all the shots and enjoyed playing them, though at times one felt their cutting edge might have been more sharply honed. Nor did he volley enough. But on and off court, he was always lively company. The contrast between Corby and Barrington was interesting. They were kindred spirits in that both refused to submit to the tyranny of convention. But whereas Barrington was formerly an extremist in his professionalism, Corby was an extremist in his free and easy amateur approach.

He was something of a playboy sportsman, a throwback to a great British tradition in that he regularly represented his country at two different games — hockey (96 international appearances) and squash (34). Because he was the last of a dying line, he was something of a misfit in an age of single-minded specialists: and his efforts to fit both sports into his schedule led to a few lively tiffs with officials. His independent spirit and sense of mischief were not always calculated to calm troubled waters.

The early rounds of the British amateur championship used to be played at the Royal Automobile Club, which had (and possibly still has) some strange and strict rules concerning clothes. Some of the customs of society can, if surviving into an alien age, serve purposes directly opposed to those they were intended to serve. This applied to the RAC ban on women wearing trousers. The galleries behind the squash courts are steeply tiered. In the years when trouser suits and 'minis' were equally fashionable, the RAC rule had spectacularly immodest consequences. Every time a player looked up to confer with the match officials, he had to sort them out from an array of sleek legs and underwear. Players tended to be remarkably inventive in devising trivial appeals. And their eyes wanderd. They could never remember exactly where the referee and marker were sitting . . .

In 1970 Valerie Turley came down from Leicester to watch her husband, Ian, play Dick Carter (the Middlesex edition, rather than the better-known Australian). Refused admittance because she was wearing a trouser suit, she dashed out, spent £10 on a dress, and was back in time for the match. 'She needn't have bothered,' said Ian. He scored six points.

There was also a lot of fuss that season over the rule barring men who were not wearing ties. Corby was one of them. As he entered the club his coat swung open and the hall porter spotted the omission and challenged him. But Corby could not hang about for a debate or a shopping expedition. He was due on court. Then ensued a chase reminiscent of the silent movies: down and up the wide, curving staircases, with Corby in the lead and the hall porter in pursuit calling 'Man with no tie!' The sportsman, of course, had an unfair advantage. Corby emerged on the landing as the lift doors were opening. He leaped in, plunged into the dressing-room, and was almost changed when the hall porter turned up with the accusation: 'That's him — the man with no tie'. John

Horry (the SRA secretary) was summoned and pacified the hunter while the quarry nipped on court. The next season, Corby was banned from the RAC and had to play at the Junior Carlton Club instead. When he eventually returned to the RAC he wore a white silk tie — on court. As I said, Corby had a sense of mischief. Nowadays he runs the London Bridge Sports Centre. I must check the dress regulations.

A contemporary of Corby's, Peter Stokes, has made more amateur international appearances than any other British player: and Wales may not have done with him yet. The records suggest that his best season was 1966-7, in which he reached the last eight of both the open and amateur championships and then played for Britain in the inaugural world amateur championships in Australia. Long-limbed and bony, Stokes always looked slightly undernourished. But he lasted well because he was fit, travelled light, and had the kind of reach that conveniently reduced pedal mileage. We used to call him 'The Spider'. His reactions were fast. He volleyed well and played to a length at a hot pace. But his short game was not punishing enough to make much impression on the kind of men he had to play in the later rounds of major championships.

Stokes drifted in and out of squash like a sporting Pimpernel. He changed his address so often that we began to wonder if he had trouble with tradesmen. But he just happened to be in the Royal Air Force. He knew about orbital forces, and once offered to instruct me in the workings of the binary scale. In 1968 he reached the last eight of the amateur championship while intermittently engaged in snow-clearing operations on the airstrip at RAF Benson. But he had a head-on collision while driving to London for the quarter-final, and was taken back to base. That year he was posted to Cranwell in Lincolnshire, which is renowned for its RAF College and, a mile or so away, the site of Bayard's Leap, where the legendary horse covered a prodigious amount of ground without touching any of it. But Cranwell was bleakly remote from the sort of competition a squash player needed if he was in the Stokes class. He was short of match play when he was beaten by Mohamed Saleem in the first round of the 1969 world amateur championship. In *The Times* the following morning I referred to Stokes as 'a rusty British international'. The next day's post contained a sheet of slightly alarming red notepaper inscribed with the words:

'Rex — My husband's not rusty. Everything is in perfect working order. Lynette S.'

They spent two years in Paris, where Stokes was assistant air attaché at the British Embassy, and then went to ground somewhere in Oxfordshire. Always the Pimpernel. Always moving. No chance of getting rusty.

A player with almost as much amateur international experience as Stokes was Paul Millman, whose early career had something in common with Barrington's in that both went to Cheltenham College and later assisted John Horry in keeping the wheels of the SRA turning. Millman was heavily influenced by Barrington's example and methods. Their close association was an inspiration to the younger man. But one suspects that eventually Millman became a little disheartened by the pace Barrington was setting and the disruptive social cost of maintaining it, and decided that in his case there had to be a distinction between work and play — that squash could not dominate his life as it was dominating Barrington's. For a time he was assistant secretary to Middlesex County Cricket Club (he might have become a first-class cricketer but for the fact that squash was his preferred sport). Then he joined Harp Lager and immersed himself in a comprehensive study of the beer business. This job also strengthened the squash connection, because Harp — under the guidance of his father, Ted, who was something of an impresario as well as a coach — were pioneers of squash sponsorship in Britain.

Meantime Millman Junior was enjoying his squash, enlivening the scene with his wit and the entertaining resources of a retentive memory, and acquiring a respectable playing record. In addition to his international career, he twice reached the last four of the British amateur championship and in 1969 he beat Sharif Khan to earn a place in the quarter-finals of the open championship. His disposition insisted that squash must be imaginative and interesting. So he took risks and made mistakes. Millman had a strong wrist and a reverberating backhand — whether it hit the wall or the tin. He was also the first Gloucestershire man to marry a girl called Devon.

The unusual thing about Philip Ayton and John Easter was the enduring parity of their level of performance. They played five games in the 1967 match between the universities of Cambridge and Oxford and almost a decade later there was still nothing to choose between them.

Ayton was born in London but spent his infancy in South Africa — and it was by winning the 1970 South African amateur championship that he established his international reputation. He reached the quarter-finals of the British amateur championship six times and in 1974 Ayton and Peter Verow (whose medical studies retarded the maturity of his uncommon flair for squash) gave Britain two places in the semi-finals for the first time since 1968. Ayton was tall and lean, bespectacled and bewhiskered. But at his prime he was a much tougher competitor than a casual glance might suggest. He did not carry a heavy enough punch to worry the leading professionals. But the tactical structure of his game was an exemplary model for the aspiring young. He was always thinking, and seldom wasted a shot. With angles and drops, drives and lobs, he mixed the long and short games with a smooth facility that sent his opponents on ever more urgent errands.

Ayton is an investment analyst and succeeded Corby as Britain's leading amateur. Easter, who represented Oxford University at both cricket and squash, drifted amiably through his twenties while preparing for — or at grips with, or recovering from — a series of widely spaced accountancy examinations. By the time this book is published, the last of them should be behind him. In 1974, at the age of twenty-eight, he became a squash professional. Barrington had just lost the British open championship (that was the year Mohamed Yasin beat him) and the confidence had drained out of him. He needed another dose of Africa and suggested that Easter should join him on a seven-match tour of Kenya. 'I hadn't had a consistent job for a couple of years. Very little income. And prospects in the amateur game were pretty bleak, with Mohibullah and Zaman still around. I'd represented Great Britain and England as often as I really wanted to. I had no more goals as an amateur — and it looked as if the professional game was expanding and there might be some money around.'

So Easter went to Kenya and the professional circuit thus acquired a crowd-pulling new recruit who looked as if he might be killing time between heroic film roles. I once referred to him in *The Times* as a 'matinée idol', and the label stuck. Easter is 6ft 3in tall with a build to match. But there is so much of him that the task of keeping all of it in peak condition presents him with more fitness problems than most players have. The leading professionals mercilessly exploit the fact that he needs more breathers than they do. But he counter-attacks in exciting bursts — because he is a strong man, a fine player, and has guts. His long reach is an advantage and his assurance on the high backhand volley (a devilishly awkward shot) is impressive.

An even better volleyer is that gloriously gifted stroke-player, Stuart Courtney (like Easter, a good cricketer too). During the 1973-4 season the left-handed Courtney took over from Ayton as Britain's leading amateur and in each of the next two seasons he reached the final of the national amateur championship. His touch is superb and he can crush a man — briefly, anyway — with a rain of volleyed nicks. But Courtney lives in Cardiff, which is a little remote from first-class competition, and is seldom as match fit as he needs to be when playing the top men. Even such talents as his are frail flowers unless fertilized by fitness.

Another good amateur, continually snapping at the heels of Britain's top men, is John Richardson, whose advance owed much to his own application and, initially, the help Richard Boddington gave him at Ealing. In January, 1975, Richardson had the distinction of taking part in an important original fixture: an open international match between Britain and Pakistan at Wembley, with professionals and amateurs lining up together in their national teams.

By the end of 1976 a new name had leapt to the top of Britain's amateur ranking list — that of Jonathan Leslie, a barrister, whose law studies had obviously been more assiduous than Barrington's. This gifted all-rounder represented Oxford University at five sports and decided that he would try to reach international level at one of them. It was just a question of selecting the best brief before going into court. Tucked in behind Leslie at No. 2 in the rankings was that bold young shot-maker, Philip Kenyon. Both were members of Lord Burnham's club at Beaconsfield, which had risen from the ground only three years and six months earlier.

New players at the top. New clubs. Yes, the British amateur game is flourishing. But the leading professionals are all over thirty. Apart from Barrington and Easter, the best known are

Bryan Patterson and Clive Francis. Patterson, like Barrington, is a left-hander and a former schoolmaster. Though somewhat out of his depth in the higher reaches of the professional game, he is an accomplished player with a formidably physical court presence — muscular and tenaciously combative. Patterson sprang to prominence in September, 1973, when he beat three seeds (Roland Watson, John Easter, and Dave Wright) to reach the final of the world amateur championship in South Africa. He then made a farewell appearance in the British amateur championship, turned professional, and beat Ken Hiscoe in the British open championship. Francis is a quick, bouncy little chap. He used to be on the staff of the Atomic Energy Commission. This was apt, because Francis himself is a lot of explosive vigour packed into a small area. He is restlessly aggressive, never happier than when whacking the ball into the nick. Like Jack Giles before him, he has made the professional championship of the United Kingdom something of a private domain.

Reluctantly, though, we must admit that the Barrington breed have not been the Cornishman's most distinguished disciples. The finest representatives of the school he founded, the men who not only respected his example but were effectively responsive in learning from it, were of a different racial stock. At first they regarded Barrington and Geoff Hunt as leaders of redoubtable stature. But they did not accept the continuance of Anglo-Saxon rule as inevitable. They were fired by patriotism and a desire to restore an earlier dynasty. They had a dream.

They came from a long, long way south-east of Morwenstow.

Eleven

An Eye For An Eye

Street, a town in Somerset, produces footwear and — by way of Millfield School — educated sportsmen and sportswomen. Millfield has a history master, named Michael Thurgur, who is also a squash professional, inured to the 250-mile round trip that London competition demands of him. In 1954 Hashim and Roshan Khan visited Millfield during an exhibition tour and a year later Hashim's son, Sharif, became a pupil there. He knew little English and for a time, predictably, was unhappy. But eventually he settled down, and there was always Uncle Azam to visit in London. In 1963 he won the British junior championship and it seemed possible that, after a few years of Abou Taleb, Sharif might put his famous family on top of the heap again. It was not to be, however. He was always an exciting player, violently venturesome in playing a wide range of shots. He made a lot of noise and had a lot of fun. But he was wild and spent his energy too prodigally. In 1966 he became a professional in Canada. It was difficult to estimate how much farther he might have progressed in the softball game. But from 1969 onwards he won the North American open championship eight times in nine seasons. In the *United States Squash Racquets Association Yearbook* he was described as 'a superb and improving stroke-maker, as well as probably the most devastating slugger in the American game's history'. In 1970 he briefly returned to the softball game, joining Barrington's trailblazing tour of the East and then reaching the semi-finals of the British open championship. Sharif's exact position in the hall of fame is debatable, but this deceptively fierce-looking chap (he has a joyously friendly nature) has certainly honoured the Khan tradition.

In terms of softball squash, Pakistan never forgot the revenge clause in the Pathan code: 'An eye for an eye, a tooth for a tooth.' They wanted the British open championship back. Aftab Jawaid and Mohamed Yasin were keeping the pot on the boil, but there was nothing special cooking. Yasin's brother, Mohamed Saleem, was vastly entertaining: an ungainly left-hander with a short grip, flat feet, an explosive forehand, and a good drop shot. But he lacked the class to win the big one. It was a transitional period for Pakistani squash. The game was languishing.

It was in the late 1960s that the first shots of a new growth gradually began to emerge. Squash was lucky in that it attracted the patronage of one of the most powerful men in the country, Nur Khan, who recognized the game's past and potential importance to a young and prestige-conscious nation. He had squash centres built at Peshawar in 1967 and at Karachi in 1976. One of the local lads to benefit from the coaching scheme at Peshawar was Mohibullah Khan Junior. Jawaid's nephew, Qamar Zaman, was brought in from Quetta. They came under Yasin's tutelage, then that of Omar Draz, who was to tour with them and ensure that their practice was diligent and constructive. While the paint was still fresh on the new courts at Peshawar, it seemed that the Karachi group — Jawaid, Yasin, Saleem, and one or two more — might soon have a local problem on their hands. Roshan's son, Torsam, was growing up. But a much more urgent challenge, creating an inter-city rivalry that could almost be described as hostility, was taking shape in the country's sporting and educational capital, Lahore. Three young men from Lahore were to form the vanguard of Pakistan's second major assault on the strongholds of world squash.

In alphabetical order, they were Gogi Alauddin, Hidayat ('Hiddy') Jahan, and Sajjad Muneer. Alauddin and Muneer were Punjabis, Jahan a Pathan. They were the same age.

Lahore, the city of Kipling and Kim and the gun Zam-Zammah, is a breath-taking blend of beauty and dinginess, dignity and hugger-mugger, opulence and indigence, repose and restlessness. Its contrasts are exciting. Pick your way past the letter-writers and palmists, the orange-presses, the donkeys and goats, and you may find your way to a five-court squash centre in Old Club Road. The floors are cemented (though there is talk of putting wood down on two new courts, to save wear and tear on shoes and rackets). The gallery is open to a usually burnished sky. The professional is a slim, gentle man called Ahmad Din. He is Alauddin's father. In the 1960s Sajjad's father, Muneer Ahmad, chairman of the regional Squash Rackets Association, lost a lot of sweat on those courts. The boys were chums and they were soon on court themselves, using sawn-off rackets. That was the beginning of a coaching scheme for the young. Jahan used to come down from Quetta (where his father, Mumtaz Khan, is a club professional) for junior tournaments — and eventually settled in Lahore to pursue his studies and his squash.

Thus was formed a trinity of friends who, collectively and individually, showed Pakistan the way ahead at the beginning of the present decade. Muneer's path diverged from that of the others when he became a civil engineer. But in the early years they were a team both on and off court. Their characters differed yet were complementary: Alauddin serene and self-effacing, Jahan hearty, Muneer suave. The common factor was that all were charming. Their playing methods, reflecting their personalities in every case, also had a common factor: although Alauddin was slightly ahead in terms of concentration, their levels of ability were very close indeed. Because they played contrasting games yet were equally effective, their combined practice and competition over a long period achieved two things: it raised their standard in every way, and prepared them for any kind of opposition the luck of the draw could throw at them.

The first to the fore was Alauddin, who weighs in at 8st 12lb and has a 28in. waist. 'The Pipecleaner', as Jonah Barrington dubbed him, made one false start as a tourist. In 1966 he and two friends decided to go to Europe. They travelled by bus — or rather buses, one after another — from Lahore to Kabul and then to Tehran. Whereupon Alauddin, having put 1,500 rugged miles behind him, lost his money and had to turn back. This could have been awkward. Such journeys are tricky for those with empty pockets. Luckily he met an English couple who were pointing in the right direction, and they drove him to Lahore. But Alauddin had not been sleeping well for two or three weeks. He had to go to hospital and could not resume his squash career until he had been injected with vitamins.

In 1967 Alauddin was to make a more conventional and comfortable trip. As Pakistan junior champion he was chosen to represent his country in the world amateur championships in Australia. He was seventeen years old. In 1969 he went to England for the second championship series (this time Muneer was in the team too). The next year, Barrington's touring circus turned up in Lahore. Alauddin, Jahan, and Muneer played so well against Rainer Ratinac, Sharif Khan, and Barrington respectively that the Punjab Sports Control Board decided to sponsor all three youngsters through the next British season. Thus, in 1970-1, the trio launched their first combined invasion of Britain and their first challenges for its major championships. In the amateur event, all three confounded the seedings: Jahan by reaching the last eight (when he ran into Alauddin), Muneer by advancing to the semi-finals, and Alauddin by winning the tournament at his first attempt, without losing a game, and becoming the youngest amateur champion since Nigel Broomfield thirteen seasons earlier. All things considered, it was a satisfactory start.

Technically and tactically, Alauddin's performance against Bill Reedman in the final was remarkably mature for a twenty-year-old newcomer to the tournament. In the entire championship, Kim Bruce-Lockhart was the only man to take more than six points from Alauddin in a single game. Alauddin's anticipation was sharp and his retrieving nimble. He was so agile, so lightly built, that he seemed to float about the court — and he made the ball do the same. He seldom played a thoughtless shot and his ball control was superb, even when he was volleying under pressure. He softened up his opponents with a carefully composed strategy: drives (often clinging to the walls) and lobs to a length, and the contrasting thrusts of drops and angles. Having thus sapped their energy, Alauddin hurt them even more by raising the pace while playing to the same basic pattern. When they were reeling, he would often toy with them for a while, like a cat playing with a helpless bird. He has improved since then, notably in his capacity for deception and for varying the pace. But the subtle design of his squash is unchanged. More than any other player in the modern game, he quietly and fluently demonstrates the enormous amount of damage that can be done without any overt violence.

Alauddin retained his amateur title the following season, though in the final he was not at his best and had to come from behind against Mohamed Asran. He then turned professional and in the next five British open championships he was twice runner-up and three times in the semi-finals. During this sequence his most memorable win occurred at Sheffield in 1973 when he beat Geoff Hunt. Alauddin's game, like Barrington's in earlier years, is a severe test for Hunt's patience and concentration, discretion and ball control. Especially when Alauddin is playing well on a warm court, which in any case makes it more difficult for Hunt to put the ball away. Alauddin gives him nothing and Hunt cannot maintain a consistent attack when the ball is clinging to the walls or humming over his head. There are times when Alauddin's touch and masking reduce even Hunt to spinning perplexity. 'He's got a beautiful backhand boast,' said Hunt, after winning their semi-final in the first world open championship at Wembley in 1976. 'Not many people can play a slow boast like that.' But the shot that stirs Alauddin to his very bones is obviously the backhand cross-court drop. He caresses the ball as if afraid of hurting it. His body stiffens, his left arm is extended, and he momentarily holds the position — a balletic pose — as if the slightest disturbance of air currents might deflect the ball from its course.

Alauddin's squash is geometry with movement. Craft and gentle precision. The emphasis is on placing rather than power. Half the time he seems to be nudging the ball rather than hitting it. Ahmed Safwat told me once: 'Gogi gives you plenty of time but plays very tight. He gets there comfortably, returns them very accurately, and doesn't take too many risks — a safe boast, a safe drop, a safe lob. He kills you . . .'

In April, 1976, Alauddin won what was then the richest tournament in the softball game. The new squash complex in Karachi had not yet been equipped with air-conditioning and the heat and humidity were debilitating. In his last two matches, at the cost of only one game, the slim little Punjabi disposed of Hunt and Mohibullah — the men who had contested the final of the world open championship only two months earlier. And Ahmad Din, who had flown down from Lahore, was there to see it happen.

Jahan's story reads like a film scenario. But at first it was uneventfully itinerant. He was born in Lahore but was still a boy when the family moved to Nowshera (Yusuf Khan country) before settling at Quetta, which is tucked away in the mountains on the road to Kandahar. The leading players up there were Jawaid and Hidayat's older brother, Shan Jahan. They were coached by Mumtaz Khan and another local professional, Ghulam Hussain, a relative of Jawaid and Zaman. As we know, Hidayat later went down to Lahore. He played a lot of badminton, which explains why he has one of the best wrists in the business, and as a cricketer he was an all-rounder good enough to captain his school. But squash was becoming his main sport and in 1967 he was in the running for a place in Pakistan's team for the world amateur championships in Australia. He was in Quetta when a summons to the final trials told him he had to be in Karachi next day. By slow train, that 600-mile ride takes a day. But he set off, economy class, on a journey that almost cost him his life.

'It was really crowded. After about ten hours of sitting, I came off to stretch my legs and lie on a bench on the platform at a small stop-over called Habib Kot. It was three o'clock in the morning. Suddenly the horn went and I tried to get back into the train. But it had got more crowded and I couldn't get through. There were two more in front of me and the door was blocked with cans of cooking oil. I was pretty sleepy. But I struggled for about a mile, holding the handles and trying to get in. I was hanging out, standing on the steps. And the signal hit me. Luckily it was the last bogie. Otherwise the train would have been on top of me. When I fell, I hit the person in front of me. He started screaming and stopped the train. I was unconscious. They picked me up and put me in hospital. I said, "I'm leaving," and went to Karachi the next day. Roshan couldn't believe what had happened when he saw the bandages on my head. I couldn't give my proper trial. I had been beating Gogi, but I lost to him. He went to Australia and I went back to Quetta — by train. I was in hospital for about three and a half months. A head injury, and my eyesight was affected. Pressed nerves. I still have scars on my head. And my back (the inside was mincemeat). A steel rod or something went into my leg, and limping is now a habit.'

All Jahan had to show for that final trial was a spectacular passport photograph. And scars. It was eight months before he was back in action.

Act Two of the offstage Jahan drama was both personal and political. He was runner-up to Geoff Hunt in the 1974 and 1975 finals of the South African open championship. His presence there contravened the Pakistan government's policy concerning sporting contacts with South Africa. Jahan is a superb ambassador for his country, wherever he goes, and in this case he achieved practical results by introducing Asians to squash and the clubs in which it was played. No matter. He was suspended by the Pakistan Squash Rackets Federation and feared that, if he returned home, he might not be allowed to leave the country again (he was to be separated from his family for two years and a half before the suspension was lifted). Superficially, his decision to go to South Africa seemed headstrong. But there was more to it. His father, Mumtaz Khan, had lost his job (it was later restored to him) and had been told to leave the house that went with it. A family running to double figures needed a new home and it was up to Jahan and his brother Shah — professional at a genteel, cosy club in Paris — to help raise the funds to buy it (which they did). But Jahan's only job was playing squash: and South Africa was an integral and lucrative segment of the professional circuit. There was nothing else going on at the time. Jahan had refused previous invitations to go to South Africa. But in the circumstances of 1974 he accepted. And with that the die had been cast.

The anguish such a dilemma can cause occurred in an even more acute form during the world open championship at Wembley in February, 1976. The Squash Rackets Association rejected a request from the Pakistan SRF that Jahan should be barred from the championship. Jahan was also aware that his sister was ill. He was in no mood for squash. But he beat Mike Donnelly and Kim Bruce-Lockhart in straight games — and then he received a telephone call. His sister was dying. He knew that he dare not fly home but he was under so much stress that he did not want to play another match. His wife, Sue, and his brother, Shah, told him to play on. Jahan beat Bill Reedman in straight games but, in the best of the quarter-finals, lost to Mohibullah in the fifth game after being poised two points from success in the fourth. Back in Pakistan, one or two bureaucrats presumably read the news and smiled.

But that South African episode did have its lighter moments. There was, for example, an incident that occurred on a hot evening outside a house at Durban after the inhibitions of the squash set had been lubricated by lavish hospitality. The parties concerned are coy about discussing the details. But I understand that Jahan and Safwat were playing table tennis on the veranda when three of the players' wives dashed past, went into a corner, emerged naked and plunged into the swimming pool. Submerged streakers.

Then there was a brief encounter subsequently construed as a romance justifying front-page headlines in South Africa. Jahan's virile squash made a big impression on a Stellenbosch University student whose family had a certain amount of political prominence. They had dinner one evening and she said that she hoped to go to Europe and might see him there. That was that: until Jahan visited Paris for a brief stay with Shah. A South African newspaper telephoned Shah's club, Eurosquash, and then sent their Paris man to interview Hidayat. Thus the headlines. After his marriage, Jahan (who now had Sue with him) had a chance meeting with the same young lady. 'She had a boyfriend who was a discus thrower. About 7ft. tall. And wide . . .'

Sue Bullmore, a Londoner, was working for an insurance company who were sponsoring squash. She was introduced to Jahan when the firm threw a party for the players ('I took her out to dinner and got the job for good'). They married in 1975 and settled in London.

Jahan is a frank, generous, occasionally impetuous extrovert. For many years one of his virtues as a man — a reluctance to dissemble his feelings — was perhaps his most obvious defect as a match-player. When angered by a refereeing decision, he let it show. He argued. His concentration and his squash briefly suffered. But after his marriage he learned to control, if not dispel, any fleeting bouts of indignation. This, together with his maturing sense of purpose as a professional and the discipline this brought to his game, made him a sounder competitor. From 1975 onwards he was firmly established in the top five and became increasingly capable of beating any of the other four.

In 1970 the initiative of Ahmed Nadi, the club's professional, led to the promotion of an open tournament on the cool courts of West Wycombe SRC, tucked away between stables and meadows on the Dashwood estate in the Chilterns. Jahan was to play some thrilling squash there, beating Alauddin in two finals and Mohibullah in another. But the same two players stopped Jahan in two semi-finals of the British amateur championship (in 1973 Mohibullah came from behind and luckily survived a match point — and Jahan was then afflicted by cramp). Jahan turned professional. In February, 1975, he celebrated his engagement by beating Mohibullah to reach the semi-finals of the British open championship.

This was one of the finest matches he had played. His cross-court backhand drop was unerring and he showed us side wall shots that he usually reserves for the privacy of the practice court. But in his next match he was tormented by Zaman and allowed himself to be disconcerted by the refereeing.

Since they were young together, up in the mountains, the rivalry between these two has always been curried. For this reason (and, even more important, because he was playing in his homeland for the first time in two years and a half) there was much satisfaction for Jahan when he crushed Zaman by the astonishing margin of 9-1, 9-3, 9-4 in only twenty-nine minutes to reach the semi-finals of the Pakistan Masters at Karachi in November, 1976. What an emotional occasion that was. Zaman's artistry was destroyed by such ruthlessly sustained ferocity, such violent splendour, that the total effect induced a degree of shock. In the dressing-room the usually buoyant Zaman was ashen, subdued, shaken, like a soldier just back from the front line on a day that had been nothing but bad news. Spectators — including hardened professionals who thought they had already seen it all — were wandering about the best tournament complex in the world groping, as if dazed, for words that might express the way they felt about Jahan's performance. 'Never I have seen such a game,' gasped Alauddin. 'That was a holocaust,' said John Easter. All over the premises little knots of people were spluttering with incredulity.

We knew about the blistering, reverberating ferocity of Jahan's hitting. We knew that, on the backhand, he could do wondrous things with his strong and flexible wrist. We knew of his ceaseless aggression, his capacity for hitting a stream of winners — most of them brutal, but some as gentle as leaves drifting on the wind. We knew that at times he could be irresistible. But for three games in a row, against Zaman? This was ridiculous. But it kept on happening. The court seemed to shake and rattle in the echoing din that always tells everybody where Jahan is playing.

Geoff Hunt beat Jahan in straight games, though they were hotly contested and imposed a terrible physical burden on both men. From the start Hunt played as if fighting for his life. Jahan had the utmost difficulty in putting the ball away. The sustained pace took the edge from Jahan's speed and Hunt exploited this with short, clinging drops. The court became too large for the big, heavy Pathan. But he did hit the most remarkable winner of the match, a cross-court forehand kill that threatened to perforate racket, wall, and floor without losing momentum.

Jahan's wrist and touch make him enviably versatile and deceptive. But his game is essentially based on powerful, thrilling savagery — and this, together with his impressive build and strikingly handsome looks, makes him the most stirring sight in modern squash. He and Alauddin are perfect in their complementary contrasts. When these to go on court together (the wispy Alauddin tends to look like a sapling bending in a gale) they can show us everything the game has to offer.

While Jahan was out of favour, a Karachi newspaper published a mollifying article, liberal in its tone and reasonable in its construction, advocating that the suspension be lifted. The writer was Sajjad Muneer, who was still torn between the pleasures of squash and the responsibilities of a career in civil engineering. During the middle 1970s he transferred his attention from demolition to construction, as it were. But in squash he was not forgotten. 'What's Muneer doing these days?' was a familiar question on the circuit. His abilities had been so promising that, in view of the way Alauddin and Jahan had progressed, there was some disappointment that Muneer's potential had not been fully explored. But he is an educated Punjabi from a well-to-do family and one suspects that by nature and background he is not ideally suited for the unremitting hard work and inevitably restricted life-style of a professional sportsman. In his early years he represented Pakistan in the world amateur championships, reached the quarter-finals of the British amateur championship in four successive seasons (in two of them he advanced a round farther), won the Australian amateur title and once figured in the last eight of the British open championship. For a time the civil engineer replaced the squash player. But in January, 1975, Muneer popped out of the blue to represent his country against Britain at Wembley in two international matches: the first an amateur event, the second open. In 1976 he became a professional and, fluently demonstrating that his talents were unimpaired, beat Rehmatullah and John Easter in the first major open tournaments to be played in Karachi.

Like Jahan, Muneer is heavily built, could not accurately be described as nimble, and must be more diligent than most players in maintaining his basic fitness. The punishing rallies he must play against the top men tend to break down his physical resources and provoke errors. But when the pressure is less severe he emerges as a superb striker of the ball with a straight-backed yet flowing and orthodox style. His backhand is powerful. But the outstanding feature of his game is his effectively facile use of the side walls. It will be interesting to see if he can spare the time for the intense practice and match-play that further improvement would demand.

But none of these three was to become the first Pakistani since Mohibullah, in 1962, to win the British open championship. Nor was it to be Mohibullah Junior (no relation), though this precocious young man has the right name and has established himself as Hunt's heir-apparent. So far as one can know the truth of these things, he appears to have been born in January, 1956. It follows that Mohibullah won the British junior championship and played the world amateur championships at the age of fifteen, that he won the British amateur championship at seventeen (which in retrospect made Broomfield, Hunt and Alauddin look relatively retarded), that he was nineteen when he won the 1975 Australian open championship without losing a game (beating Jahan, Hunt and Hiscoe in his last three matches), and that he was twenty when he led Hunt by two games to one in the final of the first world open championship. He has yet to pass the test of greatness by dominating his contemporaries. But he is heading in the right direction and travelling unusually fast.

Mohibullah was one of eleven children born in Peshawar to a poor family with no squash-playing background. Until 1968 he was a 'tennis boy' at the officers' club where Hashim had his first job as a professional. But his flair for squash was already evident and he was just the kind of lad they were looking for at the new coaching centre. From 1968 onwards, his future was secure as long as he was prepared to work. And he was. By 1971, as we know, he was ready to be launched on the international circuit. Mohibullah beat Zaman in two consecutive finals of the British amateur championship. In April, 1975, they both became professionals. This was an event of historic significance because it meant that the upper crust had now been completely removed from amateur competition. Muneer was the only amateur who could feel confident of a place in any sixteen-strong draw featuring the top men: but he was not competing much and, in any case, was to turn professional a year later.

Mohibullah has a high-pitched voice that might be issuing from a record played at too many revolutions per minutes. His English and his moustache have been audibly and visibly struggling. He is broad in the shoulder but otherwise slim and loose-limbed: beautifully balanced and somewhat bandy-legged, like many fine athletes. He and Hunt are taking agility, speed and stamina to levels that have not been attained since the peak years of Hashim and Azam. In 1976 Mohibullah repeatedly showed us that his strategy, tactics and ball control were becoming sounder yet more flexible. In the world open championship he beat Jahan and Zaman after being within two points of defeat in each match. Then he led Hunt by two games to one. But it is doubtful if Mohibullah has produced a better match-winning performance than his 9-3, 9-3, 9-0 success against Alauddin in a semi-final of the Pakistan Masters. He was so fast that he managed to divert most of Alauddin's sharpest thrusts. He offered Alauddin nothing loose. Using the side walls neatly, he rallied patiently and tidily, waiting for the right openings — which he exploited with the right shots. When given the chance to finish a rally, he finished it. His drops were short clingers and his nicked kills were so powerfully accurate that — especially when he let himself go on the backhand — one suspected it might be necessary to chisel the ball out of the crack. And all the time, as usual, he looked slightly bored and worried. There is no gaiety in Mohibullah's squash and he does nothing that others cannot do. He just does everything faster.

Zaman, his friend and practice partner for almost a decade, is a total contrast both on and off court. This explains why they have been of such mutual benefit. Each feeds on the fruits of the other's character and ability. On and off court, Zaman is a deadpan entertainer bubbling with impish humour. He has the true comedian's natural sense of timing and can raise a laugh merely with a shrug, a glance, or a sudden shift of the eyebrows. If his moustache was mobile he would use it for the same purpose. Socially he has an instinctive *savoir-faire*, a ready smile, and the gift of pleasing. All his most attractive qualities are on the surface, which is no bad place for a professional sportsman to have them. On court, he is rather flat-footed and walks with awkward deliberation. Not a natural athlete, by any means. But his pride, together with the stimulus of Mohibullah's company and the urging of Omar Draz, have brought him to a degree of quickness and fitness that few players surpass. His reactions are like lightning. Eyes, mind, and wrist achieve instant co-ordination. Then his ball sense, racket work, and astonishing certainty of touch on the volley enable him to express the artistic virtuosity that is always bursting out of the man. He has a superb wrist and a remarkable capacity for masking his intentions. His game is devilishly difficult to read. At times his opponents all come up with the wrong guesses (except for Mohibullah, who knows him too well). Crafty and imaginative, Zaman produces all kinds of trickery, much of it impromptu. He transforms the animated geometry of squash into a spectacle of dazzling beauty. 'I enjoy watching Zaman,' says Ken Hiscoe, 'because I'd hate squash to become a running game.'

It was Zaman who put the Pathans back in power.

Zaman's family came from Peshawar. But he was born at Quetta in April, 1951. His father, Mohamed Ayub, coached tennis and squash there and hammered into him the argument that most of the time spent on training runs could be better spent on court. Zaman's early preference was for tennis and he had some encouraging successes. But at fifteen he dropped the game, concentrated on squash and was soon working alongside Mohibullah under Yasin's supervision at the Peshawar training centre. The family moved back too. Zaman never managed to beat the younger Mohibullah until the British amateur championship of December, 1972. At his first attempt, Zaman thus reached the semi-finals. But in the next two years Mohibullah reasserted his former ascendancy ('He's confident against me,' admits Zaman). Though Zaman was to win the Australian amateur and Egyptian open championships, the one that mattered most was the 1975 British open. In his last three matches he beat Hunt, Jahan, and Alauddin. Mohibullah had failed to get past Jahan.

A week earlier, Barrington had beaten Hunt for the first time since 1972. But that was in an experimental professional team series which obviously did not matter as much as the open championship. Moreover, Zaman was wandering about Wembley with a scarf round his head, looking nothing like a potential champion. He had an abscess on a wisdom tooth and was receiving treatment to reduce the pain and the swelling. Hunt took the first two games from him, surviving a game ball in the second. In the next two games Hunt collected only five points, losing his length and his momentum as Zaman set about him with some lovely squash. But Hunt let 7-5 in the fifth and Australians — especially Hunt — are not the kind to let their opponents off the hook twice. But in the crisis Zaman's squash was magic and he never muffed a trick. A heavily cut cross-court backhand kill put the champion and top seed out of business. Zaman raised his arms in triumph and his compatriots rushed on court and carried him away on their shoulders, because the road was now wide open for Pakistan.

'He played too well for me,' said Hunt. 'There were patches where he played outstanding squash. I got tentative at times, but a lot of it was due to his onslaught. I thought I'd hang out in the end. But he didn't make mistakes and he hit some tight winners.'

Until that championship, Zaman had always been prone to damage his own cause with a sudden rash of errors — arising from the fact that his heart, rather than his head, was telling him which shot to go for. He was always full of ideas but could not always sort out the good ones from the bad. Artists tend to be an undisciplined breed, the kind who serve champagne in beer glasses unless closely supervised. But during that golden phase of his career Zaman was patient and discreet in working for his openings and chose his shots with care. He remained creative and deceptive, but he was prepared to sweat for his profits. Because of that, and his breath-taking skill, he beat Hunt, Jahan and Alauddin and gave the Pathans another world champion. The previous two, Azam and Mohibullah Senior, turned up from Shepherd's Bush and Boston to see the famous dynasty restored. Nur Khan, who had dreamed of such a day but flew in from New York too late to see it happen, had to make do with a televised recording. Yes, that training centre at Peshawar had been a good move . . .

Zaman promptly beat Hunt again, this time at Stockton-on-Tees in one of the most popular tournaments on the professional calendar. After that he could not maintain his authority and for a time, doubtless because of the frustration this caused him, Zaman the entertainer subdued Zaman the competitor. But he is still teasing the tigers and remains the most enchanting shot-maker since the best years of Abou Taleb.

Torsam, Pakistan's under-sixteen champion, went to New Zealand for the 1971 world amateur championship series, and in 1973 turned professional and settled in England. He has since been nagging at the heels of the top men without quite managing to sink his teeth into them. Torsam can stretch his man with cross-court drops and hurt him with nicked kills. He gives the ball a fearful wallop. When going well he can hit some blazing winners. But his game does not flow and his stamina has often been vulnerable. It seems that he would rather play shots than rallies. His fellow professionals also find him something of a traffic hazard, and as the lets accumulate Torsam punctuates the proceedings with malevolent glares and sometimes waxes disputatious. He is a fierce-looking chap and plays the 'heavy' perfectly. But his game needs a more solid basis of fitness if it is to develop fully.

When Nasrullah went to work in England, he left his sons Amanullah and Rehmatullah in Karachi with his brother, Roshan (Torsam's father). There the boys completed their education, achieved national prominence as tennis players and played a little squash for fun. They were ready to join Naz in England, but getting the necessary permits was difficult. Barrington's temporary presence in Pakistan enabled him to unravel some of the red tape and in 1970 Amanullah and Rehmatullah travelled to Europe. They soon dropped tennis and began careers as squash professionals, a relatively easy transition because they were already familiar with squash and were unusually talented at racket games. Both had club coaching jobs, but the younger Rehmatullah later became a colourfully trendy figure on the competitive circuit and was soon chasing Torsam in the rankings. He does not have enough punch to make much impression in the later rounds of big championships. But his presence is a reminder of Pakistan's formidable depth of talent.

And back home there are a few diminutive but talented youngsters getting ready for the next assault . . .

Twelve

African Arts and Crafts

In many ways Egyptian squash mirrors that of Pakistan, which occupies a similar climatic latitude. Again it is a minority sport played mostly by rich and poor (as distinct from the middle class) at sparse and often primitive facilities. Again the heat can be oppressive and the courts are mostly open-air and have concrete floors. Again, the club professional has to struggle to make a decent living. The big difference between the two countries is that, thanks to Nur Khan and Pakistan International Airlines (who sponsor the game and give leading players financial security by employing them), Pakistani squash has begun to benefit from the official encouragement and support it has been given during the past decade. That has not happened yet in Egypt. There does not seem to be the same awareness of — or perhaps the same esteem for — the prestige a nation can gain through its sportsmen. Ahmed Safwat reckons that, other than Ismael el Shafei's tennis, squash is probably the only international sport that is providing Egypt with publicity.

'If someone would go to the Egyptian president and whisper in his ear that these boys are making a lot of publicity for Egypt and he ought to look after them . . .'

Traditionally, the special quality of Egyptian squash has always been the wrist-work of its leading exponents. Some of them, indeed, have used so much wrist that they have often been inconsistent in their ball control when confronted by less attractive but sounder players. But the products of Cairo and Alexandria have given us so much pleasure and excitement that it has been sad to see the Egyptian game at such a low ebb that, from

1974 to 1976, Aly Aziz was their only player to reach the last eight of either of Britain's major championships (and Aziz was working at a squash club in Sweden). Sherif Afifi considers that Gamal Awad, who gave Ken Hiscoe a tough match in the 1976 world open championship, is the best of the new generation. But one wonders how often such youngsters will have the chance to benefit from first-class competition.

In addition to the Egyptians we have previously discussed, Ahmed Nadi and another Aziz (Wahid) popped into the quarter-finals of the open championship often enough to show the flag. Then Galal Allam, Mohamed Asran, Aly Aziz, Abbas Kaoud, Mohamed Khalifa, and Safwat arrived. All of them became professionals and settled in Europe. 'We wouldn't dream of going back,' Safwat told me once. 'It doesn't pay. In Pakistan the professionals are looked after. The "pro" game has been recognized. But not in Egypt — they just look after the amateurs.'

The burly and genial Aly Aziz (sometimes affectionately known as 'The Gorilla') works hard at his game and in 1975, unseeded, reached the final of the British amateur championship. But the players to cause most of a stir were Asran and Safwat.

Though Asran was born in Cairo, his parents came from Kana, near Luxor (the site of the ancient Egyptian capital, Thebes). This is a wild area in which wild customs still survive. The Pathans would feel at home there. The inhabitants have strong characters, tribal traditions, blood feuds, rifles and machine-guns. 'There was no law,' says Asran. 'No one could catch them. It's better now. The law start to catch them.' When relatives read about him in the newspaper, they tend to travel to his mother's home in Cairo on the assumption that Asran may have more of the world's goods than he needs. And when the word went round that he had married a girl who did not come from the family's old stamping ground, the reaction was such that he thought it wise to cover his tracks for a while. He does not dare to go back to Kana . . .

In January, 1970, when Asran and Kaoud made their first trip to Britain, they were both twenty-one and they advanced to the last eight of the British amateur championship. The next year Asran did it again. At the third attempt he got to the final but was beaten by Alauddin after leading by two games to one and 4-1 in the fourth. In 1971 he had a satisfying trip to New Zealand, winning the national amateur title and reaching the semi-finals of the world amateur championship. The following year he and Allam surged into the last eight of the British open championship. Asran achieved all this in just over two years. He was as fast as a cat, hit hard, and played a lot of shots, though he did not volley enough.

Then he was afflicted by inertia. Nowadays he is the only leading player who smokes a lot. Under pressure, he does not have a great deal to give after a game or so. But he still has the touch of a natural racket player and uses the lob effectively to reduce the pace and earn himself momentary breathers. When sufficiently irked, he entertains the public with a voluble burst of Arabic: usually succeeded by a flashing smile and a word of apology. Off court, he goes in for baggy, lurid caps. A delightful character. But not the competitor he might have been.

Safwat, squash professional and chess player, would look equally in character playing the romantic lead in a desert drama. He has the kind of eyes that melt a woman's heart. On court, though, his head is hunched in his shoulders and his legs have exaggerated curves suggesting that he has spent a lot of time on horseback. His squash obviously fulfils some necessary aesthetic function. At times he seems to be toying with pleasing patterns rather than playing a game. His strokes are imaginative, adventurous. His touch on drops and angles is delicate and he plays the reverse angle with such casual facility that he might be banging a stamp on an envelope. Once I saw him put a reverse angle in the nick and thought it was just luck. Then he did it again. When thoroughly match-fit he is one of the quickest players in the business. But as a professional he has always combined competition with club coaching, which is hardly calculated to keep a player of Safwat's class on his toes. He is the kind of sportsman every game needs, always, because even in the biggest tournaments he will concede a rally — I have seen him do it at match point — if he knows he has not made a clean return.

The son of a diplomat, Safwat came to England in 1962 and won two county junior tournaments. In 1971 he returned, with the Egyptian amateur team, and this time he stayed. His first professional job was in Essex, where he met his future wife, Ann. With her encouragement, and the help of visiting compatriots on the practice court, he made a big advance.

Safwat has a greater capacity for work than many Egyptian players, and he compromised intelligently between Egyptian flair and Anglo-Saxon discipline. He scampered into the last eight of the 1973 British open championship and subsequently became one of the most attractive and effective players on the circuit. Early in 1975 he had a win over Hunt during an eight-man grand prix circuit and, at the end of that year, he took a highly successful promotional initiative by organizing a four-man round robin series at Sheffield. Both on and off court he has become one of the most stimulating men in British squash. But he does not seem to last the course as well as he used to. Perhaps it is time he and Ann trained another dog to nip at his heels when he slows down during training runs.

At the other end of Africa, the game has older and stronger roots, is more popular, and has a sounder, more enterprising administrative structure. Traditionally, South African squash has been an amateur game played mainly in private clubs and universities by a prosperous middle-class community of British descent. But during the 1970s this pattern has been changing. An enterprising promoter called Owen Emslie created a congenial prize money circuit for the expanding group of itinerant professionals. In 1973 South Africa's leading player, Roland Watson, a drill instructor who had been in the police force for almost ten years, gave up his job and joined them. Three years later, Ian Holding and Alan Colburn followed his example. In 1974 South Africa had their first open championship.

But the changes have not been restricted to an increasing recognition of professionalism. The amateur game itself is beginning to attract more sponsorship and it is obviously desirable that some of this be diverted to expand playing and coaching facilities for non-British sections of society. Afrikaners are becoming more interested. Indians too. But squash is alien to the cultures of most Africans and the black races have so far shown little interest in the game. Bill Emmett, who represents the SRA of Southern Africa in the deliberations of the ISRF, believes that access to facilities may be the key. 'The advent of commercial centres will bring squash much closer to everybody who can't afford to belong to a club.' In this area the pioneers were two well-known players, the brothers David and Douglas Barrow, who opened a six-court public centre at a dormitory town near Johannesburg in 1975. This was soon thriving to such an extent that the Barrows began to build elsewhere. There are plans for twenty-eight commercial centres throughout South Africa. In short, the game is slowly spreading from private clubs and universities to a wider community.

With all this going on it is hardly surprising that the SRASA (which includes Rhodesia) and many of the seventeen affiliated provinces are considering means of raising funds so that they can appoint paid officers to deal with the growing volume of administrative work. It has been estimated that the game has more participants than any other sport in Southern Africa, and it is becoming too lively for honorary officers to handle in their spare time.

All this is heartening. But South Africa's extraordinary diversity of races, tribes and cultures, together with the effect of the apartheid laws, suggests that in the foreseeable future the game is unlikely to extend far beyond its present social boundaries, however much it may flourish within them. Internationally, progress is inhibited by the fact that the national associations of such renowned squash-playing countries as Pakistan and Egypt must accede to the wishes of governments who, at least for the time being, oppose sporting competition with South Africa. The South African Ministry of Sport and Recreations insists, incidentally, that the nation's sports bodies are autonomous, administering their sports without interference.

South African teams have competed in three world amateur championship series, finishing third twice and fourth once. In the 1976 individual championship, Holding got to the semi-finals (as he did in the British amateur event five months earlier) and David Scott took Kevin Shawcross to five games in the final. In recent years Derek Broom, Selwyn Machet and Colburn have all enjoyed a fleeting prominence in the British amateur championship. The best South African amateurs have mostly been just below the top class: good craftsmen, as opposed to the artists who kept coming out of Egypt. Sensible, fit and dogged, they have commanded respect without inspiring much excitement. Watson's assault on the professional élite has been a reasonably sound example of how far such virtues can take a man against players with more versatile and punishing games. He was twenty-seven when he took the plunge, and rather too hefty (13st 8lb but working for 12st) to be ideally built for the game. But because of his immense physical and mental effort and his willingness to suffer in the cause of improvement, he made such rapid progress as a match-player that by 1976 he was ranked ninth in the world. That may be the highest level he can reasonably expect to attain. But this cheerfully combative man has been a welcome recruit to the ranks and will doubtless keep his foot on the accelerator as long as there is petrol in the tank. After that, he will go back to his wife and children, his cacti, and his coaching.

Thirteen

Janet and Heather

The women's game has had a similar growth pattern to the men's. The most obvious comparative deficiency has been the lack of any Egyptian or Pakistani influence on its development because of the restricted role women play in those societies. This may change. In 1973 Rukhsana Rashid, a graduate in applied psychology at the Lahore College of Women, competed in the British women's championship. She had been Pakistan champion for more than a decade and her game had been sharpened by a good deal of match-play with men. But she was on court for her first round match the day after she flew in, was confused by the contrast in playing conditions and, not surprisingly, was beaten in straight games by a former British international, Di Corbett. Miss Rashid cut an elegantly exotic figure in her lightweight flannels (her religion did not permit bare legs and she had found her national dress too heavy for squash). She was clearly a talented player, but she was competing under too much of a handicap.

In the British championship a more familiar indication of eastern promise has been Soraya Haye, who was born at Tabriz in Iran. Her blood is Turkish-Iranian on her father's side and Russian-Armenian on her mother's. She speaks all those languages except Russian but converses with her Iranian-Pakistani husband in English because his other language is Urdu. It seems perverse of them to live in Manchester.

These girls are exceptions and neither has achieved international eminence. The women's game is almost exclusively Anglo-Saxon and until the 1960s the leading players were exclusively British. The women took longer than the men to develop squash specialists, as distinct from tennis players enjoying a form of competitive exercise indoors. So far there is no international team championship for women. Their game is ready for it but they are wary of trouble over South Africa, one of the four strongest nations — the others are Australia, New Zealand, and Britain. Nor does the women's game have a professional circuit either. Coaches, yes. But there are not enough first-class professionals to justify a competitive circuit and, in any case, it is doubtful if this would command sufficient support from the sponsors and the public.

The British women's championship (an amateur event until the Women's SRA introduced open competition during the 1973-4 season) was inaugurated in 1922, a year before the men's amateur championship. But it was to be ten years before an expanding fixture list justified a measure of administrative independence. In March, 1932, the SRA appointed 'a ladies' committee with powers to manage and control the championship and other tournaments and to decide all questions relating solely to ladies' squash rackets' (in those days all women were assumed to be ladies, and in squash the assumption was reasonable). One of the first things the liberated women did was to get out of the country. In January, 1933, a team of seven sailed for New York, where they beat the United States in a match for a cup jointly donated by Britain's captain and champion, respectively Elizabeth Wolfe and Susan Noel. The success of this initiative was swiftly followed by total devolution. In May, 1934, the SRA approved the formation of the WSRA, with the same terms of reference as the committee it replaced, and in November of that year the WSRA held their inaugural meeting.

The first chairman, Nancy Cave, was also one of the first outstanding players. She was one of three sisters who picked up the game while dashing about with their brothers on a large court they had at home — so large that they usually played doubles. That was an era in which women's squash was mostly a family recreation played in private courts scattered about the country, and the leading players tended to spring from games-playing stock and benefit from inbred talent. The first champion was the nineteen-year-old Joyce Cave, six years Nancy's junior, who was to attain a total of six finals, winning three. Nancy won three of the nine finals she played. Their dominance was interrupted by Sylvia

Huntsman, who won the second championship and reached the semi-finals of the next nine, and Cicely Fenwick, who beat Nancy in three of their four finals but lost one to Joyce Cave.

Miss Fenwick and her sister played on the private court their father had built in Gloucestershire. She had more strokes than most players and was wristy and clever in using them. The variety and severity of her squash was matched by that of her successor, Miss Noel, an international tennis player who lived near Queen's Club, where her father was secretary. Miss Noel, who competed in 1924 at the age of twelve, was the first woman to win three consecutive championships. On that 1933 tour she also became the first overseas player to win the US title. The next champion, Margot Lumb, born three weeks after Miss Noel, was another prominent tennis player (she competed in the 1937 and 1938 Wightman Cup matches). She had something else in common with Miss Noel: the kind of squash she played. This was the era of Abdel Fattah Amr, Don Butcher, and Jim Dear. It was also an era in which the women's championship was in the hands of players who could do more than whip up and maintain a hot pace — they could also play attractively constructive squash and were not afraid to use their wrists.

Miss Lumb established a record by winning five championships in a row (Miss Noel missed the first four of these). In that sequence Miss Lumb did not lose a game until the semi-finals of her fourth championship when the enterprising Betty Cooke broke the sequence. Miss Lumb also won the 1935 US title. She was as dominant in her sex as Amr was in his, and she was only twenty-six when she won the tournament for the last time before it was suspended during the war. The players to suffer most from her supremacy were Anne Lytton-Milbanke (now Lady Lytton), a retriever of great pertinacity, and the gracefully versatile Sheila McKechnie. In harness, these two became the first British winners of the United States doubles title, in 1935.

After the war, Joan Curry followed Miss Lumb's example by playing Wightman Cup tennis and also becoming women's squash champion. But her squash broke the pattern that Miss Fenwick, Miss Noel and Miss Lumb had established. Like Norman Borrett in the men's game, Miss Curry tended to be tediously effective. She had some good strokes, notably a backhand drop. But instead of risking them she preferred to rely on her outstanding qualities as a natural athlete. She was strong, fit and quick. She had plenty of stamina, and unflinching determination. For three years, her strategy was justified by results. Then Janet Morgan moved in. At her first attempt, Miss Morgan was stopped by Alice Teague in a quarter-final. Then she was twice runner-up to Miss Curry. ('The first time I lost 10-8 in the fifth and had a black eye as well.') But she beat Miss Curry in the next three finals and, gradually improving her squash technique, won ten consecutive championships, which was arithmetically tidy, before deciding that enough was enough. She also won the United States and Australian championships. Her name will be linked with Jonah Barrington's when generations yet unborn scrutinize the records in search of Britain's most successful squash players.

Miss Morgan, now Mrs Shardlow, taught physical education for twenty years. So she was interested in fitness and was qualified to achieve and sustain it. She also played county tennis for Surrey and competed at Wimbledon for fourteen years. ('Never with any prospect of doing anything — just thoroughly enjoying it.') Her introduction to squash occurred when she joined Surbiton LTC. 'It was the usual story: a wet day, and somebody said "Let's play squash". Many of the top players were converting from tennis — and played tennis on the squash court. You can go quite far with that, even today, when both games go on twelve months a year. In those days a lot played both reasonably well. I never played squash in the summer. I packed it up and played tennis.'

Looking back after almost twenty years, Mrs Shardlow reckons that there were two reasons why she won the championship so often — an advantage in fitness and the fact that she learned to play squash. 'I attached importance to fitness. I did train, which wasn't the custom. I went running. I don't know of anybody else who did, at that time. And though I started off as a pure tennis player on the squash court (just keeping the ball going for ever), I gradually learned to play squash, to acquire squash shots.'

She did indeed. The former gymnast had the agility and stamina to play a retrieving game. But it became clear that she also had a genuine flair for squash, that besides hitting hard and low she could play drops and angles and knew when to do so. In 1954 Sheila Speight, runner-up to Miss Morgan on five occasions, joined her on a missionary tour. They wandered about Australia and New Zealand playing exhibition matches and doing all they could to promote the women's game. They were not to know that ten years later Australia would beat Britain in an international match (or that before the next ten years were out New Zealand and South Africa would do the same). They were not to know either that at a small town called Queanbeyan, in cattle country near Canberra, there was a baker's daughter called Heather Blundell who would one day surpass even Miss Morgan's mighty record. 'At that time,' Mrs Shardlow recalls, 'even the men weren't very good.'

Heather Blundell was among eleven children in a tennis-playing family (her father also played rugby league football against a British touring team). She played tennis for seven years. 'My father always said I should have stuck to it. He still thinks so. But I don't think I would have reached the heights in tennis that I've reached in squash, though financially I would have been better off as an average tennis player. I didn't have the same enthusiasm for it. A different sort of enthusiasm.' But it was another game that was to lead her to squash. At seventeen she was one of a group of teenage girls who decided that they would take up squash to improve their fitness for hockey. Two years later, a month after her nineteenth birthday, she made the name Blundell of national rather than merely local importance. She won the Australian squash championship. After five months she became a receptionist at a squash centre in Sydney. When off duty, she made the most of the practice facilities at hand. At twenty she made her first trip to Britain and in January, 1962, Fran Marshall beat her in the fifth game during the Scottish championship. That was the last time any woman beat her, anywhere — though I write this fifteen years after Mrs Marshall's success.

Miss Blundell gave up her Sydney job in December, 1965, shortly before her marriage to Brian McKay, a professional coach. In 1969 they went to Canberra to manage a squash centre. 'It's seven miles from Queanbeyan — and my parents and all my brothers and sisters except one live in Queanbeyan or Canberra. But we said that if the chance came to try to break Janet's record, we would come across together: and we did. That meant giving up the job. We didn't do much for the rest of that year, except for a tour. Then we went to work in a nine-court squash centre in Brisbane owned by the late Charles Butcher, who did a lot for squash in Queensland. That's where we were until we moved to Canada

— Toronto Squash Club — in June, 1975.'

She became a professional in January, 1974. 'The biggest factor was that the British went open. After twelve years I didn't see why I should stay amateur. Turning "pro" limited me very much in what I could play. I couldn't play in any of the major tournaments in Australia. But to me the British open was more important. I could still play the No. 1 tournament in the world. As long as I won that, I thought I was still the No. 1 player. Turning "pro" made life a lot easier. Having Brian as a "pro" squash-playing husband. Travelling. Giving demonstration clinics. Racket endorsements. Not a terrific amount. But we could do it and hold down a job. We had much more freedom to do what we wanted to do for squash. I could put a little bit back into the game.'

While she was touring Britain after turning professional, The Valley WHC (Brisbane) asked her if she would be playing hockey — she was their left inner — she she got back. 'I said I would, so they registered me in the club team in the Brisbane women's hockey league, who didn't kick up any fuss. I got back and trained, and turned up for my first match. I heard a rumour that six of the other team, Taxation, refused to play because they felt it would infringe their amateur status if women's hockey ever attained Olympic status (the Olympic federation in Melbourne originally said it would). We were lined up, ready to go on. And they brought in six from their No. 2 team. Then the Olympic federation said it was OK to play. The decision was reversed. So I finished the season playing hockey.'

In sixteen consecutive British championships Mrs McKay lost only two games. One went in February, 1964, against Anna Craven Smith of Wolverhampton, as English a rose as ever graced a squash court. Miss Craven Smith played squash, tennis and golf for Staffordshire and once confessed that she was also a 'fromologist', which meant that she collected cheese labels. The most tenacious of Mrs McKay's other British rivals was Mrs Marshall, who spent the first twenty years of her life in Kenya. At the age of eighteen she was thrown from a rhinoceros (what on earth was she doing there, anyway?) and was introduced to squash as a means of working off the stiffness. The lighting and the floor were such that she had to watch the ball very closely. She still does. Mrs Marshall and Sheila Speight (Mrs Macintosh by that time) were the champions who intervened between Miss Morgan and Miss

Blundell. In sixteen finals Mrs McKay had four wins over Mrs Marshall, three over Miss Craven Smith, and one each over Bev Johnson, Jenny Irving, Marion Jackman, Sue Newman, Barbara Wall (all Australians), Marcia Roche, Kathy Malan (South Africans), Cecilie Fleming (a New Zealander) and Sue Cogswell (Britain), who also played with overwhelming brilliance to take a game from the champion in a 1977 semi-final. Miss Cogswell and Angela Smith should ensure continuing prominence for Britain at the highest level of international competition. Miss Roche and Miss Fleming were the first players from their respective countries to reach the final. Mrs McKay's most extraordinary win was that over Miss Johnson, who was on court for only fifteen minutes, did not score a point, and lost the last eighteen in one hand. This was the first all-Australian final. The match with Miss Wall was the first all-professional final.

When asked in 1976 to list the opponents she most respected, Mrs McKay named four. 'Anna [Craven Smith] always worried me when I played her. She was such a natural player and made me a bit envious, because she never trained — just played lovely squash and moved very well. Her biggest undoing was that she wasn't as fit as she could have been. Then Fran [Marshall]. When I started and she was playing particularly well, I always took her very seriously. She used all the court very well. Used her head. And there was Dot Linde, a Queenslander. I played her way back, in the final of the Australian, and for the next three or four years she played good squash. But she never got a chance to come outside Australia, so she didn't get known overseas. She was always one of the very fit girls, and played shots. She stroked the ball very nicely. Of today's girls, Marion [Jackman]. I make sure I'm fit and playing well when I come up against Marion. Because she has a good all-round game, can play all the shots, and moves beautifully.'

A pleasing sequel to the Shardlow-McKay story is the close friendship between them. I once asked Mrs Macintosh, who played both, what the result might have been had rivalry preceded amity. It was all guesswork, she said. She thought that Mrs Shardlow ('incredibly astute') might have outmanoeuvred Mrs McKay in their first match because of her initial advantage in reading the game, but that Mrs McKay might have won the second time ('she's one of the quickest learners I've known — she only needs telling once, or showing once'). They had similarities, she added, in their powers of concentration, their ability to turn quickly, and the fact that both went for kills at the front of the court.

The capacity for learning was to some extent inborn. But it was developed by Mrs McKay's remarkable concentration. Other natural talents were her athleticism and agility (she is 5ft 6in. tall and usually weighs about 9st 4lb), her flair for striking a moving ball, and the basis, at least, of her superb competitive temperament. She refined all this with a severe programme of fitness training and regular match practice with men. She accepted the need to watch the ball — all the time — and this fed a shrewd and active mind with the information that is the essence of anticipation.

She was, therefore, completely equipped with the fundamental virtues of squash. She knew where the ball was going and she was fast enough to get there with time to spare for a balanced, controlled return. Later she acquired more shots, more variety and the experience to exploit to the full everything she had learned. The outstanding qualities of her game were still its persistent power and precision. But like Miss Morgan before her she kept on improving *after* reaching the top. She did so because a bright flame of enthusiasm warmed all her endeavours — in training, practice, and competition. She told me once: 'I don't go on court and slave. I enjoy playing. I love the game — and this is why I keep at it.'

The first international match with Britain happened by chance. Four of the leading Australian players were in England on private tours and Miss Blundell had official backing to defend her championship. The only leading player missing was the No. 2, Dot Linde, who was working in New Zealand. So a fixture was arranged with Britain at the Lansdowne Club in February, 1964. Each team won two of the first four matches, all of which went to five games. Trish McClenaughan (later Mrs Faulkner), who had really come over to play the tennis circuit, survived a match point in the fourth game and won the fifth from 4-7 down against Miss Craven Smith. In the deciding match, Miss Blundell lost only one point to Mrs Marshall. So Australia won 3-2 and Britain's traditional supremacy had been shattered. Since then Britain have beaten Australia only once: on a cool, sweating court at Sheffield in 1967.

The 1971 Australian touring team stopped at Karachi on the way to Europe and played at Roshan Khan's club, the Fleet. 'They didn't have changing facilities for women,' Mrs McKay recalls, 'so they let us change in a little room. There was this young bloke standing guard outside, looking after the place while we were playing. When I came over to England a year or two later, there he was on court. It was Torsam.' The manager of that 1971 team was the joyously lively Jean Walker. Five years later I bumped into her in Paris (her daughter was playing in the French tennis championships) and we went up to Montparnasse to have a hit and a chuckle with Shah Jahan. She said that the world championship everybody had been talking about for years was going to happen at Brisbane in August and that, because Heather McKay was a professional, it was to be an open event. 'It would be a crime to restrict it and exclude the best player in the world.'

Mrs McKay won it, of course. And in the absence of a world team championship, that meant all her competitive ambitions had been fulfilled. If you asked me to count, on the fingers of one hand, the greatest sportsmen and sportswomen I have known, two of them would be Australian women. Margaret Court and Heather McKay.

Fourteen

A Professional Approach

The most startling development in modern squash was illustrated by the line-up for the last sixteen in the first world open championship, played at Wembley in 1976. All but one of those players was a professional — and the exception, Ian Holding, joined them before the year was out. There has never before been such a depth of professional talent in the competitive game, never a time when the leading players spent so much of the year touring the world and playing for prize money. And it has all happened since Jonah Barrington flung the door open and stood out in the cold, feeling rather lonely, in 1969. Ken Hiscoe and Geoff Hunt turned professional in 1971, Gogi Alauddin in 1972. By 1976 every other prominent player had joined them. It was almost true to say that an amateur needed a lucky draw if he was to have much chance of reaching the last thirty-two of a major tournament.

'I was always searching for a break-through,' says Barrington. 'Trying to persuade leading players that there was tremendous potential. Imagine my delight when the two leading Australians turned "pro" together. This was good news and bad news. The good news was that there was a lot of publicity, and it undoubtedly accelerated the turning towards professionalism of a lot of other players. The bad news was that they excluded me totally from their activities in this first phase of their new careers. This I found disappointing and disheartening. At the same time it probably added at least one British open to my belt. I was full of fury. When you win the first time it's like climbing Everest. You have to do it a second time to prove it wasn't a one-off job. The third time is not too difficult. After that, one has to create artificial motivations. One has to start disliking a person, thinking financially, et cetera. Geoff and Ken really created my incentive for about two years. I had very little communication with either of them. Now we commune together frequently. We have a lot in common, having waged war against each other for a decade or more. It's like battling your brother in the formative years. You have both respect and affection for him.

'Then we had three front runners and — lo and behold! — we suddenly collected a fourth when Gogi decided there was no way he would play for nothing. So we played a round robin in Australia, the Grandee circuit in Britain, the two-man team series . . .

'The next really significant development was the advance of Pakistan International Airlines into both the amateur game and the professional game, the employment of certain players within the PIA organization — and allowing those players to pursue their professional careers as squash players. Because of its close involvement with a number of sports, PIA constantly has teams travelling overseas and has built up a tremendous number of contacts. It can help find sponsors in new areas and create a new market for sponsorship.

'But the most significant thing could be the way squash and TV are developing. This is going to have an incredible effect in an enormous number of countries. I want to see the sport in every outpost. I want professionals to be on the same financial level and have the same status as top golfers, tennis players, soccer players. If squash was now to stagnate (having advantages it never had when I came into the game in 1964) those who lead the sport, including myself, should be arraigned for some kind of treason. It has always given me a great deal of satisfaction to say I am a professional sportsman. There's a lot of hardship attached to it. But it's a damned sight better than the way a lot of people are forced to occupy their lives. One of the fortunate aspects of my life — apart from the fact that I rather luckily came into squash and it suited me and I've had a lot of success — is that the sport itself has never stopped growing from the time I came in. It's incredibly satisfying, being involved in — and committed to — something that thrives by the day. As far as I'm concerned it has been summer since 1966. We don't go into an autumn.'

'Jonah started the ball rolling,' admits Hiscoe. 'But a hell of a lot of the development was due to Geoff and me. If we hadn't turned "pro" the game wouldn't be in the position it is today. We've played in the most unbelievable places, promoting and exposing the game. Squash has really got off the ground. We've gone from nothing to £10,000 in the British open, $8,000 in the Australian, $13,000 in the North American — in three years. Kramer and Gonzales were both "pros" by 1950, but how long did it take tennis? And Arnold Palmer played his first "pro" golf tournament at Winnipeg for $150. In the next couple of years the game's going to grow a little bit quicker than a lot of people think. We have a problem because of spectator viewing. But there's going to be a few things happen. Tournaments are going to clash. The "pros" can be split out. There's nothing wrong with that. Some in Amsterdam, some in London. That will happen.'

For Heather McKay it is a different story. 'Whereas the top men play the circuit and make a living, I have to coach full-time. If six of the top women got themselves into a group, I think they would find sponsors. But we would have to get ourselves organized and be prepared to work very hard to get it off the ground. We could do it. Women's squash is very entertaining.' Her main income, and Brian's, comes from 'a small retainer at the club and all the money from the coaching — so the harder we work, the more money we make.' Their earnings from exhibitions and endorsements are modest. At the moment she believes that there is not enough incentive for women to become professionals. 'Normally if you turn "pro" you do it with the idea of making money out of it — but there's no way, even for myself . . .'

The men have more scope. 'But unless you're in the top few players,' says Hunt, 'endorsements are not going to be the highest part of your income. And it depends on what nationality you are. For a British player who's good, a much higher proportion would come from endorsements. And it's the same with me. Once you go out of the top six, you get small sums to play with equipment, et cetera. Someone just going in would have to rely on tournament money, coaching.' As potential income sources he lists prize money, endorsements (including advertisements), exhibitions, private coaching, clinics, agency work for manufacturers, or the managing, owning, or leasing of squash courts. Hiscoe refers to fees for television work and when Barrington mentions books they have, between them, covered just about everything a man might do to earn a living from squash.

Prize money will increase, of course. In 1976 Barrington told me: 'The ISPA is looking for a level of £7,500 for twenty-four players, with eight locals joining in. This provides a return of £100 for a first round loser, which is a great deal sounder than the proposition that has been facing us for the last three or four years. When we think of that kind of money we are not in cloud-cuckoo-land. It's going to happen.'

Would they recommend squash as a career?

'There's a good opportunity for any young bloke at the moment,' says Hiscoe. 'Let's take Europeans. Who's coming up? There's nobody.' But Barrington, in spite of his enthusiasm for the game, cannot recommend squash as a career for a middle-class Englishman. 'It would not be responsible for me to do so. There are too few people making money out of the game. And the talent in England is unlikely to find itself in the top twenty-five players in the next few years.'

'If a youngster had the opportunity to attain a high standard educationally, a degree or something, he'd be silly to give it away,' asserts Hunt. 'The rewards from squash are not high enough. But in three years I might tell him the opposite. I would tell him to train and practise and get experience — but not to neglect the other side. I'm talking about Europeans, Australians . . . It would be a different thing for some of these Pakistani lads. The opportunities are probably better in squash. Look at the players in top squash. The sort of money some of the Pakistani players are earning is a lot — on their standards at home — and can buy plenty. But the same amount falls far short in Australia or England.'

Hidayat Jahan enjoys being a professional sportsman, an entertainer. He sometimes finds it more fun to play as a professional than it was as an amateur. 'You're playing for something and pushing for it. When you're playing with someone you know you can beat, you can play to the gallery. Wear coloured clothes. Joke with opponents. As an amateur you don't have the experience to do those things.' But he does not deny the price he sometimes has to pay, the effect of continual competition. 'It's mostly physical. What is happening is that we're not getting enough of a break. Playing Geoff, Zaman, Mohibullah on successive days really takes a lot out of you. By the end you feel physical pain, and tired of the game, and want to go away.'

'When I first started to play for a living,' says Hunt, 'I went to

South Africa to play Ken in a fifteen-match series. At the end, I'd had it. But now I could do it. I enjoy competition, particularly if it's tournament squash. I thrive on it. Continual competition keeps you in shape. Your body can stand a hell of a lot. But it's possible to pick up injuries, which continual play doesn't necessarily help.' Over to Hiscoe: 'The older you get, the more you travel, the better players you play, you do have a few more lows. The younger guys don't. They can handle it better.'

'Squash at the very highest level is probably one of the most perverse exercises ever devised,' suggests Barrington. 'It's a consuming torture. Very draining, mentally and physically. Whoever a man may be, at the end he will be found out — unless he withdraws for two weeks or so to recharge his batteries. It shows in his psychology. There are a lot of signs. Irritability. Loss of control on the court. You become agitated over trivial things. You have no appetite for playing. Your quality of performance goes down. Liveliness of personality is eroded.'

All condemn smoking but agree that, in moderation, beer can be relaxing and healthy, settling the nerves and replacing lost liquid. Barrington reminds us that 'some of the best racehorses in the world have done well on a drop of Guinness now and then.' And listen to Hiscoe: 'Beer's a food. There's a lot of goodness in beer. Malt and yeast and all that stuff. I've always said to Jonah that if he had one or two beers at night he'd sleep a lot better. If you're pretty fit, you'll run it out the following day. A few beers are good for you, providing you don't have eight every night. If you have a good thrash once a month, there's nothing wrong with that. But you don't go and iron yourself out two or three times a week.'

The playing conditions in which the professionals do their stuff are ludicruously varied. By common consent Salisbury, Rhodesia, has the best spectator arena in the world. 'For viewing, as well as numbers — it's beautifully designed,' says Hunt. But Karachi has the finest tournament complex. 'There's nowhere else,' Barrington points out, 'where there are five courts with glass back walls, two with excellent galleries, and good areas for TV. And it has a nice open design, a feeling of belonging — which you never have at Wembley.' In Britain, according to Hunt, 'the best by far is Abbeydale Park, Sheffield' and Hiscoe says: 'The court and the club are a hell of a lot better than Wembley'. Another popular arena is that at Albert Park, Melbourne, though this has no glass back wall. 'It was an innovation,' says Hunt. 'It's cut away at the red line, except for the front wall — so you don't practise there by yourself, without someone in the gallery . . .'

Peshawar has one mighty arena, and I have heard players speak well of the Wanderers Club and Witwatersrand University, both in Johannesburg. Sherif Afifi reckons the best spectator courts in Egypt are those at Alexandria Sporting Club and, in Cairo, at the Heliopolis and Heliolido clubs and Cairo University. 'They are planning an extension at Gezira, to incorporate the best spectator court in Egypt.'

So much for the good news. There are courts that stick in the mind for other reasons. Hunt recalls playing an exhibition with Hiscoe on a South African court that had lateral floorboards — which had warped. 'The ball either kicked up or kept low and in the hit-up we both had some air swings, which we rarely ever do.' They also played an exhibition at Shabani, an asbestos-mining town in Matabeleland. 'When we walked up to the gallery to watch the first match,' says Hiscoe, 'everybody was sneezing and coughing and had red eyes. We thought they had flu. It was the same with the players when they came off court. Then we started sneezing too. There were insects coming up through the floor. They'd put repellent down.' ('That,' adds Hunt, 'was bloody awful.') Heather McKay remembers another African court. 'They'd painted the front wall for an exhibition and it hadn't dried. So they put talcum powder on it. The stuff flew all over the court. It was like a skating-rink. Deadly. But the wall dried out somewhere along the line.'

Not that Africa has a monopoly of such bizarre episodes. Hunt will never forget an exhibition he played with Hiscoe in an English farmhouse. 'Right next to the courts is an old barn. It was winter and the barn was full of cows. The smell was terrible. Imagine — when you're doing a bit of running and begin to breathe heavily . . .'

Barrington once played Aftab Jawaid in Dacca. 'Prior to our visit the courts were the home of the professional. Accommodation for the family in one court and the fowls in the other. I'm not sure whether the family moved, or the fowls, or both. The floor had holes in it and one bit of concrete higher than another. The great object was to volley everything. Not to let the ball fall — because if it hit the surface it didn't follow the course it was travelling. And when the ball hit the front wall we had no idea where it was going. After a few interesting rallies I went to the front wall and looked along it. Extraordinary. It was like the face of the moon.'

Barrington vividly recollects a match he refereed in Lahore. Rainer ('Rattles') Ratinac, who graduated to squash via the Sydney fire brigade, had persistent diarrhoea and had not won a match for weeks. But against Sajjad Muneer he seemed to be on the point of doing so when — from a mosque next door — the piercing wail of a muezzin suddenly ululated through the balmy evening air. Ratinac was dumbfounded, incredulous. What the **** was going on? he asked. It was prayer-time, Barrington told him. Everything had to stop. But Ratinac did not want to stop. His language was unprintable. He lost the match and was last heard of heading for the Mormon sanctuary of Salt Lake City.

Let that serve as a cue for an American aside. Our story began with amateurs and we will end it in the same company. For many of us Stewart Brauns of Manhattan is the strongest and most tenacious link between the hardball and softball games. He talks as fast as he thinks, which is going some. Out of habit, I will allow him to have the last word. Brauns recollects a tri-city team match for the Lockett Cup, played at Boston. A muscle-bound New York lawyer, Joseph Barbash, was playing a gentlemen called Red Herpst. Barbash was in trouble and tried a back-wall boast. But the back wall had a small hole in it — and the ball disappeared (it went through the wall and across a corridor into a snow-covered parking lot). Whereupon Herpst, stupefied, sat on the floor and gazed at the gallery with the eyes of a man stricken by the ultimate frustration of all squash players. No ball.

'This guy,' he gasped, 'is doing *everything*.'

A Chronicle of Squash

1815-20 A primitive form of rackets played in the walled yards of a few London taverns and prisons (especially the Fleet), was introduced at Harrow School, north-west of London.

1820-40 Squash, using a softer ball, developed as a variant of rackets at Harrow. Both were still 'yard' games. Similar games were probably being played at other schools, including Elstree, Rugby and Winchester.

1850 The construction of two roofless rackets courts at Harrow confirmed the growing distinction between this game and squash.

1853 The old Prince's Club, London, originated the concept of covered courts, though this first example was for rackets.

1864 Four squash courts were built at Harrow: the first recorded case of courts created specifically for squash. Thus squash assumed a separate identity from rackets. It can be said that this was the year in which squash was 'born'.

1883 Vernon Harcourt, an old Harrovian, had a squash court constructed as part of his house on the banks of the Cherwell at Oxford. This was the first private court, and other than those at Harrow, the first built especially for squash.

1891 Philadelphia Racquet Club added a squash court to their premises and instituted a championship. Though there had been earlier experiments with the game, this marked the birth of squash in North America.

1907 The United States Squash Racquets Association was formed and held an inaugural championship. This was the first national association and the first national championship. In Britain the Tennis and Rackets Association was formed and appointed a sub-committee to administer squash and draw up rules.

1908 The USSRA held the first national team championship.

1910 South Africa formed the first national association to conform to the rules of the game as played in Britain (which had no association of its own) and inaugurated a national championship. Theirs was the first association and the first championship other than those in the United States.

1911 Canada formed a national association and inaugurated a national championship.

1912 Charles Arnold, of the Bath Club, London, became the first British professional concerned solely with squash.

1918 It was probably in this year that the first Australian court was constructed, at Sydney.

1920 Charles Read beat 'Oke' Johnson in the first two-match challenge for the professional championship of the British Isles, which thus preceded the inauguration of amateur and open championships.

1922 The first British women's championships were held: two in the same year. The Bath Club cup competition was instituted, stimulating competition in general and between London's West End social clubs in particular. Henry G. Lapham, of Boston, presented a trophy for annual competition between Canada and the United States — the oldest international fixture.

1923 The British men's amateur championship was inaugurated. The Tennis and Rackets Association, which had been studying the question of squash court dimensions since 1911, standardized courts, balls and rackets. As the USSRA already had standards of their own, this was the year in which the international softball game clearly diverged from the North American hardball game. The first British touring team went to North America for the 1923-4 season, and, at Philadelphia, finished second to the United States in the Lapham match, with Canada third.

1924 The Tennis and Rackets Association standardized the rules of squash.

1925 The nature of the game's expansion was indicated by the first public schools match (Haileybury *v.* St Peter's, York), the first Cambridge *v.* Oxford universities match, and the inauguration of Army and Royal Navy championships.

1926 Britain discarded the 15-point scoring system in favour of a 9-point system.

1927 Britain again accepted an invitation to compete in the Lapham match, which they won, with the United States second and Canada third.

1928 The Squash Rackets Association was established, taking over the management of the British game from the Tennis and Rackets Association. Until 1967 the SRA was also, *de facto*, the governing body of the international game.

1930 Charles Read was designated British open champion but was beaten by Don Butcher in the first challenge series.

1931 The Australian amateur championship was inaugurated.

1932 The New Zealand amateur championship was inaugurated. The SRA appointed 'a "ladies" committee' to manage the British women's game.

1932-3 Amr became the first player to win the British open and amateur championships in the same season.

1933 A British women's touring team went to the United States and won the first Wolfe-Noel Cup match.

1934 The Women's SRA was established and, like the SRA, was to serve as an unofficial governing body for the international game.

1935 An Australian association was formed.

1936 The committee of the Bath Club Cup competition decided that matches should be contested over the best of three games instead of the best of five (later the SRA made this optional). Anne Lytton-Milbanke and Sheila McKechnie won a women's doubles tournament — the first doubles event played in Britain — on an improvised court at Prince's Club, Knightsbridge.

1937 The SRA adopted the standard USSRA dimensions for double courts.

1939 The Australian open championship was inaugurated.

1947 The SRA discarded the challenge system in favour of a knock-out tournament to decide the British open championship.

1948 The SRA appointed a full-time secretary, and revised rule seventeen to incorporate what has become known as a 'penalty point'.

1954 The Women's SRA sent Janet Morgan and Sheila Speight, their leading players, on a tour requested by Australia and New Zealand to help develop the women's game. At this time there was a rapid increase in the construction of public courts in Australia. More than 20 per cent of the English clubs experimented with the American scoring system but opposed change by a majority of seven to one.

1955 For the time time for twenty-eight years an SRA team went overseas, touring South Africa, Rhodesia and Kenya.

1959 An SRA team toured Australia and New Zealand, winning every international match and both national championships.

1962-4 Australia won every international match during two tours of Britain.

1964 Australia beat Britain in their first women's international match, in London.

1966 The North American open championship was inaugurated, replacing separate national open tournaments for countries playing the hardball game.

1966-7 Jonah Barrington became the first player since Amr to win the British open and amateur championships in the same season.

1967 The International Squash Rackets Federation was established, taking over from Britain the task of making and maintaining the rules. The first ISRF amateur championship series was played in Australia.

1969 The Women's SRA appointed a full-time secretary.

1970 An Australian-type ball was introduced in Britain.

1973 The Women's SRA approved open competition between professionals and amateurs in Britain. The International Squash Players' Association was formed. An inaugural European amateur team championship was played in Edinburgh and the European SRF was established.

1975 Pakistan beat Britain at Wembley in the first open international match. Banbury Squash Courts Ltd. sold approximately ten times as many courts as they had done in 1970.

1976 The first official world open championships were held. Both were won by Australians — Geoff Hunt at Wembley and Heather McKay at Brisbane. The first open team tournament was played in Karachi.

Appendix 1: *Men's Results*

WORLD OPEN CHAMPIONSHIP
1976 (February)
Wembley, London

Quarter-finals
Q. Zaman beat J.P. Barrington
9-0, 9-1, 9-6.
Mohibullah Khan Jun. beat H. Jahan
6-9, 9-1, 4-9, 9-7, 9-1.
G. Alauddin beat K.J. Hiscoe
5-9, 9-0, 9-2, 9-1.
G.B. Hunt beat C.J. Nancarrow
9-5, 9-6, 9-4.

Semi-finals
Mohibullah beat Zaman
6-9, 9-5, 3-9, 9-2, 9-7.
Hunt beat Alauddin
9-2, 9-5, 1-9, 9-5.

Final
Hunt beat Mohibullah
7-9, 9-4, 8-10, 9-2, 9-2.

Note: This event was incorporated in the 1976 British open championship.

1977 (October)
Adelaide

Quarter-finals
G.B. Hunt beat B. Brownlee
9-2, 9-7, 9-3.
G Alauddin beat H. Jahan
7-9, 9-3, 5-9, 10-9, 10-8.
Q. Zaman beat J.P. Barrington
9-1, 9-5, 9-5.
Mohibullah Khan beat R. Watson
9-4, 9-6, 9-5.

Semi-finals
Hunt beat Alauddin
9-6, 5-9, 9-2, 9-6.
Zaman beat Mohibullah
5-9, 9-4, 9-6, 8-10, 9-1.

Final
Hunt beat Zaman
9-5, 10-9, 0-9, 1-9, 9-4.

BRITISH OPEN CHAMPIONSHIP

1930 (December)
D.G. Butcher beat C.R. Read
9-6, 9-5, 9-5 (Queen's Club) and 9-3, 9-5, 9-3 (Conservative Club).

1931 (November)
D.G. Butcher beat C. Arnold
9-0, 9-0, 9-0 (Conservative Club) and 9-3, 9-0, 9-5 (Bath Club).

1932 (October)
A.F. Amr beat D.G. Butcher
9-0, 9-7, 9-1 (Conservative Club) and 5-9, 5-9, 9-2, 9-1, 9-0 (Bath Club).

1933
A.F. Amr was not challenged.

1934 (November)
A.F. Amr beat D.G. Butcher
9-4, 8-10, 10-8, 9-0 (Conservative Club) and 9-6, 6-9, 9-2, 0-9, 9-5 (Bath Club).

1935 (November-December)
A.F. Amr beat J.P. Dear
9-3, 6-9, 8-10, 9-2, 9-4 (Bath Club, November) and 9-4, 9-7, 3-9, 9-7 (RAC, December).

1936 (November)
A.F. Amr beat J.P. Dear
9-7, 7-9, 9-7, 5-9, 9-6 (RAC) and 9-6, 8-10, 9-1, 9-6 (Bath Club).

1937 (November)
A.F. Amr beat J.P. Dear
10-8, 10-8, 4-9, 1-9, 9-4 (RAC) and 9-7, 8-10, 9-6, 9-5 (Bath Club).

1938 (December)
J.P. Dear beat A.E. Biddle
5-9, 9-6, 5-9, 9-6, 9-5 (Junior Carlton Club) and 6-9, 9-1, 9-2, 9-6 (RAC).

1947 (December)
M. el Karim beat J.P. Dear
9-4, 9-1, 9-3 (Lansdowne and Royal Aero Clubs) and 5-9, 7-9, 9-8, 9-7, 9-4 (RAC).

Note: These matches had been postponed the previous season. This was the last championship contested on a two-man challenge basis.

1948 (March)
Lansdowne and Royal Aero Clubs, London

Quarter-finals
M. el Karim beat J.F. Stokes
5-9, 9-0, 9-1, 10-8.
B.C. Phillips beat L.R. Hamer
6-9, 9-1, 9-4, 10-8.
A.E. Biddle beat L.W.R. Keeble
10-8, 9-7, 9-2.
J.P. Dear beat P.J. Phillips
9-7, 3-9, 9-3, 9-1.

Semi-finals
Karim beat Phillips
9-1, 2-9, 10-8, 9-3.
Dear beat Biddle
9-4, 9-4, 9-2.

Final
Karim beat Dear
9-5, 9-3, 5-9, 1-9, 10-8.

1949 (April)
Lansdowne and Royal Aero Clubs, London

Quarter-finals
M. el Karim beat E.S. Hawes
9-0, 9-0, 9-2.
N.F. Borrett beat N.E. Hopper
9-1, 9-3, 9-2.
B.C. Phillips beat R.M. Boustead
6-9, 9-4, 10-8, 8-10, 9-4.
L.W.R. Keeble beat W.E. Clements
9-7, 9-3, 9-0.

Semi-finals
Karim beat Borrett
9-2, 9-4, 9-0.
Phillips beat Keeble
9-0, 4-9, 9-3, 9-7.

Final
Karim beat Phillips
9-4, 9-2, 9-10, 9-4.

1950 (April)
Lansdowne and Royal Aero Clubs, London

Quarter-finals
M. el Karim beat A.A.T. Seymour-Haydon
8-10, 9-5, 9-2, 9-6.
J.P.Dear beat B.C. Phillips
9-0, 9-0, 9-3.
G.J. Watson beat W.E.J. Gordon
9-1, 9-7, 7-9, 10-9.
A. Bari beat W.D. McLaggan
9-2, 9-1, 9-1.

Semi-finals
Karim beat Dear
9-0, 9-6, 10-8.
Bari beat Watson
9-2, 9-2, 10-8.

Final
Karim beat Bari
9-4, 9-2, 9-7.

1951 (April)
Lansdowne and Royal Aero Clubs, London

Quarter-finals
M. el Karim beat L.W.R. Keeble
9-4, 9-0, 9-1.
R.B.R. Wilson beat A. Bari
9-6, 7-9, 4-9, 9-1, 9-4.
G. Hildick-Smith beat R.M. Boustead
9-4, 9-5, 9-2.
Hashim Khan beat W.E.J. Gordon
9-3, 9-3, 9-0.

Semi-finals
Karim beat Wilson
9-2, 8-10, 10-9, 9-5.
Hashim beat Hildick-Smith
9-6, 9-2, 9-4

Final
Hashim beat Karim
9-5, 9-0, 9-0.

1952 (April)
Lansdowne and Royal Aero Clubs, London

Quarter-finals
Hashim Khan beat A. Fairbairn
9-4, 9-0, 9-0.
G. Hildick-Smith walkover, N.E. Hooper scratched.
B.C. Phillips beat Sir Charles McLeod
6-9, 9-1, 9-2, 9-5.
M. el Karim beat R.B.R. Wilson
9-3, 9-1, 9-6.

Semi-finals
Hashim beat Hildick-Smith
9-2, 9-0, 9-2.
Karim beat Phillips
9-2, 9-4, 9-3.

Final
Hashim beat Karim
9-5, 9-7, 9-0.

1953 (March)
Lansdowne and Royal Aero Clubs, London

Quarter-finals
Hashim Khan beat J.H. Giles
9-4, 9-5, 9-3.
Azam Khan walkover, A.A.T. Seymour-Haydon scratched.
R.B.R. Wilson beat A. Bari
2-9, 9-1, 9-2, 2-9, 9-2.
Safirullah walkover, M. el Karim scratched.

Semi-finals
Hashim beat Azam
9-6, 4-9, 9-7, 8-10, 9-4.
R.B.R. Wilson beat Safirullah
1-9, 9-7, 9-3, 9-4.

Final
Hashim beat Wilson
9-2, 8-10, 9-1, 9-0.

1954 (March)
Lansdowne and Royal Aero Clubs, London

Quarter-finals
Hashim Khan beat J.H.Giles
9-1, 9-2, 9-4.
A. Bari beat A. Fairbairn
6-9, 9-3, 9-2, 9-10, 9-7.
Azam Khan beat I.C. de Sales la Terrière
9-1, 7-9, 9-2, 9-2.
Roshan Khan beat Sir Charles McLeod
9-3, 9-3, 9-6

Semi-finals
Hashim walkover, Bari scratched.
Azam beat Roshan
9-2, 6-9, 10-8, 9-3.

Final
Hashim beat Azam
6-9, 9-6, 9-6, 7-9, 9-5.

1955 (March)
Lansdowne and Royal Aero Clubs, London

Quarter-finals
Hashim Khan beat J.H. Giles
9-4, 9-5, 9-4.
Roshan Khan beat A.A.T. Seymour-Haydon
9-1, 9-0, 9-4.
R.B.R. Wilson beat A.P. Doggart
9-7, 9-5, 9-2
Azam Khan beat D.B. Hughes
9-4, 9-0, 9-3.

Semi-finals
Hashim beat Roshan
9-2, 7-9, 2-9, 9-2, 9-5.
Azam beat Wilson
9-0, 9-1, 9-3.

Final
Hashim beat Azam
9-7, 7-9, 9-7, 5-9, 9-7.

1956 (March)
Lansdowne and Royal Aero Clubs, London

Quarter-finals
Hashim Khan beat Jamal Din
9-4, 10-9, 7-9, 9-5.
Azam Khan beat S.J.S. Lam
9-0, 9-1, 9-0.
R.B. Hawkey beat J.H. Giles
9-1, 2-9, 8-10, 9-7, 9-0.
Roshan Khan beat M. Dardir
9-2, 9-6, 9-2.

Semi-finals
Hashim beat Azam
10-9, 10-9, 4-9, 9-3.
Roshan beat Hawkey
9-1, 9-2, 9-0.

Final
Hashim beat Roshan
9-4, 9-2, 5-9, 9-5.

1957 (March)
Lansdowne and Royal Aero Clubs, London

Quarter-finals
Hashim Khan beat J.H. Giles
9-5, 9-2, 10-8.
Azam Khan beat R.B. Hawkey
9-0, 9-3, 9-2.
Mohibullah Khan beat D.B. Hughes
9-5, 9-0, 9-2.
Roshan Khan beat M.J. Perkins
1-9, 9-4, 9-1, 9-4.

Semi-finals
Hashim beat Azam
9-4, 4-9, 9-6, 9-5.
Roshan beat Mohibullah
10-8, 9-0, 9-5.

Final
Roshan beat Hashim
6-9, 9-5, 9-2, 9-1.

1958 (March)
Lansdowne and Royal Aero Clubs, London

Quarter-finals
Hashim Khan beat Nasrullah Khan
9-3, 9-2, 9-0.
Mohibullah Khan beat J.H. Giles
9-4, 9-3, 6-9, 9-3.
D.B. Hughes beat Yusuf Khan
10-8, 3-9, 3-9, 9-6, 9-4.
Azam Khan beat R.B. Hawkey
9-0, 9-3, 9-3.

Semi-finals
Hashim beat Mohibullah
6-9, 9-7, 9-3, 9-3.
Azam beat Hughes
9-2, 9-0, 9-0.

Final
Hashim beat Azam
9-7, 6-9, 9-6, 9-7.

1959 (March)
Royal Automobile Club, London

Quarter-finals
Nasrullah Khan beat Jamal Din
9-7, 9-4, 9-2.
Mohibullah Khan beat D.B. Hughes
9-2, 9-6, 9-3.
Ali Akbar Khan beat R.B. Hawkey
9-5, 9-3, 9-1.
Azam Khan beat W.J. Ashford
9-3, 9-6, 9-2.

Semi-finals
Mohibullah beat Nasrullah
9-1, 9-0, 9-5.
Azam beat Akbar
9-1, 9-1, 9-1.

Final
Azam beat Mohibullah
9-5, 9-0, 9-1.

1959 (December)
Royal Automobile Club, London

Quarter-finals
Azam Khan beat M. Dardir
9-2, 9-5, 9-2.
Hashim Khan beat Nasrullah Khan
9-6, 9-5, 9-6.
M.A. Oddy beat Mohibullah Khan
9-3, 6-9, 9-3, 9-0.
Roshan Khan beat Jamal Din
9-7, 9-4, 2-9, 9-7.

Semi-finals
Azam beat Hashim
9-6, 5-9, 9-6, 9-6.
Roshan beat Oddy
6-9, 9-6, 9-3, 9-3.

Final
Azam beat Roshan
9-1, 9-0, 9-0.

1960 (November-December)
Royal Automobile Club, London

Quarter-finals
Azam Khan beat Jamal Din
9-1, 9-4, 9-4
D. Hughes beat I. Amin
4-9, 9-5, 9-6, 2-9, 9-4.

Mohibullah Khan beat M.A. Oddy
9-4, 9-5, 9-7.
Roshan Khan beat M. Dardir
9-2, 0-9, 9-6, 4-9, 9-2.

Semi-finals
Azam beat Hughes
9-0, 9-3, 9-2.
Mohibullah beat Roshan
9-7, 9-0, 9-0.

Final
Azam beat Mohibullah
6-9, 9-1, 9-4, 0-9, 9-2.

1961 (November-December)
Royal Automobile Club, London

Quarter-finals
Azam Khan beat M.A. Oddy
9-3, 9-5, 9-4.
Roshan Khan beat K. Zaghloul
9-1, 9-0, 9-2.
M. Dardir beat I. Amin
9-5, 9-1, 3-9, 10-8.
Mohibullah Khan beat A.F. Taleb
9-1, 9-2, 9-3.

Semi-finals
Azam beat Roshan
9-5, 9-3, 4-9, 1-9, 9-0.
Mohibullah beat Dardir
9-6, 9-6, 9-4.

Final
Azam beat Mohibullah
9-6, 7-9, 10-8, 2-9, 9-4.

1962 (November-December)
Lansdowne and Royal Aero Clubs, London

Quarter-finals
Mohibullah Khan beat A.W.A. Aziz
9-0, 9-0, 9-5.
A.A. Jawaid beat K. Zaghloul
9-1, 6-9, 9-1, 6-9, 9-2.
A.F. Taleb beat T. Shafik
9-4, 9-0, 2-9, 9-3.
Roshan Khan beat G.R. Chisholm
9-4, 9-5, 9-3.

Semi-finals
Mohibullah beat Jawaid
10-8, 9-3, 9-3.
Taleb beat Roshan
2-9, 9-7, 9-0, 9-6.

Final
Mohibullah beat Taleb
9-4, 5-9, 3-9, 10-8, 9-6.

1963 (November-December)
Lansdowne and Royal Aero Clubs, London

Quarter-finals
Mohibullah Khan beat T. Shafik
9-1, 4-9, 9-5, 9-5.
M.A. Oddy beat K. Zaghloul
9-5, 9-5, 9-3.
A.A. Jawaid beat M. Yasin
10-9, 9-6, 7-9, 10-8.
A.F. Taleb beat I. Amin
9-3, 9-2, 9-0.

Semi-finals
Oddy beat Mohibullah
9-1, 9-6, 9-2.
Taleb beat Jawaid
9-3, 9-7, 9-1.

Final
Taleb beat Oddy
9-3, 9-7, 9-0.

1964 (December)
Lansdowne and Royal Aero Clubs, London

Quarter-finals
A.F. Taleb beat D.R. Woods
9-2, 9-1, 9-3.
T. Shafik beat K. Zaghloul
9-2, 9-4, 9-0.
I. Amin beat A.W.A. Aziz
9-6, 2-9, 9-6, 9-7.
A.A. Jawaid beat J.G.A. Lyon
9-0, 9-6, 9-4.

Semi-finals
Taleb beat Shafik
9-2, 9-3, 9-3.
Amin beat Jawaid
1-9, 9-4, 6-9, 9-6, 9-6.

Final
Taleb beat Amin
9-0, 0-9, 9-1, 9-6.

1965 (December)
Lansdowne and Royal Aero Clubs, London

Quarter-finals
A.F. Taleb beat J.N.H. Smith
9-7, 9-6, 9-7.
T. Shafik beat J.P. Barrington
9-6, 9-6, 9-6.
K. Zaghloul beat A.W.A. Aziz
9-2, 9-4, 9-3.
A.A. Jawaid beat J.G.A. Lyon
6-9, 9-0, 9-1, 9-6.

Semi-finals
Taleb beat Shafik
6-9, 9-7, 7-9, 9-2, 9-3.
Jawaid beat Zaghloul
9-7, 9-4, 9-6.

Final
Taleb beat Jawaid
9-6, 5-9, 9-3, 9-1.

1966 (December)
Lansdowne and Royal Aero Clubs, London

Quarter-finals
J.P. Barrington beat A.F. Taleb
9-4, 9-1, 8-10, 9-5.
I. Amin beat P.D. Stokes
9-6, 7-9, 9-5, 9-4.
M. Yasin beat K. Zaghloul
9-2, 9-1, 9-2.
A.A. Jawaid beat A. Nadi
9-10, 9-4, 9-6, 9-2.

Semi-finals
Barrington beat Amin
9-4, 4-9, 9-5, 9-3.
Jawaid beat Yasin
4-9, 9-6, 9-2, 2-9, 10-8.

Final
Barrington beat Jawaid
9-2, 6-9, 9-2, 9-2.

1967 (December)
Lansdowne and Royal Aero Clubs, London

Quarter-finals
J.P. Barrington beat D.R. Brazier
9-2, 9-7, 9-5.
K. Zaghloul beat R.M.H. Boddington
9-7, 2-9, 9-5, 4-9, 9-3.
J.G.A. Lyon beat A. Nadi
9-0, 10-8, 9-7.
A.F. Taleb beat D.B. Hughes
8-10, 9-2, 9-5, 5-9, 9-3.

Semi-finals
Barrington beat Zaghloul
9-2, 9-2, 9-0.
Taleb beat Lyon
5-9, 9-4, 7-9, 9-4, 9-2.

Final
Barrington beat Taleb
9-6, 9-0, 9-3.

1969 (January)
Sheffield, S. Yorkshire

Quarter-finals
J.P. Barrington beat A.M.H. Hill
9-3, 9-4, 9-2.
C.J. Nancarrow beat K.J. Hiscoe
9-4, 9-1, 2-9, 9-7.
A.F. Taleb beat R. Carter
1-9, 10-9, 9-6, 9-4.
G.B. Hunt beat M.W. Corby
9-4, 9-7, 3-9, 9-7.

Semi-finals
Nancarrow beat Barrington
9-4, 9-5, 10-8.
Hunt beat Taleb
9-5, 9-2, 9-5.

Final
Hunt beat Nancarrow
9-5, 9-4, 9-0.

1969 (December)
Birmingham, W. Midlands

Quarter-finals
G.B. Hunt beat P.E. Millman
9-3, 10-8, 10-9.
A.A. Jawaid beat M.W. Corby
7-9, 10-8, 9-1, 9-4.
M. Yasin beat A.F. Taleb
9-6, 9-0, 5-9, 9-2.
J.P. Barrington beat J.N.C. Easter
9-6, 9-1, 9-4.

Semi-finals
Hunt beat Jawaid
9-7, 2-9, 9-1, 9-6.
Barrington beat Yasin
9-5, 6-9, 9-5, 9-3.

Final
Barrington beat Hunt
9-7, 3-9, 3-9, 9-4, 9-4.

1970 (December)
Birmingham, W. Midlands

Quarter-finals
J.P. Barrington beat M.Z. Hepker
9-2, 9-1, 9-0.
Sharif Khan beat P.N. Ayton
9-0, 5-9, 9-2, 3-9, 9-5.
M. Yasin beat R. Ratinac
2-9, 9-5, 9-3, 3-9, 9-5.
A.A. Jawaid beat J.N.C. Easter
9-4, 10-9, 9-6.

Semi-finals
Barrington beat Sharif
9-0, 9-7, 3-9, 9-3.
Jawaid beat Yasin
9-1, 9-2, 9-0.

Final
Barrington beat Jawaid
9-1, 9-2, 9-6.

1972 (January-February)
Sheffield, S. Yorkshire

Quarter-finals
J.P. Barrington beat G. Allam
9-6, 9-3, 9-7.
G. Alauddin beat A.A. Jawaid
9-5, 9-4, 9-4.
K.J. Hiscoe beat M. Asran
9-6, 3-9, 9-6, 9-3.
G.B. Hunt beat H. Jahan
9-7, 10-9, 9-10, 9-1.

Semi-finals
Barrington beat Alauddin
10-8, 9-7, 9-2.
Hunt beat Hiscoe
9-7, 10-9, 9-4.

Final
Barrington beat Hunt
0-9, 9-7, 10-8, 6-9, 9-7.

1973 (January-February)
Sheffield, S. Yorkshire

Quarter-finals
J.P. Barrington beat A. Safwat
9-3, 9-4, 9-10, 9-0.
K.J. Hiscoe beat H. Jahan
2-9, 9-5, 9-0, 9-7.
G. Alauddin beat M. Yasin
6-9, 9-2, 9-3, 9-3.
G.B. Hunt beat A.A. Jawaid
9-6, 9-6, 9-3.

Semi-finals
Barrington beat Hiscoe
3-9, 9-1, 7-9, 9-1, 9-2.
Alauddin beat Hunt
1-9, 9-7, 9-1, 10-8.

Final
Barrington beat Alauddin
9-4, 9-3, 9-2.

1974 (February)
Sheffield, S. Yorkshire

Quarter-finals
M. Yasin beat J.P. Barrington
1-9, 9-4, 10-8, 9-2.
Q. Zaman beat S. Muneer
9-6, 9-2, 9-2.
G. Alauddin beat C.J. Nancarrow
9-7, 9-7, 9-2.
G.B. Hunt beat H. Jahan
9-4, 9-3, 9-6.

Semi-finals
Yasin beat Zaman
5-9, 9-7, 10-9, 9-7.
Hunt beat Alauddin
9-4, 9-7, 9-3.

Finals
Hunt walkover, Yasin scratched.

1975 (February)
Wembley, London

Quarter-finals
Q. Zaman beat G.B. Hunt
4-9, 8-10, 9-3, 9-2, 9-7.
H. Jahan beat Mohibullah Khan Jun.
10-8, 9-3, 7-9, 10-8.
G. Alauddin beat J.P. Barrington
9-3, 9-6, 9-0.
H.J. Hiscoe beat C.J. Nancarrow
9-4, 3-9, 6-9, 9-2, 9-6.

Semi-finals
Zaman beat Jahan
9-4, 9-2, 6-9, 9-4.
Alauddin beat Hiscoe
9-3, 9-5, 9-5.

Final
Zaman beat Alauddin
9-7, 9-6, 9-1.

1976 (February)
Wembley, London

Note: see world open championship.

1977 (March-April)
Wembley, London

Quarter-finals
G.B. Hunt beat B. Brownlee
9-4, 9-1, 9-4.
J.P. Barrington beat R. Watson
10-8, 9-1, 5-9, 9-6.
C.J. Nancarrow beat J.C.A. Leslie
9-4, 7-9, 9-3, 9-5.
A. Safwat beat M. Asran
9-6, 9-0, 9-7.

Semi-finals
Hunt beat Barrington
9-5, 9-2, 9-0.

Nancarrow beat Safwat
9-1, 9-6, 6-9, 9-1.

Final
Hunt beat Nancarrow
9-4, 9-4, 8-10, 9-4.

UNITED STATES OPEN CHAMPIONSHIP

1954 (January)
New York, N.Y.

Quarter-finals
G.D. Mateer beat C. MacCracken
15-5, 15-12, 15-8.
Hashim Khan beat D. McLaggan
15-13, 15-7, 15-8.
M. el Karim beat C. Brinton
15-12, 11-15, 15-13, 15-11.
H.R. Salaun beat R.M. Bakey
15-8, 15-8, 15-12.

Semi-finals
Hashim beat Mateer
12-15, 12-15, 15-8, 15-5, 15-11.
Salaun beat Karim
15-9, 15-1, 15-5.

Final
Salaun beat Hashim
15-7, 15-12, 15-14.

1955 (January)
New York. N.Y.

Quarter-finals
Azam Khan beat H.R. Salaun
15-16, 11-15, 15-3, 15-12, 15-8.
Roshan Khan beat E. Howard
15-10, 15-10, 14-15, 15-5.
G.D. Mateer beat D. Bocquet
15-5, 15-6, 15-3
Hashim Khan beat C. MacCracken
15-10, 17-18, 11-15, 15-2, 15-10

Semi-finals
Azam beat Roshan
15-12, 15-8, 10-15, 15-9.
Mateer walkover, Hashim scratched.

Final
Mateer beat Azam
15-9, 15-5, 15-10.

1956 (January)
New York, N.Y.

Quarter-finals
G.D. Mateer beat D. McLaggan
15-10, 15-7, 15-9.
Azam Khan beat Roshan Khan
15-7, 15-10, 18-14.
H.R. Salaun beat G. MacCracken
10-15, 15-8, 15-8, 15-8.
Hashim Khan beat C. Fergusson
15-10, 15-9, 15-9.

Semi-finals
Azam beat Mateer
15-9, 15-11, 15-9.
Hashim beat Salaun
15-6, 15-11, 15-7.

Final
Hashim beat Azam
18-16, 12-15, 16-18, 15-4, 15-9.

1957 (January)
Cedarhurst, N.Y.

Quarter-finals
Hashim Khan beat J. Warzychi
15-5, 15-9, 15-12.
G.D. Mateer beat B.H. Heckscher
18-16, 13-15, 15-8, 12-15, 15-8.
Roshan Khan beat Azam Khan
10-15, 15-4, 15-14, 15-9.
H.R. Salaun beat C. MacCracken
15-6, 15-9, 18-16.

Semi-finals
Hashim beat Mateer
8-15, 15-13, 15-9, 15-13.
Roshan beat Salaun
15-7, 12-15, 15-13, 13-15, 15-13.

Final
Hashim beat Roshan
12-15, 15-5, 15-3, 15-9.

1958 (January)
Detroit, Michigan

Quarter-finals
Roshan Khan beat D. McLaggan
15-8, 15-13, 15-10.
C. MacCracken beat A.E. Chassard
18-13, 15-17, 15-10, 15-9.
Azam Khan beat M. el Karim
15-10, 15-9, 15-9.
H.R. Salaun beat C. Fergusson
11-15, 15-10, 15-3, 15-5.

Semi-finals
Roshan beat MacCracken
15-13, 15-4, 15-11.
Salaun beat Azam
8-15, 15-10, 9-15, 15-12, 15-11.

Final
Roshan beat Salaun
14-18, 15-7, 18-17, 18-16.

1959 (January)
Pittsburgh, Pennsylvania

Quarter-finals
H.R. Salaun beat B.H. Heckscher
15-7, 15-12, 15-10.
Hashim Khan beat R. Widelski
13-15, 15-13, 16-15, 15-8.
G.D. Mateer beat M. Dardir
15-8, 18-14, 15-9.
Roshan Khan beat C. MacCracken
15-10, 14-17, 13-15, 15-9, 15-7.

Semi-finals
Hashim beat Salaun
16-17, 10-15, 15-11, 17-16, 15-12.
Mateer beat Roshan
15-5, 18-15, 15-8.

Final
Mateer beat Hashim
6-15, 15-9, 15-17, 15-9, 15-5.

1960 (January)
Hartford, Connecticut

Quarter-finals
G.D. Mateer beat R. Widelski
15-6, 8-15, 10-15, 15-7, 15-7.
Azam Khan beat Hashim Khan
15-9, 15-10, 18-17.
H.R. Salaun beat B.H. Heckscher
15-14, 15-13, 15-12.
Roshan Khan beat A.E. Chassard
15-12, 15-6, 15-11.

Semi-finals
Azam beat Mateer
14-16, 15-5, 11-15, 15-7, 15-11.
Roshan beat Salaun
15-7, 15-4, 9-15, 15-8.

Final
Roshan beat Azam
15-7, 11-15, 15-11, 11-15, 15-7.

1961 (January)
Indianapolis, Indiana

Quarter-finals
G.D. Mateer beat R. Widelski
15-11, 12-15, 15-6, 10-15, 15-8.
Azam Khan beat D. Watts
15-8, 15-11, 15-8.
Mohibullah Khan beat C.W. Ufford
15-10, 15-11, 15-4.
Roshan Khan beat Hashim Khan
17-14, 15-7, 7-15, 15-9.

Semi-finals
Azam beat Mateer
15-10, 15-12, 15-10.
Roshan beat Mohibullah
18-17, 15-9, 15-8.

Final
Roshan beat Azam
15-6, 15-4, 15-8.

1962 (January)
Atlantic City, New Jersey

Quarter-finals
B.H. Heckscher beat A.E. Chassard
17-14, 15-16, 4-15, 18-14, 15-13.
Azam Khan beat Mohibullah Khan
15-11, 15-17, 15-13, 10-5 retired.
Hashim Khan beat C.W. Ufford
15-12, 7-15, 15-13, 15-7.
Roshan Khan beat R. Widelski
15-9, 15-11, 13-15, 15-6.

Semi-finals
Azam beat Heckscher
9-15, 15-6, 15-9, 15-14.
Roshan walkover, Hashim scratched.

Final
Azam beat Roshan
15-9, 15-7, 15-11.

1963 (January
New York, N.Y.

Quarter-finals
R. Widelski beat H.R. Salaun
11-15, 15-7, 16-13, 15-12.
Hashim Khan beat Roshan Khan
15-6 retired.
Mohibullah Khan beat A.E. Chassard
15-11, 18-17, 17-18, 15-10.
C.W. Ufford beat J. Zug
15-7, 15-13, 15-7.

Semi-finals
Hashim beat Widelski
15-7, 12-15, 7-15, 18-17, 15-8.
Mohibullah beat Ufford
11-15, 15-8, 15-13, 15-2.

Final
Hashim beat Mohibullah
15-6, 10-15, 15-10, 11-15, 15-12.

1964 (January)
Buffalo, N.Y.

Quarter-finals
Hashim Khan beat R. Hetherington
15-12, 15-8, 15-11.
V. Niederhoffer beat H. Conlon
15-10, 15-14, 15-6.
Mohibullah Khan beat R.E. Howe
15-4, 15-11, 15-8.
A.E. Chassard beat A.F. Taleb
15-10, 16-15, 15-3.

Semi-finals
Hashim beat Niederhoffer
10-15, 15-7, 15-18, 15-3, 15-5.
Mohibullah beat Chassard
15-10, 15-7, 15-12.

Final
Mohibullah beat Hashim
15-10, 15-7, 15-12.

1965 (January)
Wilmington, Delaware

Quarter-finals
Mohibullah Khan beat V. Niederhoffer
18-13, 15-5, 15-6.
S.P. Howe beat A.E. Chassard
15-9, 15-9, 17-14.
Hashim Khan beat R.E. Howe
14-18, 17-14, 15-7, 15-11.
C.W. Ufford beat R. Hetherington
15-9, 15-7, 15-7.

Semi-finals
Mohibullah beat S.P. Howe
15-11, 15-2, 15-4.
Hashim beat Ufford
9-15, 15-5, 15-11, 15-4.

Final
Mohibullah beat Hashim
15-11, 15-10, 15-9.

Note: The United States and Canadian open championships were then combined to innovate the North American open championship, an umbrella title covering the entire northern continent.

NORTH AMERICAN OPEN CHAMPIONSHIP

1966 (January)
Detroit, Michigan

Quarter-finals
Mohibullah Khan beat D. Pemberton-Smith
15-10, 15-6, 15-8.
R. Hetherington beat C.W. Ufford
15-10, 18-15, 15-12.
S. Vehslage beat S.P. Howe
17-16, 15-5, 10-15, 15-14.
V. Niederhoffer beat R. Widelski
15-10, 14-15, 18-17, 17-14.

Semi-finals
Mohibullah beat Hetherington
15-10, 18-17, 18-13.
Niederhoffer beat Vehslage
15-10, 13-15, 15-6, 15-8.

Final
Mohibullah beat Niederhoffer
15-2, 15-3, 12-15, 15-10

1967 (January)
Montreal, Quebec

Quarter-finals
Mohibullah Khan beat R. Hetherington
15-2, 15-8, 15-6.
R.E. Howe beat R. Widelski
16-14, 15-12, 15-11.
V. Niederhoffer beat Sharif Khan
15-9, 14-15, 16-14, 14-15, 17-15.
S.P. Howe beat A.E. Chassard
16-13, 15-14, 16-13.

Semi-finals
R.E. Howe beat Mohibullah
11-15, 15-12, 18-15, 9-15, 15-12.
S.P. Howe beat Niederhoffer
16-18, 15-13, 13-15, 15-3, 15-12.

Final
R.E. Howe beat S.P. Howe
15-12, 15-13, 5-15, 13-15, 15-13.

1968 (January)
Indianapolis, Indiana

Quarter-finals
R.E. Howe beat A. Nayar
15-13, 15-9, 15-7.
Mohibullah Khan beat P. Martin
15-6, 15-7, 15-6.
S.P. Howe beat R. Widelski
15-10, 15-11, 15-6.
Sharif Khan beat R. Hetherington
15-13, 18-15, 15-9.

Semi-finals
Mohibullah beat R. Howe
15-4, 16-14, 15-10.
Sharif beat S. Howe
11-15, 15-2, 15-6, 15-10.

Final
Mohibullah beat Sharif
15-9, 15-13, 15-2.

1969 (January)
Cincinnati, Ohio

Quarter-finals
Mohibullah Khan beat P. Martin
15-11, 15-9, 15-10.
Hashim Khan beat L. Terrell
15-12, 15-8, 15-9.
Sharif Khan beat A. Nayar
12-15, 15-13, 15-12, 15-11.
K. Binns beat R. Hetherington
15-11, 15-7, 12-15, 15-5.

Semi-finals
Mohibullah beat Hashim
15-5, 15-13, 15-11.
Sharif beat Binns
15-12, 15-6, 15-7.

Final
Sharif beat Mohibullah
15-9, 15-6, 13-15, 15-7.

1970 (January)
Chicago, Illinois

Quarter-finals
Sharif Khan beat Yusuf Khan
15-5, 15-5, 15-8.
Hashim Khan beat A. Nayar
15-10, 15-11, 7-15, 17-14.
Mohibullah Khan beat L. Terrell
15-7, 16-14, 15-12.
K. Binns beat T. Poor
9-15, 15-12, 15-11, 10-15, 18-14.

Semi-finals
Sharif beat Hashim
15-14, 15-13, 9-15, 15-11.
Mohibullah beat Binns
15-9, 15-9, 15-5.

Final
Sharif beat Mohibullah
17-16, 15-5, 15-12.

1971 (January)
Toronto, Ontario

Quarter-finals
Sharif Khan beat C. Adair
15-12, 15-3, 8-15, 15-10.
L. O'Loughlin walkover, Hashim Khan scratched.
Mohibullah Khan beat R. Hetherington
15-9, 11-15, 15-9, 15-3.
K. Binns beat P. Martin
11-15, 15-9, 15-13, 7-15, 15-12.

Semi-finals
Sharif beat O'Loughlin
15-9, 15-6, 15-11.
Binns beat Mohibullah
18-16, 8-15, 11-15, 18-15, 15-10.

Final
Sharif beat Binns
15-11, 15-9, 15-10.

1972 (January)
Louisville, Kentucky

Quarter-finals
Sharif Khan beat Khalid Mir
9-15, 15-9, 15-11, 15-12.
L. Terrell beat S. Moysey
15-5, 15-10, 15-13.
Mohibullah Khan beat R. Ratinac
9-15, 8-15, 15-3, 15-8, 15-11.
V. Niederhoffer beat K. Binns
15-11, 15-6, 15-8.

Semi-finals
Sharif beat Terrell
14-15, 15-9, 15-9, 15-3.
Niederhoffer beat Mohibullah
18-17, 15-12, 18-17.

Final
Sharif beat Niederhoffer
15-11, 14-17, 15-7, 15-6.

1973 (January)
Pittsburgh, Pennsylvania

Quarter-finals
Sharif Khan beat K. Binns
15-12, 15-12, 9-15, 15-11.
R. Ratinac beat R. Hetherington
15-12, 15-7, 15-14.
Mohibullah Khan beat F.P. Satterthwaite
15-9, 15-10, 18-16.
Yusuf Khan beat G. Anderson
8-15, 18-15, 15-7, 15-7.

Semi-finals
Sharif beat Ratinac
18-14, 15-8, 12-15, 15-8.
Mohibullah beat Yusuf
15-11, 7-15, 13-15, 15-6, 15-6.

Final
Sharif beat Mohibullah
11-15, 12-15, 15-8, 15-3, 15-10.

1974 (January)
Toronto, Ontario

Quarter-finals
Sharif Khan beat R. Hetherington
15-7, 15-11, 15-5.
K. Binns beat C. Caldwell
15-12, 15-11, 15-6.
R. Ratinac beat G. Anderson
15-11, 15-13, 10-15, 15-8.
V. Niederhoffer beat Yusuf Khan
15-9, 18-15, 15-9.

Semi-finals
Sharif beat Binns
15-11, 15-7, 16-17, 15-10.
Ratinac beat Niederhoffer
15-9, 12-15, 15-5, 15-11.

Final
Sharif beat Ratinac
17-14, 15-8, 15-12.

1975 (January-February)
Mexico City

Quarter-finals
Sharif Khan beat K. Binns
15-10, 10-15, 15-2, 15-8.
P. Briggs beat G. Anderson
16-13, 9-15, 15-7, 15-12.
J. de Villafranca beat Yusuf Khan
18-15, 15-8, 15-13.
V. Niederhoffer beat Mohibullah Khan
12-15, 15-8, 15-7, 15-10.

Semi-finals
Sharif beat Briggs
15-10, 15-8, 17-18, 15-8.
Niederhoffer beat de Villafranca
18-15, 15-7, 15-6.

Final
Niederhoffer beat Sharif
15-9, 15-7, 4-15, 15-11.

1976 (January)
New York, N.Y.

Quarter-finals
V. Niederhoffer beat J. Reese
15-9, 12-15, 15-12, 15-12.
C. Caldwell beat Gul. Khan
15-11, 15-4, 15-6.
R. Ratinac beat Mohibullah Khan
13-15, 15-13, 15-13, 15-10.
Sharif Khan beat B. Taylor
15-12, 15-7, 15-6.

Semi-finals
Niederhoffer beat Caldwell
15-6, 9-15, 15-9, 15-12.
Sharif beat Ratinac
13-15, 15-9, 15-10, 15-11.

Final
Sharif beat Niederhoffer
15-3, 15-7, 15-5.

1977 (January)
Philadelphia, Pennsylvania

Quarter-finals
Sharif Khan beat M. Desaulniers
4-15, 15-8, 15-9, 15-11.
T. Page beat H. Jahan
15-10, 17-18, 15-9, 15-10.
G.B. Hunt beat C. Caldwell
15-2, 14-16, 15-11, 15-7.
V. Niederhoffer beat Mohibullah Khan
15-7, 15-11, 15-9.

Semi-finals
Sharif beat Page
15-12, 9-15, 15-4, 11-15, 15-11.
Hunt beat Niederhoffer
15-7, 9-15, 15-13, 15-6.

Final
Sharif beat Hunt
15-9, 11-15, 15-10, 15-13.

SOUTH AFRICAN OPEN CHAMPIONSHIP

1974 (August-September)
Johannesburg

Quarter-finals
G.B. Hunt beat R. Watson
9-3, 5-9, 9-1, 9-4.
J.P. Barrington beat K.J. Hiscoe
9-5, 9-6, 9-1.
H. Jahan beat J.N.C. Easter
9-1, 3-9, 9-5, 9-6.
C.J. Nancarrow beat A. Safwat
6-9, 9-5, 10-8, 10-8.

Semi-finals
Hunt beat Barrington
9-4, 9-7, 0-9, 9-4.
Jahan beat Nancarrow
9-1, 9-6, 9-5.

Final
Hunt beat Jahan
9-7, 9-7, 9-1.

1975 (August-September)
Johannesburg

Quarter-finals
G.B. Hunt beat I. Holding
9-5, 10-8, 9-1.
C.J. Nancarrow beat J.P. Barrington
9-6, 10-8, 5-9, 9-6.
K.J. Hiscoe beat A. Safwat
9-7, 9-0, 2-9, 9-4.
H. Jahan beat R. Watson
6-9, 9-6, 10-8, 9-4.

Semi-finals
Hunt beat Nancarrow
9-2, 9-1, 9-6
Jahan beat Hiscoe
9-5, 10-8, 9-5.

Final
Hunt beat Jahan
6-9, 9-1, 9-5, 10-8.

1976 (September)
Johannesburg

Quarter-finals
G.B. Hunt beat I. Holding
9-6, 9-3, 9-4.
R. Watson beat J.N.C. Easter
9-4, 7-9, 5-9, 9-3, 9-3.
C.J. Nancarrow beat K. Shawcross
9-6, 9-4, 2-9, 9-7.
J.P. Barrington beat A.A. Aziz
7-9, 9-4, 9-5, 5-9, 9-7.

Semi-finals
Hunt beat Watson
9-10, 9-4, 9-2, 9-7.
Nancarrow beat Barrington
9-4, 9-5, 10-9.

Final
Hunt beat Nancarrow
9-3, 9-7, 9-1.

1977 (August)
Johannesburg

Quarter-finals
G.B. Hunt beat I. Holding
9-3, 9-4, 7-9, 9-1.
A. Safwat beat A.A. Aziz
9-2, 9-3, 5-9, 10-8.
C.J. Nancarrow beat A. Colburn
10-8, 9-6, 9-7.
R. Watson beat M. Symonds
9-3, 7-9, 9-7, 9-3.

Semi-finals
Hunt beat Safwat
9-7, 9-4, 9-5.
Watson beat Nancarrow
7-9, 9-2, 9-2, 9-6.

Final
Hunt beat Watson
9-6, 9-3, 9-4.

OPEN INTERNATIONAL MATCHES

Great Britain *v.* Pakistan

1975 (Wembley, London)
Pakistan 5, Gt Britain 0

G. Alauddin beat J.P. Barrington
9-1, 9-7, 8-10, 9-6.
Mohibullah Khan beat J.N.C. Easter
9-6, 9-0, 9-0.
Q. Zaman beat P.N. Ayton
9-7, 9-1, 9-4.
M. Yasin beat M.W. Corby
9-2, 5-9, 9-3, 9-2.
S. Muneer beat J.L. Richardson
9-4, 9-3, 5-9, 9-4.

INVITATION TOURNAMENT (for Hashim Khan Trophy)

1976 (Karachi)
Winners: Pakistan Professionals

Qualifying round
India 2, Canada 1;
Hong Kong 2, Singapore 1;
Pakistan Amateurs 3, New Zealand 0;
Japan 3, Phillippines 0.

Quarter-finals
Pakistan Professionals 3, India 0.
G. Alauddin beat F. Madon
9-0, 9-2, 9-3.
Mohibullah Khan beat R. Manchanda
9-2, 9-0, 9-0.
Q. Zaman beat N. Senapati
9-0, 9-0, 9-1.

United States 3, Hong Kong 0.
W. Andruss beat J. Wasan
5-9, 9-3, 9-2, 9-1.
Mohibullah Khan Sen. beat Lai Yau Chuen
9-2, 9-1, 9-2.
Gul Ahmed beat K.K. Chan
10-8, 9-2, 5-9, 9-0.

Pakistan Amateurs 2, Gt Britain 1.
Maqsood Ahmed (P) beat M. Thurgur
9-6, 9-2, 9-2.
M. Saleem (P) lost to B. Patterson
3-9, 9-3, 5-9, 9-4, 6-9.
Atlas Khan (P) beat C. Francis
7-9, 9-1, 9-1, 9-0.

Egypt 3, Japan 0.
A.A. Aziz beat T. Ochiai
9-1, 9-1, 9-2.
A. Kaoud beat S. Sakamoto
9-4, 9-4, 9-1.
M. Asran beat M. Shida
9-1, 9-2, 9-2.

Semi-finals

Pakistan Professionals 3, United States 0.
G. Alauddin beat Yusuf Khan
9-1, 9-1, 9-0.
Mohibullah Khan Jun. beat Mohibullah Khan Sen.
9-1, 9-0, 9-0.
Q. Zaman beat Gul Ahmed
9-4, 9-2, 9-4.

Pakistan Amateurs 2, Egypt 1.
Maqsood Ahmed (P) beat M. Asran
9-2, 9-6, 9-3.
M. Saleem (P) lost to A. Safwat
3-9, 9-5, 10-9, 6-9, 4-9.
Atlas Khan (P) beat A. Kaoud
9-4, 10-8, 9-2.

Final

Pakistan Professionals 3, Pakistan Amateurs 0.
Q. Zaman beat Atlas Khan
9-2, 9-1, 9-1.
G. Alauddin beat Maqsood Ahmed
9-2, 9-2, 9-1.
Mohibullah Khan beat M. Saleem
9-4, 9-6, 9-1.

WORLD AMATEUR CHAMPIONSHIPS

1967 (August)
Australia

Team event

1, Australia; 2, Gt Britain; 3, New Zealand; 4, South Africa; 5, India; 6, Pakistan.

Australia beat GB 3-0, N. Zealand 3-0, S. Africa 3-0, Pakistan 3-0, India 3-0.
Gt. Britain beat S. Africa 21, India 3-0, Pakistan 3-0.
New Zealand beat GB 2-1, S. Africa 2-1, India 2-1.
South Africa beat India 3-0, beat Pakistan 3-0.
India beat Pakistan 2-1.
Pakistan beat N. Zealand 2-1.

Individual event

Semi-finals

C.J. Nancarrow beat J.P. Barrington
9-7, 9-6, 9-7.
G.B. Hunt beat K.J. Hiscoe
9-3, 9-7, 0-9, 10-8.

Final

Hunt beat Nancarrow
9-3, 9-2, 9-1.

1969 (February)
Gt Britain

Team event

1, Australia; 2, Gt Britain; 3, Pakistan; 4, South Africa; 5, New Zealand; 6, Egypt.

Australia beat GB 2-1, S. Africa 2-1, Pakistan 2-1, N. Zealand 3-0, Egypt 3-0.
Gt. Britain beat S. Africa 3-0, Pakistan 2-1, N. Zealand 2-1, Egypt 2-1.
Pakistan beat S. Africa 2-1. N. Zealand 2-1, Egypt 3-0.
South Africa beat N. Zealand 2-1, Egypt 2-1.
New Zealand beat Egypt 2-1.

Individual event

Semi-finals
J.P. Barrington beat C.J. Nancarrow 9-0, 9-2, 10-8.
G.B. Hunt beat K.J. Hiscoe 9-6, 9-5, 2-9, 9-7.

Final
Hunt beat Barrington 9-7, 2-9, 9-4, 9-0.

1971 (July)
New Zealand

Team event
1, Australia; 2, Pakistan; 3, Egypt; 4, Gt Britain; 5, New Zealand; 6, India; 7, Canada.
Australia beat Pakistan 2-1, Egypt 3-0, GB 3-0, N. Zealand 3-0, India 3-0, Canada 3-0.
Pakistan beat Egypt 2-1, N. Zealand 3-0, India 3-0, Canada 3-0.
Egypt beat GB 2-1, N. Zealand 2-1, India 3-0, Canada 3-0.
GB beat Pakistan 3-0, N. Zealand 3-0, India 3-0, Canada 3-0.
New Zealand beat India 2-1, Canada 3-0. India beat Canada 2-1.

Individual event

Semi-finals
G.B. Hunt beat K.J. Hiscoe 9-1, 9-3, 3-9, 9-1.
C.J. Nancarrow beat M. Asran 9-3, 6-9, 9-7, 9-5.

Final
Hunt beat Nancarrow 9-0, 9-7, 8-10, 9-5.

1973 (September)
South Africa

Team event
1, Australia; 2, Gt Britain; 3, South Africa; 4, New Zealand; 5, United States.
Australia beat GB 2-1. S. Africa 2-1, N. Zealand 3-0, USA 3-0.
Gt Britain beat S. Africa 2-1, N. Zealand 3-0, USA 3-0.
South Africa beat N. Zealand 3-0, USA 3-0.
New Zealand beat USA 3-0.

Individual event

Semi-finals
C.J. Nancarrow beat M. Donnelly 10-9, 9-2, 7-9, 9-6.
B. Patterson beat D. Wright 5-9, 9-5, 9-7, 10-8.

Final
Nancarrow beat Patterson 9-2, 9-5, 9-3.

1976 (May)
Gt Britain

Team event

1, Gt Britain; 2, Pakistan; 3, Australia; 4, Egypt; 5, New Zealand; 6, Sweden; 7, India; 8, Canada; 9, United States; 10, Kuwait.

Pool A.

Australia beat Egypt 2-1, Sweden 3-0, India 3-0, USA 3-0.
Egypt beat Sweden 2-1, India 3-0, USA 3-0.
Sweden beat India 3-0, USA 3-0.
India beat USA 2-1.

Pool B

Gt Britain beat Pakistan 3-0, N. Zealand 3-0, Canada 3-0, Kuwait 3-0.
Pakistan beat N. Zealand 2-1, Canada 3-0, Kuwait 3-0.
New Zealand beat Canada 3-0, Kuwait 3-0.
Canada beat Kuwait 3-0.

Play-off series.

Gt Britain beat Australia 2-1, Egypt 2-1.
Pakistan beat Australia 3-0, Egypt 2-1.
New Zealand beat Sweden 2-1, India 3-0, USA 3-0.
Sweden beat Canada 2-1, Kuwait 3-0.
India beat Canada 2-1, Kuwait 3-0.
Canada beat USA 2-1.
USA beat Kuwait 3-0.

Individual event

Semi-finals

K. Shawcross beat M. Donnelly 9-3, 9-4, 9-2.
D. Scott beat I. Holding 2-9, 9-3, 9-10, 9-6, 9-2.

Final

Shawcross beat Scott 9-1, 0-9, 9-6, 6-9, 9-2.

1977 (September)
Canada

Team Event

1, Pakistan; 2, New Zealand;
3, Egypt; 4, Gt Britain;
5, Australia; 6, Sweden;
7, Canada; 8, United States.

Pakistan beat Canada 3-0, Egypt 3-0, USA 3-0, GB 2-1, Sweden 3-0, Australia 3-0.
New Zealand beat USA 3-0, Sweden 2-1, Pakistan 2-1, GB 2-1, Canada 3-0, Australia 2-1.
Egypt beat GB 2-1, Sweden 2-1, Australia 2-1, New Zealand 2-1, Canada 3-0, USA 3-0.
Gt Britain beat Canada 3-0, USA 3-0, Australia 3-0, Sweden 2-1.
Australia beat Sweden 2-1, USA 3-0, Canada 2-1.
Sweden beat Canada 2-1, USA 2-1.
Canada beat USA 3-0.

Individual event

Semi-finals

M. Saleem beat G. Awad 9-7, 9-4, 1-9, 9-7.
Maqsood Ahmed beat J.C.A. Leslie 6-9, 9-2, 7-9, 9-5, 9-2.

Final

Maqsood beat Saleem 9-4, 9-7, 9-3.

BRITISH AMATEUR CHAMPIONSHIP

1923 (April)
Lord's, London

Semi-finals
J.E. Tomkinson beat S.M. Toyne
15-7, 15-7.
T.O. Jameson beat C. le C. Browning
15-6, 15-3.

Final
Jameson beat Tomkinson
17-15, 12-15, 15-0.

1923 (December)
Bath Club, London

Semi-finals
T.O. Jameson beat G. Robarts
15-6, 15-6.
C. le C. Browning beat R.H. Wethered
15-5, 15-6.

Final
Jameson beat Browning
15-11, 16-14.

1924 (December)
Bath Club, London

Semi-finals
W.D. Macpherson beat R.G. de Quetteville
15-13, 18-13.
J.E. Tomkinson beat F.W. Strawson
15-10, 15-5.

Final
Macpherson beat Tomkinson
17-14, 8-15, 15-7.

1926 (January)
Bath Club, London

Semi-finals
J.E. Tomkinson beat W.D. Macpherson
15-11, 12-15, 15-12.
V.A. Cazalet beat H.W. Backhouse
15-4, 15-10.

Final
Cazalet beat Tomkinson
15-8, 12-15, 18-17.

1926 (December)
Bath Club, London

Semi-finals
J.E. Tomkinson beat H.W. Backhouse
9-6, 9-5, 9-10, 9-4.
V.A. Cazalet beat W.L. Davis
9-2, 7-9, 9-0, 9-3.

Final
Tomkinson beat Cazalet
9-5, 9-7, 7-9, 9-6.

1927 (December)
Bath Club, London

Semi-finals
H.W. Backhouse beat P.V.F. Cazalet
9-2, 9-7, 4-9, 9-4.
V.A. Cazalet beat P.Q. Reiss
9-4, 9-4, 2-9, 9-7.

Final
Cazalet beat Backhouse
4-9, 9-6, 3-9, 10-8, 9-4.

1929 (January)
Bath Club, London

Semi-finals
W.D. Macpherson beat R.S. Wright
9-2, 10-8, 5-9, 9-4.
V.A. Cazalet beat G. d'O. Sheppard
9-0, 9-5, 9-5.

Final
Macpherson beat Cazalet
9-3, 9-1, 5-9, 1-9, 9-1.

1929 (December)
Bath Club, London

Semi-finals
W.F. Basset beat I. Akers-Douglas
5-9, 1-9, 10-8, 9-5, 9-2.
V.A. Cazalet beat P.Q. Reiss
9-2, 8-10, 9-6, 9-5.

Final
Cazalet beat Basset
9-2, 9-5, 9-7.

1930 (December)
Bath Club, London

Semi-finals
K.C. Gandar Dower beat G. d'O. Sheppard
9-0, 9-3, 9-0.
V.A. Cazalet beat A.F. Amr
6-9, 9-4, 7-9, 9-1, 9-0.

Final
Cazalet beat Gandar Dower
9-2, 6-9, 7-9, 9-6, 9-2.

1931 (December)
Bath Club, London

Semi-finals
W.D. Macpherson beat V.A. Cazalet
9-10, 9-7, 9-4, 9-0.
A.F. Amr beat G.O.M. Jameson
4-9, 7-9, 9-3, 9-0, 9-1.

Final
Amr beat Macpherson
9-7, 9-6, 4-9, 5-9, 9-0.

1932 (December)
Bath Club, London

Semi-finals
A.F. Amr beat P.Q. Reiss
9-0, 9-1, 9-5.
E. Snell beat C.P. Hamilton
9-6, 9-1, 9-3.

Final
Amr beat Snell
9-1, 9-0, 9-4.

1933 (December)
Bath Club, London

Semi-finals
A.F. Amr beat O.C. Browning
9-1, 9-3, 9-4.
G.O.M. Jameson beat J.C. Gregory
0-9, 9-6, 9-4, 2-9, 9-5.

Final
Amr beat Jameson
9-0, 9-2, 9-4.

1934 (December)
Bath Club, London

Semi-finals
C.P. Hamilton beat J.N.S. Ridgers
9-2, 9-0, 9-4.
D.M. Backhouse beat J.A. Gillies
9-3, 10-8, 0-9, 8-10, 9-4.

Final
Hamilton beat Backhouse
9-7, 9-0, 9-4.

1935 (December)
Bath Club, London

Semi-finals
E. Snell beat C.P. Hamilton
1-9, 3-9, 9-7, 10-8, 9-2.
A.F. Amr beat N.W.D. Yardley
9-3, 9-3, 9-3.

Final
Amr beat Snell
9-1, 9-0, 9-1.

1936 (December)
Bath Club, London

Semi-finals
A.F. Amr beat R. Pulbrook
9-3, 9-1, 9-0
E. Snell beat J.A. Gillies
9-2, 10-9, 9-5.

Final
Amr beat Snell
9-4, 9-0, 9-2.

1937 (December)
Bath Club, London

Semi-finals
J.F. Stokes beat F.D.M. Flowerdew
9-7, 5-9, 9-7, 10-8.
A.F. Amr beat J.W.C. More
9-4, 9-0, 9-0.

Final
Amr beat Stokes
9-3, 9-4, 9-2.

1938 (December)
Bath Club, London

Semi-finals
K.C. Gandar Dower beat E. Snell
6-9, 9-5, 9-0, 1-9, 9-2.
D.I. Burnett beat F.D.M. Flowerdew
9-3, 9-1, 9-1.

Final
Gandar Dower beat Burnett
2-9, 10-8, 9-6, 10-8.

1947 (January)
Lansdowne and Royal Aero Clubs, London

Semi-finals
N.F. Borrett beat B.C. Phillips
9-6, 9-5, 5-9, 9-4.
J.A. Gillies beat G.O.M. Jameson
9-5, 3-9, 10-8, 0-9, 9-7.

Final
Borrett beat Gillies
9-3, 9-6, 9-3.

1948 (January)
Lansdowne and Royal Aero Clubs, London

Semi-finals
N.F. Borrett beat B.C. Phillips
9-6, 9-4, 9-6.
J.R. Thompson beat A.A.T. Seymour-Haydon
7-9, 9-7, 9-1, 9-4.

Final
Borrett beat Thompson
9-2, 9-4, 9-4.

1949 (January)
Lansdowne and Royal Aero Clubs, London

Semi-finals
N.F. Borrett beat D.M. Bull
9-2, 9-1, 9-3.
B.C. Phillips beat R.M. Boustead
6-9, 9-4, 9-3, 9-3.

Final
Borrett beat Phillips
9-2, 9-4, 9-2.

1950 (January)
Lansdowne and Royal Aero Clubs, London

Semi-finals
N.F. Borrett beat R.B.R. Wilson
9-1, 9-6, 9-6.
H.J.A. Dagnall beat A.W.H. Mallett
5-9, 9-1, 8-10, 9-4, 9-6.

Final
Borrett beat Dagnall
9-4, 9-5, 10-8.

1951 (January)
Lansdowne and Royal Aero Clubs, London

Semi-finals
N.F. Borrett beat R.B.R. Wilson
1-9, 9-7, 1-9, 9-2, 9-4.
G. Hildick-Smith walkover, B.C. Phillips scratched.

Final
Borrett beat Hildick-Smith
9-6, 10-8, 9-1.

1952 (January)
Lansdowne and Royal Aero Clubs, London

Semi-finals
B.C. Phillips beat G.W.T. Atkins
9-5, 2-9, 9-3, 9-2.
G. Hildick-Smith beat A.A.T. Seymour-Haydon
1-9, 9-1, 9-3, 6-9, 9-1.

Final
Hildick-Smith beat Phillips
9-3, 9-2, 9-2.

1953 (January)
Lansdowne and Royal Aero Clubs, London

Semi-finals
A. Fairbairn beat A.A.T. Seymour-Haydon
0-9, 9-7, 6-9, 9-6, 9-5.
R.B.R. Wilson beat I.C. de Sales la Terriere
9-2, 9-3, 9-10, 9-7.

Final
Fairbairn beat Wilson
9-2, 9-2, 4-9, 9-1.

1954 (January)
Lansdowne and Royal Aero Clubs, London

Semi-finals
A. Fairbairn beat A.A.T. Seymour-Haydon
9-10, 9-5, 9-5, 9-2.
R.B.R. Wilson beat D.B. Hughes
9-4, 9-3, 9-3.

Final
Fairbairn beat Wilson
7-9, 9-1, 7-9, 9-7, 9-7.

1955 (January)
Lansdowne and Royal Aero Clubs, London

Semi-finals
A. Fairbairn beat M.J. Perkins 9-2, 9-5, 9-2.
R.B.R. Wilson beat A.A.T. Seymour-Haydon 9-10, 9-2, 9-0, 9-4.

Final
Wilson beat Fairbairn 9-7, 8-10, 9-6, 9-4.

1956 (January)
Lansdowne and Royal Aero Clubs, London

Semi-finals
R.B.R. Wilson beat N.H.R.A. Broomfield 9-1, 9-6, 9-7.
I. Amin beat M.F. Mohtadi 9-5, 9-3, 7-9, 9-7.

Final
Amin beat Wilson 4-9, 9-7, 2-9, 9-7, 10-8.

1957 (January)
Lansdowne and Royal Aero Clubs, London

Semi-finals
R.B.R. Wilson beat C. Kaplan 9-3, 7-9, 9-5, 2-9, 9-0.
D. Callaghan beat N.H.R.A. Broomfield 9-7, 10-9, 9-1.

Final
Wilson beat Callaghan 7-9, 8-10, 9-1, 9-4, 9-6.

1958 (January)
Lansdowne and Royal Aero Clubs, London

Semi-finals
N.H.R.A. Broomfield beat M.A. Oddy 9-5, 9-0, 9-1.
I. Amin beat J.G.A. Lyon 6-9, 10-8, 9-3, 9-10, 9-5.

Final
Broomfield beat Amin 9-1, 9-7, 9-4.

1959 (January)
Royal Automobile Club, London

Semi-finals
N.H.R.A. Broomfield beat T. Shafik 9-3, 9-7, 1-9, 9-7.
I. Amin beat M.A. Oddy 2-9, 9-5, 9-2, 9-7.

Final
Broomfield beat Amin 9-2, 9-6, 1-9, 9-7.

1960 (January)
Royal Automobile Club, London

Semi-finals
T. Shafik beat M.A. Oddy 9-5, 10-9, 5-9, 9-2.
I. Amin beat D.B. Hughes 9-7, 7-9, 9-5, 9-3.

Final
Amin beat Shafik 9-7, 0-9, 9-6, 9-5.

1961 (January)
Royal Automobile Club, London

Semi-finals
I. Amin beat D.B. Hughes
2-9, 9-6, 9-3, 10-9.
M.A. Oddy beat T. Shafik
9-3, 9-7, 9-6.

Final
Oddy beat Amin
9-2, 7-9, 10-8, 9-4.

1962 (January)
Royal Automobile Club, London

Semi-finals
M.A. Oddy beat T. Shafik
9-3, 9-7, 9-6.
I. Amin beat K.J. Hiscoe
6-9, 7-9, 9-3, 9-7, 9-3.

Final
Oddy beat Amin
9-5, 3-9, 10-8, 9-1.

1963 (January)
Lansdowne and Royal Aero Clubs, London

Semi-finals
T. Shafik beat A.A. Jawaid
7-9, 9-5, 9-7, 10-8.
K.J. Hiscoe beat R. Carter
7-9, 9-7, 9-7, 9-0.

Final
Hiscoe beat Shafik
9-3, 9-7, 5-9, 9-7.

1964 (January)
RAC and Lansdowne, London

Semi-finals
A.A. Jawaid beat K.J. Hiscoe
2-9, 5-9, 9-5, 9-5, 9-6.
T. Shafik beat M.A. Oddy
4-9, 0-9, 9-1, 10-8, 9-7.

Final
Jawaid beat Shafik
7-9, 9-2, 5-9, 9-4, 9-5.

1965 (January)
RAC and Lansdowne, London

Semi-finals
A.A. Jawaid beat K.J. Hiscoe
9-3, 9-1, 9-2.
G.B. Hunt beat J.G.A. Lyon
9-4, 9-1, 9-3.

Final
Jawaid beat Hunt
9-5, 8-10, 9-3, 10-9.

1966 (January)
RAC and Lansdowne, London

Semi-finals
A.A. Jawaid beat K.J. Hiscoe
9-5, 5-9, 9-2, 6-9, 9-4.
R. Carter beat G.B. Hunt
6-9, 9-6, 9-2, 8-10, 9-5.

Final
Jawaid beat Carter
7-9, 9-2, 9-2, 9-10, 9-6.

1967 (January)
RAC and Lansdowne, London

Semi-finals
R. Carter beat A.A. Jawaid
9-1, 9-7, 9-5.
J.P. Barrington beat K.J. Hiscoe
5-9, 2-9, 9-5, 9-5, 9-1.

Final
Barrington beat Carter
1-9, 9-6, 7-9, 9-7, 9-0.

1968 (January)
RAC and Lansdowne, London

Semi-finals
J.P. Barrington beat A.M.H. Hill
9-1, 9-2, 9-0.
M.W. Corby beat J.G.A. Lyon
5-9, 9-1, 9-7, 6-9, 9-7.

Final
Barrington beat Corby
9-3, 9-6, 2-9, 9-5.

1968 (December)
RAC and Lansdowne, London

Semi-finals
J.P. Barrington beat P.E. Millman
9-4, 9-0, 9-0.
M.W. Corby beat J.G.A. Lyon
9-2, 9-3, 5-9, 9-5.

Final
Barrington beat Corby
3-9, 9-1, 9-2, 9-3.

1970 (January)
RAC and Lansdowne, London

Semi-finals
G.B. Hunt walkover, D. Broom scratched.
A.A. Jawaid beat M.W. Corby
10-8, 9-5, 9-7.

Final
Hunt beat Jawaid
9-7, 9-2, 9-0.

1971 (January)
RAC and Lansdowne, London

Semi-finals
W. Reedman beat S. Muneer
9-7, 9-3, 9-2.
G. Alauddin beat J.N.C. Easter
9-5, 9-6, 9-3.

Final
Alauddin beat Reedman
9-3, 9-0, 9-5.

1971 (December)
RAC and Lansdowne, London

Semi-finals
G. Alauddin beat H. Jahan
6-9, 9-1, 9-3, 9-4.
M. Asran beat P.E. Millman
9-5, 9-4, 9-1.

Final
Alauddin beat Asran
6-9, 9-3, 7-9, 9-6, 9-2.

1972 (December)
Lambton Club, London
Semi-finals
C.J. Nancarrow beat S. Muneer
9-3, 10-9, 6-9, 9-5.
W. Reedman beat Q. Zaman
9-3, 9-5, 7-9, 1-9, 10-9.

Final
Nancarrow beat Reedman
0-9, 9-2, 9-0, 9-7.

1973 (December)
Lambton and New Croydon, London

Semi-finals
Q. Zaman beat M. Saleem
9-2, 9-3, 8-10, 9-2.
Mohibullah Khan beat H. Jahan
5-9, 8-10, 9-7, 10-8, 9-6.

Final
Mohibullah beat Zaman
9-5, 10-8, 6-9, 7-9, 10-8.

1974 (December)
Wembley, London

Semi-finals
Mohibullah Khan beat P.N. Ayton
9-10, 9-3, 9-6, 9-0.
Q. Zaman beat P.G. Verow
9-1, 9-5, 9-5.

Final
Mohibullah beat Zaman
10-8, 9-5, 5-9, 9-5.

1975 (December)
Wembley, London

Semi-finals
A.A. Aziz beat S.H. Courtney
9-5, 9-5, 9-0.
K. Shawcross beat I. Holding
9-5, 9-4, 9-3.

Final
Shawcross beat Aziz
9-2, 9-7, 9-6.

1976 (December)
Wembley, London

Semi-finals
B. Brownless beat M. Lilley
7-9, 1-9, 9-0, 9-0, 9-5.
J.C.A. Leslie beat L. Kvant
9-0, 2-9, 8-10, 9-7, 9-6.

Final
Brownlee beat Leslie
9-3, 10-8, 8-10, 9-5.

AMATEUR INTERNATIONAL MATCHES

Note: For world amateur team championship, see earlier section.

Lapham Cup and Grant Trophy
The oldest international fixture is the Lapham Cup amateur match between Canada and the United States, played in each country alternately. Of the fifty-five matches between 1922 and 1976 inclusive, the United States won thirty-five and Canada twenty. On two occasions British touring teams were invited to take part, finishing second to the United States at Philadelphia in 1924 and winning the 1927 series in Toronto.

In 1945 a corresponding amateur doubles match was instituted, for the Grant Trophy. Of the twenty-four matches between 1945 and 1976 inclusive, the United States won fourteen and Canada ten.

EUROPEAN AMATEUR TEAM CHAMPIONSHIP

Note: In this event, as in Britain's 'home' amateur international championship, England, Ireland, Scotland and Wales compete as separate teams.

1973 (April)
Edinburgh
1, England; 2, Scotland; 3, Ireland; 4, Wales.

Also competed: Sweden, Finland, Denmark, Netherlands, Greece, Monaco.

1974 (April)
Stockholm
1, England; 2, Scotland; 3, Ireland; 4, Wales.
Also competed: Sweden, Finland, Denmark, Netherlands, Greece, Switzerland, Belgium, West Germany.

1975 (April)
Dublin
1, England; 2, Scotland; 3, Sweden; 4, Ireland; 5, Wales; 6, Finland; 7, Denmark; 8, Belgium; 9, Netherlands; 10, Switzerland; 11, West Germany; 12, France.

1976 (April)
Brussels
1, England; 2, Scotland; 3, Sweden; 4, Ireland; 5, Wales; 6, Denmark; 7, Finland; 8, Netherlands; 9, Belgium; 10, Switzerland; 11, France; 12, West Germany; 13, Greece; 14, Luxembourg; 15, Monaco.

Gt Britain *v.* United States

1924 (January), Philadelphia: USA 3, GB 2.
1925 (April), Bath Club, London: GB 5, USA 0.
1927 (January), Toronto: GB 3, USA 3.
1928 (December), Bath Club, London: GB 5, USA 0.
1935 (December), Bath Club, London: GB 5, USA 0.

Gt Britain *v.* Canada

1924 (January), Philadelphia: GB 4, Canada 1.
1927 (January), Toronto: GB 4, Canada 2.

Gt Britain *v.* South Africa

1955 (August), Johannesburg: S. Africa 4, GB 1.
1955 (August), Durban: GB 4, S. Africa 1.
1955 (September), Cape Town: S. Africa 3, GB 2.
1955 (September), Johannesburg: S. Africa 3, GB 2.
1957 (January), Lansdowne Club, London: GB 3, S. Africa 2.
1957 (January), Cardiff: GB 5, S. Africa 0.
1957 (January), Edinburgh: GB 5, S. Africa 0.
1963 (January), Lansdowne Club, London: GB 3, S. Africa 2.
1965 (July), Johannesburg: GB 2, S. Africa 1.
1965 (August), Cape Town: GB 3, S. Africa 0.
1965 (August), Port Elizabeth: GB 2, S. Africa 1.
1965 (August), Durban: S. Africa 3, GB 0.
1965 (August), Johannesburg: S. Africa 2, GB 1.
1970 (July), Cape Town: S. Africa 3, GB 2.
1970 (August), Durban: S. Africa 4, GB 1.
(August), Johannesburg: S. Africa 5, GB 0.
1972 (December), Cheltenham: S. Africa 3, GB 2.
1973 (January), Halifax: GB 3, S. Africa 2.
1973 (January), Croydon: GB 3, S. Africa 2.

Gt Britain *v*. Australia

1959 (August), Sydney: GB 4, Australia 0.
1959 (August), Parramatta: GB 3, Australia 1.
1959 (September), Melbourne: GB 4, Australia 0.
1963 (January), Lansdowne Club, London: Australia 4, GB 1.
1963 (December), Lansdowne Club, London: Australia 3, GB 0.
1966 (January), Lansdowne Club, London: Australia 3, GB 0.

Gt Britain *v*. New Zealand

1959 (August), Sydney: GB 4, N. Zealand 0.
1959 (August), Sydney: GB 4, N. Zealand 0.
1959 (September), Napier: GB 4, N. Zealand 0.

Gt Britain *v*. Pakistan

1974 (December), Stockton-on-Tees: Pakistan 3, GB 1.
1974 (December), Coventry: Pakistan 3, GB 1.
1975 (January), Wembley, London: Pakistan 4, GB 0.

Appendix 2: *Women's Results*

WORLD OPEN CHAMPIONSHIP

1976 (August)
Brisbane

Quarter-finals
Mrs B. McKay beat Mrs J. Webster
9-1, 9-1, 9-1.
Miss M. Zachariah beat Mrs J. Eckstein
9-3, 9-6, 9-0.
Miss S. Newman beat Miss S. Cogswell
9-5, 9-5, 9-4.
Mrs M. Jackman beat Miss C. van Nierop
9-5, 9-5, 10-8.

Semi-finals
Mrs McKay beat Miss Zachariah
9-1, 9-4, 9-1.
Mrs Jackman beat Miss Newman
9-1, 9-5, 9-3.

Final
Mrs McKay beat Mrs Jackman
9-2, 9-2, 9-0.

BRITISH CHAMPIONSHIP

Note: The first six championships were contested in groups on an all-play-all basis, the most successful players qualifying for concluding knock-out rounds. In the second championship there were no semi-finals, because only the top player in each of two groups went forward — meeting in the final. The 1928 championship was the first played entirely on a knock-out basis. Until 1974, the championship was restricted to amateurs.

1922 (February)
Queen's Club, London

Semi-finals

Miss N.F. Cave beat Miss M. Cave
11-15, 17-16, 15-12.

Miss J.I. Cave beat Mrs C.N. Bruce
15-2, 16-13.

Final

Miss J.I. Cave beat Miss N.F. Cave
11-15, 15-10, 15-9.

1922 (November)
Queen's Club, London

Final

Miss S. Huntsman beat Miss N.F. Cave
6-15, 15-9, 17-15.

1923 (December)
Queen's Club, London

Semi-finals

Miss N.F. Cave beat Miss S. Huntsman
15-10, 15-5.

Miss J.I. Cave beat Miss P. Blake
15-1, 15-7.

Final

Miss N.F. Cave beat Miss J.I. Cave
15-8, 15-13.

1924 (December)
Queen's Club, London

Semi-finals

Miss N.F. Cave beat Miss S. Huntsman
15-11, 15-5.

Miss J.I. Cave beat Miss C.M. Fenwick
12-15, 15-8, 15-6.

Final

Miss J.I. Cave beat Miss N.F. Cave
15-3, 6-15, 16-13.

1925 (December)
Queen's Club, London

Semi-finals

Miss C.M. Fenwick beat Miss S. Huntsman
16-13, 15-3.

Miss N.F. Cave beat Miss J. Nicholson
15-6, 5-15, 15-5.

Final

Miss Fenwick beat Miss Cave
15-12, 15-11.

1926 (December)
Queen's Club, London

Semi-finals
Miss C.M. Fenwick beat Miss S. Huntsman
7-9, 9-4, 9-3, 9-3.
Miss N.F. Cave beat Mrs C.N. Bruce
9-5, 4-9, 9-7, 5-9, 9-3.

Final
Miss Fenwick beat Miss Cave
4-9, 9-6, 9-2, 9-5.

1928 (January)
Queen's Club, London

Semi-finals
Miss J.I. Cave beat Miss S.B.D. Noel
9-5, 9-4, 10-8.
Miss C.M. Fenwick beat Miss S. Huntsman
9-6, 9-3, 9-2.

Final
Miss Cave beat Miss Fenwick
4-9, 9-5, 10-9, 9-6.

1929 (January)
Queen's Club, London

Semi-finals
Miss J.I. Cave beat Miss S. Huntsman
0-9, 9-4, 9-0, 9-4.
Miss N.F. Cave beat Mrs C.N. Bruce
9-0, 9-0, 9-3.

Final
Miss N.F. Cave beat Miss J.I. Cave
9-6, 3-9, 9-2, 3-9, 9-6.

1930 (January)
Queen's Club, London

Semi-finals
Miss C.M. Fenwick beat Miss A. Lytton-Milbanke
9-3, 9-6, 6-9, 5-9, 9-2.
Miss N.F. Cave beat Miss S. Huntsman
9-2, 9-2, 7-9, 9-3.

Final
Miss Cave beat Miss Fenwick
10-8, 9-1, 7-9, 9-5.

1931 (January)
Queen's Club, London

Semi-finals
Miss C.M. Fenwick beat Miss A. Lytton-Milbanke
9-6, 9-0, 10-8.
Miss N.F. Cave beat Miss S. Huntsman
10-8, 9-7, 9-6.

Final
Miss Fenwick beat Miss Cave
9-7, 10-8, 9-10, 9-1.

1932 (February)
Queen's Club, London

Semi-finals
Miss S.D.B. Noel beat Miss A. Lytton-Milbanke
5-9, 9-6, 9-4, 10-8.
Miss J.I. Cave beat Miss S. Huntsman
9-2, 10-8, 9-2.

Final
Miss Noel beat Miss Cave
9-5, 9-7, 9-1.

1933 (April)
Queen's Club, London

Semi-finals
Miss S.D.B. Noel beat Miss M.E. Lumb
9-5, 9-1, 9-5.
Miss S. Keith Jones beat Miss P. Blake
9-5, 9-0, 9-5.

Final
Miss Noel beat Miss Keith Jones
9-4, 9-0, 9-2.

1934 (February)
Queen's Club, London

Semi-finals
Miss S.D.B. Noel beat Mrs I.H. McKechnie
9-2, 9-7, 5-9, 9-1.
Miss M.E. Lumb beat Miss A. Lytton-Milbanke
9-2, 9-2, 9-1.

Final
Miss Noel beat Miss Lumb
9-7, 9-0, 9-6.

1934 (December)
Queen's Club, London

Semi-finals
Miss M.E. Lumb beat Mrs J.B. Pittman
9-2, 9-0, 9-2.
Miss A. Lytton-Milbanke beat Mrs I.H. McKechnie
9-4, 5-9, 10-8, 9-5.

Final
Miss Lumb beat Miss Lytton-Milbanke
9-4, 9-0, 9-1.

1936 (March)
Queen's Club, London

Semi-finals
Miss M.E. Lumb beat Miss F.B. Cooke
9-1, 9-0, 9-3.
Miss A. Lytton-Milbanke beat Mrs I.H. McKechnie
0-9, 9-3, 9-6, 4-9, 9-0

Final
Miss Lumb beat Miss Lytton-Milbanke
9-5, 9-5, 9-4

1937 (January)
Queen's Club, London

Semi-finals
Miss M.E. Lumb beat Miss E.E. Knox
9-0, 9-2, 9-2.
Mrs I.H. McKechnie beat Miss A. Lytton-Milbanke
9-2, 9-3, 1-9, 9-5.

Final
Miss Lumb beat Mrs McKechnie
9-3, 9-2, 9-0.

1938 (February)
Queen's Club, London

Semi-finals
Miss M.E. Lumb beat Miss F.B. Cooke
9-1, 9-4, 6-9, 9-3.
Mrs I.H. McKechnie beat Miss A. Lytton-Milbanke
9-4, 6-9, 9-3, 9-0.

Final
Miss Lumb beat Mrs McKechnie
9-3, 9-2, 9-1.

1939 (March)
Queen's Club, London

Semi-finals
Miss S.D.B. Noel beat Miss A.D.S. Page
9-0, 9-4, 9-2.
Miss M.E. Lumb beat Miss A. Lytton-Milbanke
9-6, 5-9, 9-5, 9-2.

Final
Miss Lumb beat Miss Noel
9-6, 9-1, 9-7.

1947 (January-February)
Lansdowne and Royal Aero Clubs, London

Semi-finals
Miss P.J. Curry beat Miss M.E. Piper
9-1, 9-2, 9-2.
Mrs R.J. Teague beat Mrs G.F. Powell
8-10, 9-1, 9-1, 9-4.

Final
Miss Curry beat Mrs Teague
9-3, 10-9, 9-5.

1948 (January)
Lansdowne and Royal Aero Clubs, London

Semi-finals
Miss P.J. Curry beat Miss A.M. Carlisle
9-2, 9-3, 9-4.
Miss J.R.M. Morgan beat Mrs R.J. Teague
9-1, 7-9, 9-6, 9-1.

Final
Miss Curry beat Miss Morgan
9-5, 9-0, 9-10, 6-9, 10-8.

1949 (January)
Lansdowne and Royal Aero Clubs, London

Semi-finals
Miss P.J. Curry beat Miss A.M. Carlisle
0-9, 9-2, 9-0, 9-0.
Miss J.R.M. Morgan beat Mrs B.E. Hilton
9-1, 9-3, 9-2.

Final
Miss Curry beat Miss Morgan
2-9, 9-3, 10-8, 9-0.

1950 (February)
Lansdowne and Royal Aero Clubs, London

Semi-finals
Miss J.R.M. Morgan beat Miss A.M. Carlisle
9-3, 9-2, 9-4.
Miss P.J. Curry beat Mrs B.E. Hilton
10-8, 9-5, 9-2.

Final
Miss Morgan beat Miss Curry
9-4, 9-3, 9-0.

1951 (February)
Lansdowne and Royal Aero Clubs, London

Semi-finals
Miss J.R.M. Morgan beat Miss S. Speight
9-3, 9-1, 9-1.
Miss P.J. Curry beat Miss M.E. Gowthorpe
9-3, 9-0, 9-2.

Final
Miss Morgan beat Miss Curry
9-1, 2-9, 9-3, 9-4.

1951 (December)
Lansdowne and Royal Aero Clubs, London

Semi-finals
Miss J.R.M. Morgan beat Miss A.V.M. Isaac
9-2, 9-3, 3-9, 9-0.
Miss P.J. Curry beat Mrs G.R. Turner
9-3, 10-8, 7-9, 9-2.

Final
Miss Morgan beat Miss Curry
9-3, 9-1, 9-5.

1953 (February)
Lansdowne and Royal Aero Clubs, London

Semi-finals
Mrs H.R.J. Townsend beat Miss R. Walsh
9-4, 5-9, 9-6, 9-3.
Miss J.R.M. Morgan beat Miss S. Speight
9-6, 9-1, 9-6.

Final
Miss Morgan beat Mrs Townsend
9-4, 9-2, 9-4.

1954 (February)
Lansdowne and Royal Aero Clubs, London

Semi-finals
Miss S. Speight beat Mrs R.J. Teague
9-5, 9-1, 9-2.
Miss J.R.M. Morgan beat Mrs G.R. Turner
9-1, 9-3, 9-2.

Final
Miss Morgan beat Miss Speight
9-3, 9-1, 9-7.

1954 (December)
Lansdowne and Royal Aero Clubs, London

Semi-finals
Mrs G.R. Turner beat Miss L.R. Byrne
7-9, 9-4, 9-2, 10-9.
Miss J.R.M. Morgan beat Miss R. Walsh
9-4, 9-2, 9-7.

Final
Miss Morgan beat Mrs Turner
9-5, 9-3, 9-6.

1956 (February)
Lansdowne and Royal Aero Clubs, London

Semi-finals
Miss S. Speight beat Mrs H.R.J. Townsend
9-0, 9-3, 9-6.
Miss J.R.M. Morgan beat Mrs G.R. Turner
9-2, 9-2, 9-7.

Final
Miss Morgan beat Miss Speight
9-6, 9-4, 9-2.

1957 (February)
Lansdowne and Royal Aero Clubs, London

Semi-finals
Miss S. Speight beat Mrs G.R. Turner
9-6, 9-5, 9-7.
Miss J.R.M. Morgan beat Mrs J.D. Campion
9-5, 9-0, 9-3.

Final
Miss Morgan beat Miss Speight
4-9, 9-5, 9-1, 9-6.

1958 (February)
Lansdowne and Royal Aero Clubs, London

Semi-finals
Mrs H.G. Macintosh beat Mrs J.L. Deloford
9-7, 9-6, 9-6.
Miss J.R.M. Morgan beat Miss M.E. Gowthorpe
9-5, 9-2, 9-6.

Final
Miss Morgan beat Mrs Macintosh
9-2, 9-4, 9-2.

1958 (December)
Lansdowne and Royal Aero Clubs, London

Semi-finals
Mrs H.G. Macintosh beat Miss D. Herman
9-5, 9-6, 9-4.
Miss J.R.M. Morgan beat Mrs G.E. Marshall
4-9, 4-9, 9-2, 9-3, 9-0.

Final
Miss Morgan beat Mrs Macintosh
9-4, 9-1, 9-5.

1960 (February)
Lansdowne and Royal Aero Clubs, London

Semi-finals
Mrs H.G. Macintosh beat Mrs J.L. Deloford
9-3, 9-3, 9-4.
Mrs G.E. Marshall beat Mrs F.R.D. Corbett
9-1, 9-3, 4-9, 9-0.

Final
Mrs Macintosh beat Mrs Marshall
4-9, 8-9, 9-5, 9-3, 9-6.

1961 (February)
Lansdowne and Royal Aero Clubs, London

Semi-finals
Mrs G.R. Turner beat Miss M.E. Gowthorpe
7-9, 9-5, 9-2, 9-2.
Mrs G.E. Marshall beat Mrs F.R.D. Corbett
9-5, 9-4, 9-4.

Final
Mrs Marshall beat Mrs Turner
9-3, 9-5, 9-1.

1962 (February)
Lansdowne and Royal Aero Clubs, London

Semi-finals
Mrs G.E. Marshall beat Miss A.M. Price
9-0, 9-1, 9-0.
Miss H. Blundell beat Miss E.C. Hargreaves
9-2, 9-2, 9-3.

Final
Miss Blundell beat Mrs Marshall
9-6, 9-5, 9-4.

1962 (December)
Lansdowne and Royal Aero Clubs, London

Semi-finals
Mrs G.E. Marshall beat Mrs. H.G. Macintosh
9-5, 9-4, 9-5.
Miss H. Blundell beat Miss M. Muncaster
9-3, 9-2, 9-6.

Final
Miss Blundell beat Mrs Marshall
9-3, 9-2, 9-6.

1964 (February)
Lansdowne and Royal Aero Clubs, London

Semi-finals
Miss H. Blundell beat Miss A.M. Craven Smith
9-4, 7-9, 9-1, 9-3.
Mrs G.E. Marshall beat Miss M. Muncaster
9-4, 9-6, 9-5.

Final
Miss Blundell beat Mrs Marshall
9-2, 9-2, 9-1.

1965 (February)
Lansdowne and Royal Aero Clubs, London

Semi-finals
Miss H. Blundell beat Mrs J.R. White
9-0, 9-1, 9-1.
Miss A.M. Craven Smith beat Mrs G.E. Marshall
1-9, 6-9, 9-4, 10-8, 9-5.

Final
Miss Blundell beat Miss Craven Smith
9-0, 9-1, 9-2.

1966 (February)
Lansdowne and Royal Aero Clubs, London

Semi-finals
Mrs B. McKay beat Mrs G.E. Marshall
9-6, 9-5, 9-1.
Miss A.M. Craven Smith beat Mrs J. Irving
9-5, 9-4, 9-2.

Final
Miss McKay beat Miss Craven Smith
9-0, 9-0, 10-8.

1967 (February)
Lansdowne and Royal Aero Clubs, London

Semi-finals
Miss A.M. Craven Smith beat Mrs G.E. Marshall
9-1, 8-10, 9-4, 9-3.
Mrs B. McKay beat Miss M. Hawcroft
9-1, 9-0, 9-3.

Final
Mrs McKay beat Miss Craven Smith
9-1, 10-8, 9-6.

1968 (February)
Lansdowne and Royal Aero Clubs, London

Semi-finals
Mrs B McKay beat Mrs G. Erskine
9-0, 9-0, 9-0.
Miss B. Johnson beat Miss E. Allnutt
9-10, 9-4, 9-2, 9-1.

Final
Mrs McKay beat Miss Johnson
9-0, 9-0, 9-0.

1969 (January)
Lansdowne and Royal Aero Clubs, London

Semi-finals
Mrs B. McKay beat Mrs H.G. Macintosh
9-0, 9-0, 9-0.
Mrs G.E. Marshall beat Miss S. McClure
9-4, 4-9, 9-1, 9-4.

Final
Mrs McKay beat Mrs Marshall
9-2, 9-0, 9-0.

1970 (February)
BP Club, Sydenham

Semi-finals
Mrs B. McKay beat Mrs A.L. Chapman
9-0, 9-1, 9-1.
Miss M. Roche beat Mrs G.E. Marshall
6-9, 10-8, 10-8, 9-5.

Final
Mrs McKay beat Miss Roche
9-1, 9-1, 9-0.

1971 (February)
BP Club, Sydenham

Semi-finals
Mrs B. McKay beat Mrs M. Jackman
9-7, 9-0, 9-4.
Mrs J. Irving beat Mrs G.E. Marshall
9-7, 9-5, 9-6.

Final
Mrs McKay beat Mrs Irving
9-0, 9-3, 9-1.

1972 (March)
BP Club, Sydenham

Semi-finals
Miss K. Malan beat Miss J.M. Wilson
8-10, 9-6, 9-6, 9-6.
Mrs B. McKay beat Mrs G.E. Marshall
9-1, 9-1, 9-3.

Final
Mrs McKay beat Miss Malan
9-1, 9-1, 9-2.

1973 (March)
BP Club, Sydenham

Semi-finals
Mrs B. McKay beat Miss P. Buckingham
9-2, 9-0, 9-0.
Miss C. Fleming beat Miss S. Newman
1-9, 7-9, 9-2, 10-8.

Final
Mrs McKay beat Miss Fleming
9-1, 9-0, 9-1.

1974 (March)
BP Club, Sydenham

Semi-finals
Mrs B. McKay beat Mrs G.E. Marshall
9-2, 9-1, 9-1.
Miss S. Cogswell beat Miss J. Barham
9-4, 10-8, 9-5.

Final
Mrs McKay beat Miss Cogswell
9-2, 9-1, 9-2.

1975 (February-March)
Wembley, London

Semi-finals
Mrs B. McKay beat Miss M. Zachariah
9-1, 9-0, 9-1.
Mrs M. Jackman beat Miss S. Newman
7-9, 9-4, 9-10, 9-1, 9-6.

Final
Mrs McKay beat Mrs Jackman
9-3, 9-1, 9-5.

1976 (February-March)
Wembley, London

Semi-finals

Mrs B. McKay beat Miss T. Lawes
9-2, 9-1, 9-1.

Miss S. Newman beat Miss S. Cogswell
9-0, 9-10, 9-6, 4-9, 9-6.

Final

Mrs McKay beat Miss Newman
9-2, 9-4, 9-2.

1977 (February-March)
Wembley, London

Semi-finals

Mrs B. McKay beat Miss S. Cogswell
9-5, 9-7, 5-9, 9-0.

Miss B. Wall beat Miss A. Smith
9-4, 6-9, 4-9, 9-3, 9-6.

Final

Mrs McKay beat Miss Wall
9-3, 9-1, 9-2.

AMATEUR INTERNATIONAL MATCHES

Gt Britain *v.* United States (for the Wolfe-Noel Cup)

1933 (February), Sleepy Hollow, N.Y.: GB 4, USA 1.
1934 (February), Queen's Club, London: GB 5, USA 0.
1935 (February), Boston: USA 3, GB 2.
1936 (March), Lansdowne Club, London: GB 5, USA 0.
1937 (February), New York: USA 3, GB 2.
1939 (March), Queen's Club, London: GB 5, USA 0.
1949 (February), Haverford, Pa.: USA 3, GB 2.
1950 (February), Lansdowne Club, London: GB 5, USA 0.
1952 (February, Boston: USA 4, GB 1.
1953 (February), Lansdowne Club, London: GB 5, USA 0.
1955 (February, Philadelphia: GB 4, USA 1.
1957 (February), Lansdowne Club, London: GB 5, USA 0.
1959 (February), Philadelphia: USA 3, GB 2.
1961 (March), Lansdowne Club, London: GB 5, USA 0.
1963 (February), Philadelphia: GB 4, USA 1.
1968 (February), Lansdowne Club, London: GB 5, USA 0.

Gt Britain *v.* South Africa

1963 (July), Durban: GB 5, S. Africa 0.
1963 (July), Johannesburg: GB 5, S. Africa 0.
1963 (July), Johannesburg: GB 5, S. Africa 0.
1968 (January), Leeds: GB 4, S. Africa 1.
1968 (January), Birmingham: GB 4, S. Africa 1.
1968 (February), Lansdowne Club, London: GB 3, S. Africa 2.
1973 (June), Cape Town: S. Africa 4, GB 1.
1973 (July), Durban: S. Africa 5, GB 0.
1973 (July), Johannesburg: S. Africa 4, GB 1.

Gt Britain *v.* Australia

1964 (February), Lansdowne Club, London: Australia 3, GB 2.
1965 (August), Melbourne: Australia 2, GB 1.
1965 (August), Sydney: Australia 2, GB 1.
1965 (August), Hobart: Australia 2, GB 1.
1967 (January), Sheffield: GB 2, Australia 1.
1967 (February), Birmingham: Australia 3, GB 0.
1967 (February), Lansdowne Club, London: Australia 2, GB 1.
1971 (February), Sheffield: Australia 3, GB 0.
1971 (February), Birmingham: Australia 2, GB 1.
1971 (February), Lansdowne Club, London: Australia 3, GB 0.
1972 (August), Melbourne: Australia 3, GB 0.
1972 (August), Brisbane: Australia 3, GB 0.
1972 (August), Sydney: Australia 3, GB 0.
1975 (February), Bournemouth: Australia 2, GB 1.
1975 (February), Coventry: Australia 3, GB 0.
1975 (February), Wembley, London: Australia 3, GB 0.
1976 (August), Sydney: Australia 2, GB 1.

Gt Britain *v.* New Zealand

1965 (August), Auckland: GB 3, N. Zealand 0.
1972 (August), Auckland: N. Zealand 2, GB 1.
1973 (February), Nottingham: N. Zealand 3, GB 0.
1973 (February), Sheffield: N. Zealand 2, GB 1.
1973 (February), Croydon: N. Zealand 3, GB 0.
1976 (August), Gold Coast: GB 3, N. Zealand 0.
1976 (September), Sydney: GB 3, N. Zealand 1.

Index